The Illusion of Accountability in the European Union

This book examines accountability in the EU from different perspectives and considers whether EU citizens have real opportunities for holding decision-makers accountable. The volume analyses five arguments defending the current order, supporting the conclusion that there are indeed sufficient means for holding decision-makers to account in the Union. The authors examine:

- The argument that we should rethink the meaning of accountability in the EU context
- The claim that there is no accountability deficit in the EU because member states have the power to retrieve all delegated competencies
- The assertion that EU citizens have effective mechanisms for holding those responsible for legislative decision-making to account
- The contention that the arrangements that obtain at present for holding the executive power in the EU to account are acceptable
- The belief that the involvement of organised civil society can work as an alternative to traditional forms of accountability.

The main conclusion is that the current institutional set-up and practice of decision-making in the EU is one that merely creates an illusion of accountability.

Using a strict framework focusing on the difference between formal mechanisms and actual opportunities for accountability, this highly coherent volume will be of interest to students and scholars of European politics, especially those interested in the democratic foundations of the European political system.

Sverker Gustavsson is Jean Monnet Professor of European Political Integration at the Department of Government, Uppsala University, Sweden. His main research interests are European constitutional affairs, welfare state theory and research policy doctrines. **Christer Karlsson** is Associate Professor at the Department of Government, Uppsala University. His main research interests are democratic theory, European Union politics and international climate change negotiations. **Thomas Persson** is a researcher at the Department of Government, Uppsala University. His research interests include the involvement of civil society and interest groups in European Union politics, and the impact of European integration on national political systems.

Routledge Advances in European Politics

1 Russian Messianism
Third Rome, revolution, Communism and after
Peter J.S. Duncan

2 European Integration and the Postmodern Condition
Governance, democracy, identity
Peter van Ham

3 Nationalism in Italian Politics
The stories of the Northern League, 1980–2000
Damian Tambini

4 International Intervention in the Balkans since 1995
Edited by Peter Siani-Davies

5 Widening the European Union
The politics of institutional change and reform
Edited by Bernard Steunenberg

6 Institutional Challenges in the European Union
Edited by Madeleine Hosli, Adrian van Deemen and Mika Widgrén

7 Europe Unbound
Enlarging and reshaping the boundaries of the European Union
Edited by Jan Zielonka

8 Ethnic Cleansing in the Balkans
Nationalism and the destruction of tradition
Cathie Carmichael

9 Democracy and Enlargement in Post-Communist Europe
The democratisation of the general public in fifteen Central and Eastern European countries, 1991–1998
Christian W. Haerpfer

35 Britain and the Balkans
1991 until the present
Carole Hodge

36 The Eastern Enlargement of the European Union
John O'Brennan

37 Values and Principles in European Union Foreign Policy
Edited by Sonia Lucarelli and Ian Manners

38 European Union and the Making of a Wider Northern Europe
Pami Aalto

39 Democracy in the European Union
Towards the emergence of a public sphere
Edited by Liana Giorgi, Ingmar Von Homeyer and Wayne Parsons

40 European Union Peacebuilding and Policing
Michael Merlingen with Rasa Ostrauskaite

41 The Conservative Party and European Integration since 1945
At the heart of Europe?
N.J. Crowson

42 E-Government in Europe
Re-booting the state
Edited by Paul G. Nixon and Vassiliki N. Koutrakou

43 EU Foreign and Interior Policies
Cross-pillar politics and the social construction of sovereignty
Stephan Stetter

44 Policy Transfer in European Union Governance
Regulating the utilities
Simon Bulmer, David Dolowitz, Peter Humphreys and Stephen Padgett

45 The Europeanization of National Political Parties
Power and organizational adaptation
Edited by Thomas Poguntke, Nicholas Aylott, Elisabeth Carter, Robert Ladrech and Kurt Richard Luther

46 Citizenship in Nordic Welfare States
Dynamics of choice, duties and participation in a changing Europe
Edited by Bjørn Hvinden and Håkan Johansson

47 National Parliaments within the Enlarged European Union
From victims of integration to competitive actors?
Edited by John O'Brennan and Tapio Raunio

48 Britain, Ireland and Northern Ireland since 1980
The totality of relationships
Eamonn O'Kane

49 The EU and the European Security Strategy
Forging a global Europe
Edited by Sven Biscop and Jan Joel Andersson

50 European Security and Defence Policy
An implementation perspective
Edited by Michael Merlingen and Rasa Ostrauskaitė

51 Women and British Party Politics
Descriptive, substantive and symbolic representation
Sarah Childs

52 The Selection of Ministers in Europe
Hiring and firing
Edited by Keith Dowding and Patrick Dumont

53 Energy Security
Europe's new foreign policy challenge
Richard Youngs

54 Institutional Challenges in Post-Constitutional Europe
Governing change
Edited by Catherine Moury and Luís de Sousa

55 The Struggle for the European Constitution
A past and future history
Michael O'Neill

56. Transnational Labour Solidarity
Mechanisms of commitment to cooperation within the European trade union movement
Katarzyna Gajewska

57 The Illusion of Accountability in the European Union
Edited by Sverker Gustavsson, Christer Karlsson and Thomas Persson

The Illusion of Accountability in the European Union

Edited by Sverker Gustavsson, Christer Karlsson and Thomas Persson

Routledge
Taylor & Francis Group
LONDON AND NEW YORK

First published 2009 by Routledge
2 Park Square, Milton Park, Abingdon, Oxon, OX14 4RN

Simultaneously published in the USA and Canada
by Routledge
270 Madison Avenue, New York, NY 10016

Routledge is an imprint of the Taylor & Francis Group, an informa business

Typeset in Times New Roman by Taylor & Francis Books
Printed and bound in Great Britain by the MPG Books Group

British Library Cataloguing in Publication Data
A catalogue record for this book is available from the British Library

Library of Congress Cataloging in Publication Data
A catalog record for this book has been requested

ISBN 10: 0-415-48099-X (hbk)
ISBN 10: 0-203-87471-4 (ebook)

ISBN 13: 978-0-415-48099-4 (hbk)
ISBN 13: 978-0-203-87471-4 (ebook)

Contents

Notes on contributors xi
Acknowledgements xiii
Preface xiv

1 Examining the illusion of accountability 1
SVERKER GUSTAVSSON, CHRISTER KARLSSON AND THOMAS PERSSON

2 Accountability in world politics 11
ROBERT O. KEOHANE

3 Accountability and democracy 23
HEIDRUN ABROMEIT

4 Putting limits on accountability avoidance 35
SVERKER GUSTAVSSON

5 Irretrievable powers and democratic accountability 51
HANS AGNÉ

6 EU treaty reform and accountability 67
CHRISTER KARLSSON

7 Delegation to the permanent representation and mechanisms of accountability 83
THOMAS LARUE

8 European intelligence cooperation and accountability 96
THORSTEN WETZLING

9 Executive power and accountability in the European Union 111
JONAS TALLBERG

10 The European Central Bank – independent and accountable? 126
DANIEL NAURIN

11 Civil society participation and accountability 141
THOMAS PERSSON

12 Improving accountability in the European Union – the potential role of NGOs 155
LOUISA PARKS

13 Taking accountability seriously 170
SVERKER GUSTAVSSON, CHRISTER KARLSSON AND THOMAS PERSSON

Bibliography 176
Index 190

Notes on contributors

Heidrun Abromeit is Professor of Political Science at the Technical University in Darmstadt. Her main research interests are political economy, democratic theory and federalism with special reference to Germany, Switzerland and the European Union.

Hans Agné is a researcher at the Swedish Institute of International Affairs and at the Department of Political Science at Stockholm University. His research interests include transnational actors in global governance and the founding of democratic states by external powers.

Sverker Gustavsson is Jean Monnet Professor of European Political Integration at the Department of Government, Uppsala University. His main research interests are European constitutional affairs, welfare state theory and research policy doctrines.

Christer Karlsson is Associate Professor at the Department of Government, Uppsala University. His main research interests are democratic theory, European Union politics and international climate change negotiations.

Robert O. Keohane is Professor of International Affairs, Princeton University. He is the author of *After Hegemony: Cooperation and Discord in the World Political Economy* (1984) and co-author of *Designing Social Inquiry* (1994). He won the Johan Skytte Prize in Political Science, 2005.

Thomas Larue is currently employed as Committee Secretary at the Swedish Parliament's Committee on the Constitution. He received his PhD from Umeå University in 2006. His main research focuses are constitutional issues and European Union decision-making.

Daniel Naurin is Associate Professor at the Department of Political Science, Gothenburg University. His main research interests are European Union politics and democratic theory.

Louisa Parks is nearing completion of her PhD, a comparative study of the impacts of social movement campaigns in the EU, at the European University Institute in Florence.

Thomas Persson is a researcher at the Department of Government, Uppsala University. His research interests include the involvement of civil society and interest groups in European Union politics, and the impact of European integration on national political systems.

Jonas Tallberg is Professor at the Department of Political Science, Stockholm University. His principal research interests are delegation to international institutions, multilateral negotiations, and legalization in world politics, with a regional specialization in European Union politics.

Thorsten Wetzling is a PhD student at the Graduate Institute of International and Development Studies, Geneva. His research seeks to illuminate, assess and explain the paths that European parliaments have taken in their efforts to practise democratic intelligence.

Acknowledgements

The Publishers and Editors would like to thank the following for permission to reprint their material:

Wiley Blackwell Publishing for permission to reprint (as Chapter 2 in this volume): 'Accountability in world politics' by Robert Keohane in *Scandinavian Political Studies*, 29: 75–87. Copyright © 2006 Robert Keohane. Reproduced with permission of Blackwell Publishing Ltd.

Wiley Blackwell Publishing for kind permission to reprint (as Chapter 5 in this volume) material from Hans Agné 'The myth of international delegation: limits to and suggestions for democratic theory in the context of the European Union', *Government and Opposition*, 42: 18–45.

Preface

The days of the 'permissive consensus' are long gone, and concerns over the 'democratic deficit' have become a recurrent theme in the debate on the contemporary European Union. Accountability features at the centre of this debate, and there are growing concerns that the EU's political system does not provide appropriate means for holding decision-makers to account. At the same time, much of the debate seems to be occupied with finding ways for the EU to circumvent its problems in this area. We wish to contribute to this debate with a view that stresses the need to take the Union's problems in connection with accountability seriously.

The first impetus for writing a book about accountability in the European Union came from a research project, 'Reform strategies for the European Union', funded by The Bank of Sweden Tercentenary Foundation. This project, led by Sverker Gustavsson and Christer Karlsson, focused on the 2002–4 treaty-reform process that culminated with the rejection of the Constitutional Treaty by Dutch and French voters. As this project drew to a close, we became convinced it was a good idea to focus our attention on accountability, as this was emerging as one of the most prominent aspects of the debate on the democratic deficit.

Accountability in the EU was also the quintessence of a three year research project that Thomas Persson led from 2004. This project, on 'Democratic accountability and scientific expertise in EU chemicals regulation', was part of the so-called NewS programme, headed by Professor Sven Ove Hansson at the Royal Institute of Technology in Stockholm, and financed by the Foundation for Strategic Environmental Research (Mistra).

An opportunity to make contact with researchers with a similar interest in questions relating to democracy and legitimacy in the EU presented itself when, in July 2004, the CONNEX (Connecting Excellence on European Governance) network, headed by Professor Beate Kohler-Koch in Mannheim, was launched. The work carried out in its Research Group 2, 'Democratic governance and multilevel accountability' coordinated by Professor Deirdre Curtin in Utrecht, has been an invaluable source of intellectual inspiration to us. CONNEX also provided generous funding, which allowed us to organise two workshops in Uppsala. The first was held in December 2005, under the rubric, 'Democratic accountability and legitimacy in the EU'; the second took place in March 2007, on 'Delegation and mechanisms of accountability in the European Union'. We are grateful to all of the participants in these workshops for presenting papers and taking part in very fruitful discussions.

The majority of contributors to this volume were recruited at these workshops; the line-up was then completed through invitations extended to additional scholars who we thought would be able to make valuable contributions to our book. We greatly appreciate the cooperative efforts made by all contributors in putting together this volume.

We are also grateful for being part of the stimulating research environment at the Department of Government in Uppsala. In particular, we wish to thank participants in the European studies seminar at the department, who provided valuable input during the early stages of this project. In addition, we want to acknowledge the Swedish Network for European Studies in Political Science. Indirectly, it has very much supported our work through its regular conferences and the good relations it has promoted between scholars.

Finally, we would like to express our gratitude to Peter Mayers and Jörgen Ödalen who have helped in finalizing the manuscript.

Uppsala, 29 April 2009

Sverker Gustavsson
Christer Karlsson
Thomas Persson

1 Examining the illusion of accountability

Sverker Gustavsson, Christer Karlsson and Thomas Persson

Accountability features as an important – perhaps the most important –theme in the ongoing debate on the EU's democratic deficit (Curtin and Wille 2008). This seems only natural, since accountability is necessary if representative democracy is to work. Representatives must, if they are to fulfil their duties in an effective manner, be accorded independent powers to act. On the other hand, they must not forget those whom they represent.

With the use of open mandates, there will always be a need for institutional arrangements which force representatives to be responsive to the wishes of those they represent (Pitkin 1967: 233). Representative democracy is about the *controlled* transmission of power (Sartori 1987: 232–4). If there is to be any guarantee that representatives actually work to promote the interests of citizens, the latter must be able to hold the former accountable for their actions. Thus, representative political systems which lack mechanisms for holding decision-makers effectively accountable are seriously flawed from a democratic standpoint.

Do EU citizens have real opportunities to hold decision-makers accountable, or does the current institutional set-up in the Union merely create an *illusion* of accountability? That is the central question of this volume. There are widespread and growing concerns that the political system of the EU does not, in fact, afford citizens appropriate mechanisms of accountability (Schmitter 2000; Harlow 2002; Arnull and Wincott 2002; Fischer 2004; Bovens 2007a). The aim of the current study is to ascertain whether such concerns are warranted.

We thereby connect up with the ongoing debate on the EU's democratic deficit, which has been with us for almost two decades now. Concerns over accountability are an integral part of this overarching discussion on the Union's democratic credentials. Is a democratisation of the EU necessary? Is it desirable? Is there, in fact, any problem that really needs addressing here? And if there is, can it be remedied? As we understand it, there are three main positions in this huge debate:

According to the first, there is no democratic problem at the European level (Moravcsik 2002, 2008; Majone 2005). The EU works wonderfully, and the only problem is the tendency of European intellectuals and even some politicians to fuel the notion that the EU is plagued by a democratic deficit.

Proponents of the second position argue that there is indeed a democratic problem, and that it can and should be addressed. The solution is to introduce more political competition at the European level, thus establishing 'limited democratic politics' in the European Union (Føllesdal and Hix 2006; Hix 2008).

Advocates of the third position concede there is a democratic deficit, but they believe we should proceed with extreme care when deciding how or whether to address it. They warn us that the cure may turn out to be worse than the disease (Bartolini 2006, 2008; Scharpf 2008, 2009).

Taking a step back, we might ask why questions of democracy and accountability are relevant in the context of the European Union. Is not the EU, after all, just an international organisation among others, to which member states have delegated tasks which they believe are more efficiently handled at the international level? Why is there so much fuss about the EU's democratic deficit? True enough, scholars are now beginning to analyse and question the democratic status not only of the EU but of other international organisations as well (e.g. Zweifel 2006). However, the demands placed on the EU when it comes to meeting democratic criteria are far heavier than on any other international organisation. How come?

We believe that the EU (and its member states) has partly itself to blame that the debate over its democratic shortcomings has become so heated. While formally an international organisation, namely, the EU has gradually acquired an institutional structure and set of competencies that had previously been reserved for nation-states. In its current form, the EU is an extremely influential organisation, with the power to make collective decisions which are binding on all residents of its member states. When a decision-making body is that powerful, concerns over democracy and legitimacy are only natural and appropriate.

Furthermore, the EU has partly responded to the demands for democratisation that have been placed upon it. Through a series of treaty reforms over time, it has developed an institutional set-up bearing a reasonable resemblance to a democratic political system. At the international level, that makes the EU unique, as the only site today of governance beyond the nation-state where 'the incipient institutions of a "democratic" transnational political community are faintly visible' (Dahl 1994: 32). This has served to encourage the idea that a 'third transformation' (Dahl 1989: 309–21) in the history of democratic practice may be possible.

A third transformation?

Towards the end of *Democracy and Its Critics*, Robert Dahl raises the question of whether the scale of politics can remain coterminous over the long term with the scale of economics, law, and culture. Thus far we have witnessed two democratic transformations: The first took place in ancient Greece, and led to the establishment of the democratic city-state. Government by the few was replaced by government by the many. The second transformation involved the replacement of direct forms of democracy with representative forms. The democratic process could then be applied at the level of the nation-state, rather than being reserved for political systems the size of a city-state. The question now is whether a third transformation, establishing democratic governance beyond the nation-state, is in the cards (Dahl 1989: 312).

Dahl's own answer to this question is to urge his readers to be cautious. In his earlier work, Dahl seemed fairly optimistic about the possibilities for a third transformation, pointing out the EU as the most likely contender to meet the challenge of establishing democratic governance at the international level (Dahl 1989: 320). More recently, however, he seems to have become more sceptical of the possibility of democratising international organisations and achieving a third transformation (Dahl 1998: 117; Dahl 1999: 32–4).

At a more general level, furthermore, Dahl reminds us of the obstacles we always face when we try to translate visions into practice. He urges us to hold on to our sound practical judgement, and to recall the discrepancy between the ideal and the real.

> Measured against its exacting ideal, the imperfections of any actual democracy are so obvious and so enourmous that the palpable discrepancy between ideal and reality constantly stimulates unbounded hopes that the ideal may somehow be made real. But feasible solutions often prove elusive, and those who so easily construct an ideal democracy in their imaginations soon discover that it is far harder, or even impossible, to construct that ideal in the real world.
>
> (Dahl 1989: 312)

In the case of the EU, the discrepancy between democratic ideals and practices has been quite apparent, and it has given rise – as Dahl predicted – to numerous proposals on how to address the democratic shortcomings of that body (e.g. Abromeit 1998; Eriksen 2000; Føllesdal and Hix 2006; Schmalz-Bruns 2007; Hix 2008). It is also possible to point to a number of reforms – the introduction and gradual extension of co-decision, the adoption of regulation 1049/2001 on public access to documents, and the increased role of the EP in the appointment of a new Commission – that have served to close, at least in some degree, the gap between the ideal and the real, moving EU governance in a more democratic direction (Karlsson 2001: 44–103).

How should these attempts at remedying the democratic deficiencies of the EU be understood? Has the EU succeeded with the third transformation, at least in part? Or have these reforms only created a false image of a democratic political system in which citizens are able to hold decision-makers to account?

We would not, of course, expect the EU to meet the criteria of an ideal democracy fully. For the story of democracy's transformations – as Norberto

Bobbio reminds us in *The Future of Democracy* – shows that there will always be a gap between the ideal and the real, 'between what was promised and what has actually come about' (Bobbio 1987: 27). According to Bobbio, real-world democracies have failed to keep the promises inherent in democratic ideals. But the reason, he argues, why these broken promises (Bobbio 1987: 27–39) were not kept is that 'the project of political democracy was conceived for a society much less complex than the one that exists today' (Bobbio 1987: 37). It is therefore impossible for real-world democracies to meet their ideals fully. The question we should rather ask ourselves, as we set out to examine existing political systems, is to what degree they manage to meet the criteria of a fully democratic process.

An illusion of accountability?

We make no attempt, in the current study, to accomplish the monumental task of assessing whether the EU meets all of the criteria that constitute the democratic ideal. Instead, we focus exclusively on what opportunities citizens have for holding decision-makers accountable.

We believe the topic selected for this volume is a timely one, in view of the increased interest in questions of accountability in an EU context. Our choice is also justified by the fact that accountability, as argued above, is of vital importance for any representative political system that aspires to be even minimally democratic.

By accountability, we have in mind a relationship between two actors (X and Y) wherein X has the right to: (1) *monitor* the actions of Y, (2) *evaluate* the actions of Y, and (3) impose *sanctions* on Y (cf. Grant and Keohane 2005: 29; Bovens 2007a: 450–1).

Our concern here is with what is sometimes called 'internal accountability': i.e. a relationship whereby X has *delegated* authority to Y (who may in turn have delegated authority to Z). Some scholars also speak of 'external accountability', whereby actors are held to account by all those who are *affected* by their actions, rather than by those who have delegated power to them (cf. Keohane's contribution in this volume). Our understanding of accountability, however, presupposes an act of delegation. An accountability relationship between two actors can therefore be described in principal-agent terms (Strøm *et al.* 2004).

In the context of the EU, it is the citizens of the Union who are the ultimate principals. It is they who have delegated power to parliaments and governments. The latter in turn have empowered EU institutions and civil servants to carry out the day-to-day business of EU affairs. A chain of delegation often has more than two links, with actors in the middle playing the role of both agent and principal. Member-state governments, for example, are the agents of EU citizens and act as their representatives in Brussels. Yet they are also principals, for they delegate their own authority to civil servants.

Principals may have a number of mechanisms at their disposal for ensuring that their agents act in accordance with the mandate given them. Such mechanisms operate in an *ex post* manner: they involve monitoring, evaluating, and sanctioning after the fact. However, the impact of accountability may also be apparent *ex ante*, 'since the anticipation of sanctions may deter the powerful from abusing their positions in the first place' (Grant and Keohane 2005: 30).

A number of different accountability mechanisms are available in different contexts, including electoral contests, legal requirements, and fiscal instruments. These various mechanisms can be placed on a continuum from *weak* to *strong*. At the weak end, we find tools that merely allow for monitoring an agent's actions: e.g. the right to access documents. Then, moving along the continuum towards the other end, we find instruments that also permit principals to evaluate the actions of representatives: e.g. the right to call hearings. At the strong end of the spectrum, finally, we find mechanisms that make it possible to impose sanctions on the agent: e.g. the right of superiors to remove employees, of parliaments to call a vote of confidence, and of voters to change government on Election Day.

What sets the EU apart from other international organisations is that it offers an institutional setting that seems, on the surface, to allow the public actually to hold decision-makers accountable: indirectly through their national governments, and directly through the European Parliament. It is important to distinguish, however, between *formal* accountability mechanisms and any *real* opportunities principals may have to hold agents accountable. Consider direct accountability via the European Parliament. MEPs are directly elected by EU citizens, so there is a strong mechanism for accountability here: should EU citizens feel that 'their' MEPs have done a bad job, they can simply not vote for them at the next EP election. However, the real opportunities for citizens to hold MEPs accountable are sharply limited by the fact that EP elections are second-order national contests fought out on domestic rather than European issues (Reif and Schmitt 1980; Hix 2008). The absence of electoral contests fought on European issues undermines the ability of citizens to hold MEPs accountable for their actions, notwithstanding the existence of a strong accountability mechanism.

It is important to ascertain, then, whether the accountability mechanisms at the disposal of EU citizens are weak or strong. However, it is also necessary to know whether these powers are merely formal, or whether instead they provide real opportunities to hold decision-makers to account.

There are those, then, who are genuinely concerned that the political system of the EU does not afford citizens sufficient opportunities to hold decision-makers to account. But there are also those who deny there is any accountability deficit at all, or that the current system lacks adequate mechanisms for accountability (Moravscik 2002: 611–2). In the current debate on the democratic status of the EU, we can identify five arguments supporting the conclusion that there are indeed sufficient means for holding decision-makers to account in the Union. Taken together, these arguments paint a picture of the EU as a site for governance in which the third transformation (to democracy beyond the nation-state) has partly succeeded – at least when it comes to meeting reasonable criteria for accountability.

In this volume, we shall examine these five arguments in order to determine whether the image of the EU as offering sufficient accountability is justified, or whether the current institutional set-up and practice of decision-making is one that merely creates an *illusion* of accountability. It may well be that denials of an accountability deficit in the Union are based on a misapprehension of the true state of affairs.

Five arguments that EU accountability is sufficient

These five arguments, which claim there is no accountability deficit and that current arrangements are therefore satisfactory, will be examined under the following headings: 'rethink the meaning of accountability'; 'delegated powers and accountability'; 'hold the legislature accountable'; 'hold the executive accountable'; and 'accountability through civil society'.

Rethink the meaning of accountability

According to the first argument, we should rethink what it means to hold decision-makers to account. Where the EU is concerned, we should 'look for new standards of legitimacy and accountability' (Majone 1998: 18). We should not necessarily require that its political system provide citizens with strong mechanisms of accountability; rather, we ought to content ourselves with reforms designed to improve transparency, and we should require of decisions-makers that they give reasons for their actions (Majone 1998: 20–2).

In Chapter 2, 'Accountability in world politics', Robert Keohane notes that the lack of global democracy has become an important public issue, as interdependence and globalisation have increased the need for global governance. The problem is that the conditions for electoral democracy – much less participatory democracy – are not present on the global level. Rather than abandoning democratic principles, however, we should rethink our ambitions and look for feasible ways to strengthen mechanisms of accountability in world politics. If we are to succeed in this mission, we will need to abandon the belief that all forms of accountability require popular elections in order to be meaningful.

In Chapter 3, 'Accountability and democracy', Heidrun Abromeit criticises the notion that existing mechanisms of accountability can be taken – even when they seem to be working well enough – as a surrogate for democracy. She stresses that the view that accountability and democracy are identical involves a fair amount of concept-stretching. Rather than rethinking the meaning of accountability and democracy in the context of international politics, she argues, we should acknowledge that what is needed for true democratic accountability in the Union is a mixture of electoral and direct-democratic elements.

In Chapter 4, 'Putting limits on accountability avoidance', Sverker Gustavsson asks whether light can be shed on the basic problem if we approach the issue from the other end: i.e. if we explore different strategies for *avoiding* rather than promoting accountability. The question put in his chapter is: what are the limits of accountability avoidance? We are impelled to put a limit on the evasion of responsibility, he argues, by the need to maintain a role for legitimate opposition. For not even the most ardent believers in consensus and expert rule are completely insensitive to the risk of a constitutional breakdown. In societies with universal suffrage and political freedom, it is very risky to allow opposition to wane, or to let it take the form of principled and fundamental negativism.

Delegated power and accountability

According to the second argument, the accountability deficit is a matter of limited concern, because the member states have the power to retrieve all delegated competencies. This argument rests on the premise that authority has only been delegated – not alienated – to the Union. It is national politicians who have the final say over what competencies are to be delegated to the EU, or retrieved from it – and these decision-makers are indeed subject to strong accountability mechanisms in the member states. Since member states can retrieve delegated competencies by reforming the treaties, it is no more difficult to justify delegation to the EU than to justify delegation to domestic regulatory agencies (Kahler 2004: 135; Moravscik 2004: 356).

In Chapter 5, 'Irretrievable powers and democratic accountability', Hans Agné examines the widely held view that democratic states are able to retrieve powers they have delegated to international organisations like the EU. This capacity is cited in justification of the limited nature of present opportunities to hold international decision-makers accountable. Agné challenges this argument, by showing that the authority exercised by organisations like the EU is virtually impossible to restore to member states. He then explores the implications of the irrevocability of international powers for the meaning and normative standing of accountability. He argues that the trend whereby more and more competencies are delegated to the European level has resulted in a weaker kind of accountability. Rather than trying to obfuscate this reality by conflating what are fundamentally different concepts of delegation, scholars should help to raise awareness of what is at stake here: namely, how our ability to hold decision-makers accountable is affected when we delegate powers to international organisations like the EU.

In Chapter 6, 'EU treaty reform and accountability', Christer Karlsson asks whether EU citizens have any meaningful influence over the most fundamental decisions taken in the Union: namely, those that lay down the rules of the game. He shows that the opportunities enjoyed by EU citizens to hold treaty reformers accountable are in fact limited. Moreover, the convention method introduced by the Laeken European Council improves the situation only marginally. The fundamental problem is that neither national nor EP elections are contests over issues relating to the future design of European integration; nor are voters ever presented with alternative views on the issues decided at Intergovernmental Conferences (IGCs). In practice, therefore, EU citizens have no effective means of sanctioning those responsible for deciding on new treaties.

Hold the legislature accountable

According to proponents of the third argument, the EU has developed an institutional structure that furnishes EU citizens with two effective mechanisms for holding those responsible for legislative decision-making in the Union to account: namely, 'direct accountability via the EP and indirect accountability via elected national officials' (Moravscik 2002: 611).

As we saw above, however, the strong mechanism for accountability via directly elected MEPs is problematic in practice, due to the fact that EP elections are not fought on European issues. Extensive research has been devoted in recent years to the role of the EP in EU legislation, and to the ability of EU citizens to hold MEPs accountable through elections to that body (e.g. Hix and Marsh 2007). We prefer, therefore, to focus our attentions in this study on two areas relating to legislative accountability that have been researched far less.

First, in Chapter 7, 'Delegation to the permanent representation and mechanisms of accountability', Thomas Larue analyses and compares the delegation and accountability designs established by national governments in Sweden and France vis-à-vis their respective permanent representations in Brussels. This link is crucial for understanding and evaluating the opportunities open to national citizens to hold the Council of Ministers indirectly accountable for EU legislation. Larue argues that national bureaucrats stationed in Brussels are indeed cornerstones of our democracies, yet there are no effective mechanisms at present for holding them accountable. Back-pedalling along the chain of delegation is extremely costly, if not downright impossible – because revoking a national standpoint entails a severe loss of credibility. Thus we have a situation where accountability is a *de jure* possibility, but a *de facto* chimera.

In Chapter 8, 'European intelligence cooperation and accountability', Thorsten Wetzling seeks to shed light on accountability in relation to intelligence activities, an area increasingly characterised by European cooperation. Intelligence still figures as one of the least transparent fields; it therefore serves as a critical case for accountability in the EU. Wetzling asks what the effect is on accountability when intelligence moves to the European level. He shows that the accountability mechanisms established for intelligence under the EU umbrella suffer from major structural flaws. The European Parliament lacks an independent oversight body, and the Council has no obligation to inform the EP on intelligence matters. Wetzling therefore concludes that structures for intelligence accountability are virtually absent at the European level.

Hold the executive accountable

A defining characteristic of the EU is the delegation of powerful executive competencies to the European Commission, the European Central Bank (ECB), and independent agencies. According to the fourth argument, the arrangements that obtain at present are – even in the absence of strong mechanisms for accountability – generally acceptable. The institutions that exercise executive powers in the EU have been established through democratic procedures; their decision-making methods are reasonably transparent; they are subject to oversight by the European Parliament and the member states; and the authority delegated to them can be revoked by amending the treaties (Majone 1996b, 1998; Issing 1999).

In Chapter 9, 'Executive power and accountability in the European Union', Jonas Tallberg examines these claims. He asks what powers have been delegated and why, and to what extent the resulting pattern of delegation and control presents a problem for accountability. He concludes that executive power in the EU is subject to a variegated pattern of control and accountability. While the Commission and the European regulatory agencies operate within relatively tight constraints, the ECB enjoys far-reaching discretion in the exercise of its powers. The current state of affairs, Tallberg points out, is one which proponents of strong accountability mechanisms find most unsatisfactory. The EP's oversight of the Commission, the transparency policy of the ECB, the statutes governing the European agencies, and the general threat of treaty revision all serve to create an illusion of accountability; whereas, in practice, these institutions only can be held accountable for their actions and decisions with great difficulty, if at all.

In Chapter 10, 'The European Central Bank – independent and accountable?', Daniel Naurin puts his full focus on the ECB. He wonders whether it can reconcile the independence it requires to act credibly with the accountability it needs to be legitimate. He examines the claim that independence and accountability are 'two sides of the same coin', as well as the argument that the ECB is indeed subject to a sufficient level of democratic accountability. Naurin finds that the latter claim is founded on the unsustainable assumption that transparency – and in particular the ECB's version of it – is a sufficient condition for accountability. However, holding press conferences can never be an adequate substitute for ensuing that the people are able to sanction decision-makers.

Accountability through civil society

The fifth argument directs our interest towards civil society and organised interests, which are increasingly regarded as alternative channels for citizen participation and accountability at the EU level (Greenwood 2007; Steffek *et al.* 2008). Letting civil society and organised interests take an active part in policy-making is considered by both academic scholars and practitioners to offer a promising complement to representative democracy. According to this argument, the involvement of organised civil society can increase transparency in the EU and put policy-making under public scrutiny and control, thus facilitating accountability.

In Chapter 11, 'Civil society participation and accountability', Thomas Persson notes that participatory and deliberative arrangements are increasingly seen as having the potential to improve accountability in the EU. He sets out to assess this potential on the basis of empirical findings from a policy-making process in which new measures for societal involvement have been tested: the overhaul of European chemicals policy. The results show that this process was indeed, at least to some extent, more transparent, inclusive, and responsive than EU-level decision-making in general. And transparency, inclusiveness, and responsiveness are all prerequisites for accountability. Accountability itself, however, must be furnished primarily by the traditional representative bodies of the Union. While weak mechanisms of accountability were improved in this case, stronger mechanisms were not changed in any way. Persson therefore concludes that, despite great expectations that participatory and deliberative measures would improve EU accountability, the evidence from the chemicals-policy overhaul gives reason for caution.

In Chapter 12, 'Improving accountability in the European Union: the potential role of NGOs', Louisa Parks considers the role that non-governmental organisations can play in securing effective accountability in the Union. Her point of departure is that NGOs can contribute to weak forms of accountability, by monitoring the behaviour of EU institutions and calling attention to any wrongdoing. However, these forms of accountability presume that the quality of information-provision among the involved parties is high. Evidence from interviews with representatives of NGOs involved in four EU-level campaigns reveals that, in the eyes of these actors, the main problems have to do with transparency and access in the case of the Commission, with secretiveness in the case of the Council, and with lack of power in the case of an otherwise exemplary European Parliament. Parks accordingly concludes that, if we wish to see NGOs make their contribution to solving the EU's accountability problem, we will need to introduce greater transparency and openness – particularly in the Council and the Commission.

In Chapter 13, finally, the editors make a plea for 'Taking accountability seriously', stressing the importance of 'telling it like it is', acknowledging that the current institutional set-up in the Union merely portrays an illusion of accountability. Breaking up this illusion will allow us to see the more deep-seated underlying problem, namely the absence of opposition in the EU. Only by restoring opposition can we hope to establish real opportunities for EU citizens to hold their representatives to account.

2 Accountability in world politics

Robert O. Keohane

World politics has never been a democratic realm. Now, with interdependence and globalisation prompting demands for global governance, the lack of global democracy has become an important public issue. Yet the domestic analogy is unhelpful since the conditions for electoral democracy, much less participatory democracy, do not exist on a global level. Rather than abandoning democratic principles, we should rethink our ambitions. First, we should emphasise, in our normative as well as our positive work, the role played by information in facilitating international cooperation and democratic discourse. Second, we should define feasible objectives such as limiting potential abuses of power, rather than aspiring to participatory democracy and then despairing of its impossibility. Third, we should focus as much on the powerful entities that are the core of the problem, including multinational firms and states, as on multilateral organisations, which often are the focus of criticism. Finally, we need to think about how to design a pluralistic accountability system for world politics that relies on a variety of types of accountability: supervisory, fiscal, legal, market, peer and reputational. A challenge for contemporary political science is to design such a system, which could promote both democratic values and effective international cooperation.

Much of the work for which you honour me with the Skytte Prize[1] derives from my critique of a conventional view of the study of international relations that was more common 35 years ago than now. In this perspective, world politics is essentially a matter of interstate competition, which breaks out occasionally in warfare. The role of students of world politics, in this view, is to understand the causes of war and the conditions of peace. Without denying the importance of this subject, I have sought to redefine the study of world politics by broadening its scope. I have sought to analyse transnational relations and interdependence, and to explore the conditions under which institutionalised or legalised cooperation takes place among states. I have also investigated the implications of such cooperation for outcomes that we care about, ranging from the maintenance of alliances, to security against terrorism to environmental protection.

The most comprehensive statement of my perspective on world politics is in my 1984 book, *After Hegemony: Cooperation and Discord in the World Political Economy* (Keohane 1984). My argument builds explicitly on realism, particularly Kenneth Waltz's neorealism (Waltz 1979), but goes beyond it. States do not typically cooperate out of altruism or empathy with the plight of others, nor for the sake of pursuing what they conceive as 'international interests'. They seek wealth and security for their own people, and search for power as a means to these ends. The key to my argument is the 'functional theory of international regimes', according to which states build international regimes in order to promote mutually beneficial cooperation. The international trade regime of the General Agreement on Tariffs and Trade (GATT), now the World Trade Organisation (WTO), is the closest real-world example to the model that I construct. In my view, international regimes – clusters of principles, norms, rules and decision-making procedures – reduce transaction costs for states – that is, the costs of making and enforcing agreements. They also alleviate problems of asymmetrical information and enhance the credibility of states' commitments. Their existence can be explained in terms of self-interest; yet the resulting institutions exert an impact on state policies by changing the costs and benefits of various alternatives, and over time have often unforeseen effects.

It is important to note that although my view of world politics is based on rational-choice theory, and relies heavily on microeconomic analogies, it is not inconsistent with what has become known as 'constructivist' thinking in world politics. According to constructivists, interests are derived not merely from material identities, but are also constituted by ideas and norms (Jepperson *et al.* 1996: 53; Wendt 1999: 113ff.). As Judith Goldstein and I have written, this view 'is irrefutable in the abstract and reminds researchers to investigate not just what strategies are devised to attain interests but how preferences are formed and how identities are shaped' (Goldstein and Keohane 1993: 5–6).

Constructivism and my version of rationalist theory are not only compatible, but are also in some ways complementary. Both rationalism and constructivism focus on the beliefs of agents *prior to* the strategic calculus that these agents employ. In game theory, it is important to understand what beliefs are common knowledge; 'constructivism analyzes discourses and practices that continuously recreate what rationalists refer to as common knowledge' (Katzenstein *et al.* 1999: 41). The point is that although their languages are different, rationalism and constructivism have more in common than stylisations of them as containing different ontologies would suggest. In my view, students of world politics should be seeking to integrate their insights rather than pitting them against one another in a gladiatorial contest. At any rate, that is the spirit of my inquiry in this chapter into issues of accountability – which can be well-understood only by comprehending both the strategic interactions between those in authority and those to whom they are supposedly accountable ('principals' and 'agents' in rational-choice language), and the underlying norms and identities that define what is considered to be appropriate behaviour for global rule-making (March and Olsen 1999). My argument about international cooperation and institutions emphasises that information is a *variable*. It is not just that world politics is uncertain; institutionalisation can provide information, increase credibility and generate focal points, thus reducing uncertainty.

Recently, I have been trying to understand the normative implications of the patterns of complex interdependence and institutionalised cooperation that my work describes. Since information is at the core of my positive theory of international regimes, it makes sense that it should be central to my normative theory as well. Since I am a liberal democrat by conviction, I have been particularly interested in the information that is available to the governed in democratic societies – that is, in issues of accountability. To what extent can democratic principles of accountability be applied to world politics, and what are the implications – for our own actions – of the answer to this question?

The democracy dilemma

An accountability relationship is one in which an individual, group or other entity makes demands on an agent to report on his or her activities, and has the ability to impose costs on the agent. Democratic accountability within a constitutional system is a relationship in which power-wielders are accountable to broad publics through a variety of means including elections with a universal franchise. A system of democratic accountability in world politics would be one in which power-wielders would have to report to people whose actions they profoundly affected, and be subject to sanctions from them (Held 2004: Chapter 6). For someone who believes in liberal democracy like me, it would be pleasant to imagine that such a system could be constructed for world politics.

Unfortunately, such a vision would be utopian in the sense of illusory – impossible of realisation under realistically foreseeable conditions. There is no coherent global government and none is likely to emerge within the next few decades. There is a loose global civil society, with many voluntary groups, but there is no global public in a sense parallel to the concept of a Swedish public or an American public. A global public requires two conditions. First, it requires a political structure to define who was entitled to participate, and on what issues. Second, a global public requires a large 'imagined community' – people who share a sense of common destiny and are in the habit of communicating with one another on issues of public policy. The fate of the European constitutional treaty shows that even in the European Union, such a sense of common destiny is not yet widespread.

So we cannot resort to an analogy with domestic politics. Should we then abandon the notion of accountability at a global level? Doing so would be to accept as a fact that international organisations are undemocratic bureaucracies, as Dahl (1999) has characterised them. If we were to accept the inherently undemocratic nature of international organisations, we would be left with two alternatives, both unpalatable. We could accept arbitrary rule, with attendant abuses of power, at the global level as the price of managing interdependence and resign ourselves to the demise of democratic practices as globalisation proceeds. In this case, we could put our hopes in governmental networks of elites (Slaughter 2004a), 'clubs' of negotiators working on specific issues (Keohane and Nye 2001) and wise arbitration by experts. The WTO, writ large, would provide the vision of our future. The second alternative would be to demand the maintenance of national sovereignty, at least for constitutional democracies, on the premise that democracy can flourish only within the boundaries of a nation-state (Rabkin 2005). On both the Right and the Left, voices have been raised to limit, in the name of national democracy, one or another form of globalisation.

I am not willing to accept either horn of this dilemma. Even institutions established with the best intentions in the world can foster corruption – as we have seen recently in the United Nations Secretariat – or oppression. The political theorist Judith Shklar enunciated what she called the 'liberalism of fear', and stated memorably that 'no liberal ever forgets that governments are coercive' (Shklar 1984: 244). So extension of power without constraints on abuses of power (i.e. procedures for accountability) is unacceptably dangerous. On the other hand, the world is increasingly interdependent with respect to our personal physical security as well as economically, socially, militarily and ecologically. To combine interdependence with lack of governance is to create an explosive and deadly compound – as deadly as suicide bombs. Trusting national states to manage interdependence without international institutions is like trusting a four-year-old boy to play with real guns. Since neither of these alternatives makes sense in the twenty-first century, we must, I believe, figure out ways to gain benefits from governance at a global level while protecting ourselves against its abuse. In other words, we need urgently to seek innovative ways to hold potential abusers of power, at a global level, to account; otherwise, we risk discrediting global governance and fostering a reversion to national sovereignty, with disastrous consequences for cooperation, for peace, and for our own prosperity and personal security.

Accountability and abuses of power

At the global level it is difficult to answer two fundamental questions about accountability. First, what constitutes an abuse of power, and why? Second, who is entitled to hold power-wielders accountable, and why? We need to recognise that people dislike being held accountable. Everyone seeks to hold others accountable, but few of us really want to be held accountable ourselves. The reason is that accountability is a *power relationship*. To be held accountable is to have one's autonomy and one's power over others, constrained. Since few of us like to be held accountable, we must expect leaders of organisations – whose drive for power is greater than that of the average person – to resist accountability, especially when they can do so without jeopardising other goals. Establishing accountability relationships necessarily implies conflict.

With this general sketch of accountability at a global level in mind, I will next distinguish between external and internal accountability, and discuss accountability in comparison with other ways to limit abuses of power. Then I will outline various elements of what I call a '*pluralistic accountability system*'. Accountability can be internal or external. The most common type of internal accountability occurs through delegation. People or groups create organisations that depend on those who created them for financial support, legitimacy or other resources. Corporate CEOs are responsible to their boards of directors, who are responsible to stockholders; in congregational churches, pastors are accountable to the church members, in episcopal churches, to diocesan bishops. External accountability is quite different. Where external accountability is at issue, organisations are held accountable not to those who delegated power to them, but to those affected by their actions. The World Bank is internally accountable to its rich and powerful shareholders; but we might think it should also be accountable to poor farmers in developing countries. If the world were a liberal democratic state and the World Bank an agent of the government of this state, the internal and external models would be fused. Through democratic elections, people affected by its actions would be able to choose between candidates with alternative platforms on what the Bank's policies should be, but in the world as it is, this prospect is unrealistic. States with funds are not going to provide them unless they have substantial control over their use. We could preach global democracy to the G8 until we were exhausted, but it would change nothing. Yet it is external accountability that matters most to us in normative terms. Only experts will worry much about whether the boards of the World Bank or the International Monetary Fund (IMF) can control the executive heads or staffs of these organisations. People outside the United States are less concerned with limitations from American public opinion on the President with the effectiveness of constraints on the United States from the rest of the world. Does the United States have to display 'a decent respect to the opinions of mankind', in the words of the Declaration of Independence?

Consider the entities conventionally held accountable on a transnational basis. The most prominent, judging from demonstrations, press coverage and even scholarly articles, are major intergovernmental organisations, including the United Nations (UN), the European Union (EU), The World Bank, the IMF and the WTO. These organisations do not meet democratic standards of accountability as applied in the best-functioning democracies of our era. Their internal accountability is often very weak, as indicated by the recent oil-for-food scandals at the UN. The UN secretariat has been supervised by multiple states, most of which have little financial stake in efficiency and often a significant stake in placing their nationals, often incompetent or troublesome ones, in the UN bureaucracy. The states have their own interests, leading them to overlook irregularities or even corruption.

The external accountability gaps are even greater. Indeed, many poor people affected by the policies of the IMF, The World Bank and the WTO have no ability to hold these organisations accountable. Nevertheless, many people feel that these organisations should be externally as well as internally accountable, and many non-governmental organisations (NGOs) purport to speak for the poor. One result of their endeavours is that the decision-making processes of the IMF, The World Bank and WTO have become more remarkably transparent. Indeed, in transparency they now compare well to the decision-making processes of most governments, even some democratic governments – and of many of the NGOs that demand transparency!

When the processes of major multilateral organisations are not transparent, the chief source of non-transparency is governmental pressure for confidentiality. Their leaders spend much of their time seeking to persuade constituencies that the organisations are actually both constructive and responsive. These organisations are therefore anything but 'out of control bureaucracies', accountable to nobody. They are much too weak to be so arrogant. Indeed, the real problem of external accountability seems to me quite different. The IMF, The World Bank and WTO are chiefly accountable to the governments whose support they need – not necessarily to the people most affected by their actions. NGOs claim to speak for these people, but in fact heavily over-represent liberal, professional elites in the rich countries. These NGOs demand accountability, but they are not even representative of dominant opinion in many of their own countries – such as the United States. The NGOs are therefore weak compared to governments. Yet when the NGOs lose the battle due to their institutionally weak positions, they condemn the organisations as 'unaccountable', rather than the governments – which then weakens the perceived legitimacy of the multilateral institutions in the eyes of members of national publics who should most support them. The discourse is therefore perverse, strengthening the hand of those, such as the Right Wing in the United States, who seek to ignore the views of people elsewhere in the world.

What the controversies also indicate is that accountability is a distributional issue. The issue is not so much: are these organisations accountable? The answer to that question is 'yes'. They are accountable to the states that authorised their creation and that provide financial support. The real issue is: are they accountable to the right groups? NGOs make a normative claim for accountability to groups that are affected or for accountability to principles such as 'sustainable development' or 'human rights'. These are serious issues, but they are not so much issues of 'lack of accountability' as issues of 'accountability to whom?' Different types of accountability favour different accountability-holders. Once again, accountability is largely a matter of power.

Why is accountability important? Essentially, in my view, accountability helps prevent abuses of power. A critic might say, however, that it is a category mistake to talk about accountability in world politics. The only realistic way to limit abuses of power in world politics, in this view, would be to impose coercive constraints on the potential abuser: to rely on the balance of power, or on economic constraints. There is something in this objection. Not all entities whose actions we may fear in world politics can be held accountable in a meaningful sense. For instance, the Roman Catholic Church is deliberately structured as a closed hierarchy to resist human external accountability. Conversely, mass religious movements, whether Islamic or evangelical Christian, are difficult to hold accountable since they are so decentralised. Who is to be held accountable? At the extreme, al-Qaeda cannot be held accountable by their potential victims since al-Qaeda does not share values or even a common normative language with its victims. Sometimes, in world politics, limiting abuses of power requires the use of legitimate force, or the wielding of material resources controlled by states. Such limitations on power should not be confused with accountability. Nevertheless, accountability relationships, when institutionalised, regularise restraints on power without imposing the tremendous costs involved in the application of coercion. If feasible, they are therefore a superior means of preventing abuses of power. Consider two examples of powerful entities whose potential abuses of power could be limited either through coercion or through accountability relationships.

Multinational corporations

Multinational corporations are held internally accountable, with more or less success, to their shareholders, who authorise action and provide support. Yet their actions also have enormous effects on other people. Multinational corporations should not be demonised – indeed, studies in various issue areas show that brand-name corporations often act in more socially responsible ways than anonymous local firms in the same industry (e.g. sweatshops, tankers, the environment). However, when they act only in their own interests and those of their shareholders, they may do enormous damage. One response would be to weaken them, but for one or a few states to attempt this strategy would probably be unsuccessful, and for many to do so could well destroy the economic and technological benefits that size and global integration can bring. Arrangements for accountability could provide early warning of problems, institutionalising what Albert Hirschman referred to as 'voice'. They could also impose moderate reputational costs on corporations for anti-social behaviour, which could have the effect of leading the firms themselves to institutionalise controls to avoid this, and in the process to become routinely more sensitive to the interests of people outside the firm itself. Conversely, firms that were sensitive to the public interest would gain reputational benefits. The UN's 'Global Compact' seeks to institutionalise relationships between the UN and major multinational firms that will improve accountability and reward firms for being responsible corporate citizens (Ruggie 2004). It remains to be seen how effective these arrangements will be.

Powerful states

The doctrine of sovereignty has traditionally served to protect states from external accountability. It has not prevented occasional resort to war and other coercive measures as means of control, with enormously destructive results. Multilateral institutions are designed to make states accountable to each other, if not to outsiders, by institutionalising a pattern of questioning and making it possible to withhold approval from coercive actions. The result will not be harmony, but it can be the emergence of patterns of cooperation that benefit all or most participants and prevent a spiral of misperceptions and misjudgements that can lead to war. The problem, of course, is that extremely powerful states seem virtually immune from accountability if they refuse to accept it. The United States is of course the chief case in point, demanding more rope with which to hang itself, as in Iraq. On any given issue, the United States can typically act unilaterally, dismissing demands for accountability. However, as I will argue below, even the United States needs to worry about its reputation.

A pluralistic accountability system for world politics

I do not have a normatively satisfactory solution for these failures of external accountability. In my view, the unevenness of arrangements for external accountability is caused by the power asymmetries of world politics and cannot therefore be rectified by any academic formula. Yet we do need to recognise that non-electoral mechanisms of external accountability do exist, although they are often weak. They need to be strengthened. Not surprisingly, the issues are easiest with respect to formal intergovernmental organisations, since two accountability mechanisms for these institutions are already in place. *Supervisory mechanisms* exist by which those entities that delegated powers – states or larger-scale multilateral organisations – supervise the exercise of those powers. And *fiscal mechanisms* exist, ensuring that the organisation will respond to its supervisors for fear of having funding cut off. The various measures now being taken by the United Nations to ensure that its financial procedures provide for more accountability reflect the impact of supervisory and fiscal mechanisms.

Legal accountability mechanisms are expanding in world politics. The legalisation of world trade makes national leaders with responsibility for trade policy accountable to tribunals applying an expanding body of law. If the International Criminal Court succeeds in establishing jurisdiction over accused war criminals, it will constitute another expansion of legal accountability mechanisms. Insofar as those who control those mechanisms act responsibly, and are themselves accountable to others, such an expansion promises to create a set of welcome restraints on the ability of national leaders to commit abuses of human rights.

Corporations and governments can both be held accountable by *markets*. The processes by which financial markets constrain the actions of democratic governments are inherently undemocratic: almost by definition, financial markets are controlled by the rich. Yet democracies have strong tendencies to put future generations at risk, or under debt burdens, for the sake of gratifying current voters and interest groups. By increasing the costs of debt beyond a certain point, financial markets may constrain this particular abuse of the power of adults now over succeeding generations. Accountability to consumer markets, on the other hand, is inherently more democratic. It does not imply accountability to the poor, but may involve accountability to a transnational middle class. Nike, Coca-Cola and McDonald's all have to be concerned about the possibility of consumer boycotts, even if such boycotts are discussed more often than they are implemented. So do Exxon-Mobil and British Petroleum: it is not accidental that tankers owned by brand-name corporations are safer, on average, than those owned by anonymous entities (Mitchell 1994).

Two other forms of accountability may exert some impact even on powerful states. *Peer accountability* refers to ways in which organisations may criticise the operations of similar organisations, often through multilateral organisations. National financial policies are subject to criticism by other states, directly and in the context of organisations such as the Organisation for Economic Cooperation and Development (OECD) and Bank for International Settlements. Governmental networks of security regulators, standard-setters and accounting experts collectively develop 'best practice' standards that are often costly to disavow or evade (Slaughter 2004a). The EU has multiple processes to facilitate for its Member States both criticism of each other's policies and the sharing of information about best practices.

Finally, reputation matters, so we can speak of *reputational accountability*. To be accepted into the right 'clubs', one has to behave in appropriate ways. Such a process of socialisation is often conflictual, but over time its impact can be enormous. China's efforts to change its practices in order to be accepted into the world economy provide fascinating indicators of how reputational accountability works, as well as its limitations. So do the efforts of Secretary of State Condoleezza Rice to restore America's reputation as a cooperative member of what Hedley Bull called 'international society'. Her efforts are indicated not only by her fence-mending trip to Europe but by American acceptance of a central role for the UN in tsunami relief efforts, its agreement that the International Criminal Court may have jurisdiction over crimes of genocide in the Sudan, and its greater cooperation with others in dealing with North Korea and Iran. Reputation is a form of 'soft power', defined as 'the ability to shape the preferences of others' (Nye 2004: 5). No intelligent statesperson is likely to discard it lightly.

When we evaluate institutions – states, NGOs or multilateral organisations – one of our criteria should be whether they provide accurate information about their own processes as well as about their accomplishments. Accountability is only possible with information, much of which has to be provided by the organisation in question. Hiding information is endemic to organisations, even when their leaders do not engage in systematic deceit. It is not a trivial standard, therefore, to demand truth-telling and transparency as a condition for legitimacy. Taking this standard seriously would have made many well-meaning people more sceptical during the Cold War of the Soviet Union, which would have been well-founded in view of subsequent discoveries about such matters as environmental degradation and biological weapons programmes. It would make us critical of the UN bureaucracy now. And it would make us even more critical of the current United States government.

Institutions should be judged not merely by their transparency, but by the *epistemic quality* of our understanding of them. Too much information, without coherent interpretation, is merely confusing noise. We also need the capacity to interpret information intelligently, which entails the ability to ask pointed questions of power-holders and to demand answers. For that capacity, we need a vibrant global civil society, with many groups, from different perspectives, investigating and criticising the actions of states, multilateral institutions and other powerful entities. A pluralistic accountability system will depend on many kinds of accountability: supervisory, fiscal, legal, market, peer and reputational. In world politics, such forms of accountability will not come from a centralised hierarchy, but from a pluralistic, often discordant system of NGOs and networks among them.

Often the fragmentation of world politics is lamented because it implies a lack of well-structured, coherent global governance. Yet from an informational standpoint such fragmentation is beneficial since it ensures that Gramscian structures of hegemonic discourse and consequent false consciousness are very unlikely to emerge. Too many actors, with both different normative perspectives and interests, can exercise voice in the world. The global media, including the new Internet-based media, are capable of transmitting a huge volume and variety of messages. The results often appear chaotic, and there may be no way to focus and aggregate concerns about the behaviour of power-wielders. Yet it is less likely in world politics than in a more hierarchical structure that nefarious behaviour will continue to be hidden, or its discussion repressed. The reaction of the American public to human rights abuses by the United States at Abu Graib and Guantanamo was remarkably muted, presumably by a combination of patriotism and fear. The stronger global reaction kept these issues alive, and even made them resonate more among the American public than would have been the case had the United States been closed to outside influences.

The most effective institutions for enhancing global accountability may well be those that create ripple effects within powerful democratic states. If states were monolithic, it would be much more difficult to hold them accountable.

Yet when a powerful democracy engages in behaviour that is censured by people in other societies, some members of the democracy will be affected. The mechanisms may include persuasion, and will almost certainly include bolstering. In other words, opponents of the state's policies, in a minority at home, will be provided with arguments and moral support by the outside reaction. Furthermore, some other people, who might not be normatively moved by the criticism, will worry about its effects on the reputation and soft power of the state, and may therefore act to check abuses that they otherwise would have overlooked. As in so much else in world politics, the interaction between inter-state behaviour and domestic politics is crucial for the outcomes that eventually result.

Conclusion

If we are to work effectively to improve accountability in world politics, we need to abandon the domestic analogy: the belief that meaningful accountability has to be democratic, entailing popular elections. We need to devise and strengthen mechanisms of accountability that are feasible, given the continuing power asymmetries of world politics. Although the world today does not have a global public, those of us involved in transnational conversations and concerned about global institutions can readily talk to one another. Democrats around the world can draw on common democratic values that have become widely, although not universally, accepted in principle, albeit less realised in practice. In the age of the Internet, we have the great advantage over previous generations that information is much easier to discover and harder to conceal. The decentralisation and diversity of world politics make transparency easier to achieve since a variety of voices can express themselves, and these voices can be heard at low cost. No single state or coalition of states can prevent the organisation and operation of a networked system of pluralistic accountability, with the potential to limit abuses of power.

I believe that people committed to democracy and international cooperation around the world should be taking advantage of the opportunities we have to build, piece by piece, a pluralistic accountability system in world politics. I also believe that political science has a special responsibility to help construct institutions that would both be accountable and that would hold other powerful entities accountable. We could do much more as a discipline to integrate our descriptive and normative work by posing ourselves questions about how to design international regimes that are effective, relatively efficient and legitimate.

Legitimacy has two dimensions: sociological and normative. Political scientists have tools for assessing the sociological legitimacy of institutions: the degree to which they are accepted by relevant constituencies as having the right to rule. Political theory contains substantial resources for assessing normative legitimacy: whether institutions have the right to rule according to a coherent and defensible set of normative principles. Normative legitimacy requires a consistent pattern of institutional outputs that meet both epistemic and performance tests. The epistemic dimension of legitimacy means that for powerful institutions to be legitimate, they need to generate correct information, both about the problems they purport to solve and about their own practices. They need to be transparent and accountable, and located in the context of independent monitoring agents that can interrogate their behaviour. The performance dimension of legitimacy – what Fritz Scharpf (1999) calls 'output legitimacy' – is also crucial since institutions are created, and their costs borne, to solve problems. Political scientists are in a good position to help design more effective institutions and assess their normative quality. Doing so is a task worthy of our best efforts in the twenty-first century.

Notes

1 This chapter is an amplification of my Skytte Prize lecture, presented at Uppsala University, Sweden, on 1 October 2005. It was first published in the 2006 volume of *Scandinavian Political Studies*, 29: 75–87. Parts of it draw on two earlier papers: Keohane (2003) and Grant and Keohane (2005).

3 Accountability and democracy

Heidrun Abromeit

In this chapter, I criticise the way in which the twin problems of accountability and democracy are discussed in recent research on the European Union. I take particular exception with the assumption, frequently made, that 'working' systems of accountability can serve as a satisfactory surrogate for democracy. Thus my first point is that the concepts of accountability and of democracy are by no means identical, and that treating them as interchangeable requires a fair amount of concept-stretching.

My second point is that European political scientists, with rare exceptions, take an overly narrow view of democracy, by restricting it to its electoral form. The European political system presents too many obstacles – namely its 'multiple demoi' and its complex institutional structure – to be rendered democratic by means of elections alone. More will be needed if the EU is to be democratised: first of all an inventive mind; second, clarity about the 'why' of democracy and about its essence.

The argument unfolds in four steps: first, I describe the EU's 'democratic problem', which is not one that gradually and inevitably evolved; rather, it resulted from deliberate action on the part of national political leaders whose object was to evade the constraints of democracy. Second, I highlight the difficulties experienced even by 'experts' from different national backgrounds in trying to agree on the essentials of democracy, which mean quite different things to them. Hence, the failure to come to grips with the European democratic problem is rooted, at a theoretical level, in the lack of an 'all-European' understanding of democracy. Third, I analyse what accountability has to do with democracy, and what conditions must obtain if a given arrangement for ensuring accountability is to qualify as 'democratic'. And fourth, I suggest a plausible way of identifying the essence of democracy (understood as a system of collective decision-making): by searching for that *objective* which can be achieved by democratic means *alone*, and which can*not* be achieved by autocratic means. That objective is individual self-determination. For it to be given effect, however, these democratic means (i.e. participatory instruments) must fit the societal and political context, and vary along with it. In conclusion, finally, I argue that what is needed to render the EU truly democratic is a mixture of electoral and direct-democratic elements.

Europe's democratic problem

In self-congratulatory speeches at the time of its passage, European politicians celebrated the Maastricht Treaty as an important step towards democracy. Political scientists took a closer look and discovered Europe's democratic deficit, which before Maastricht had widely gone unnoticed but which now – with the Union apparently approaching statehood – had become a problem. A conundrum dominated the academic debate on Europe for some decade thereafter: on the one hand, one would expect a federation of democracies to be democratic itself; on the other, the multiple societies making up the Union seemed to lack all requisites for democratisation at a common level. Few observers noticed that the conundrum was a consequence, at least in part, of the inadequate way in which the question had been framed.

Researchers were agreed that the Union was sadly lacking in 'electoral accountability': although the European Parliament was elected by European voters in common elections, these elections were not 'meaningful', because (1) the Commission was not responsible to the Parliament, and (2) no truly European parties existed for politicising European issues. European politicians were thus elected, but they could not claim a mandate. Voters' choices were made at random, and they were in any case completely irrelevant for the choices made by MEPs; and the choices made by the latter were, if not altogether, at least in large measure irrelevant for the decisions taken by the Commission and the Council. Vivien Schmidt (2006) sums up the findings as follows: the political system of the EU, she avers, presents the singular picture of 'policy without politics'.

There was broad consensus on the diagnosis, but not on the remedy. The academic community was split in two, with one half urging a full parliamentarisation of the EU, the other stating the impossibility thereof and refusing to discuss any remedy at all. As the first half saw it, the road to a full-fledged parliamentary (or perhaps presidential) system stood open; it could be embarked upon with comparative ease. All that was needed was some constitutional engineering: the EP would have to be upgraded and a firm link established between voters, parliamentarians, and the executive; and it would be necessary to provide – by means of some suitable clause in the rules for the European electoral system (see, for example, S. Wolf 2000) – incentives strong enough to induce national parties to unite or truly European parties to evolve. Why should the model of representative (party) democracy that had been a success story all over the world not perform properly in a union of democracies?

Because – or so the other half argued – this union was unique and *sui generis*, and not just institutionally but also socially. The peoples making it up lacked a common culture, language, and history; and not being united by common experiences, they could not constitute a *demos*. The question of democracy was moot in the absence thereof: 'no demos, no democracy – quite simple' (Neunreither 2000: 148). A government could not be held responsible – or accountable – to the public when no such thing as *a* public existed, but rather a multitude of publics speaking different languages and adhering to different values. The Union was united at the top, but it lacked the social infrastructure required for representative democracy. Nor could such an infrastructure be created by force. It was as simple as that.

Yet, if Peter Mair is to be believed, the lack of a public and collective identity – a *demos* – is not the main hindrance to the construction of a European democracy. As things now stand, he contends, conflicts over the shape and reach of Europeanisation can only be fought out (effectively, that is) within the political arena of each member state, because it is at that level that decisions are made as to how far integration shall go. Actually, conflicts of this kind are not 'politicised' at that level, but rather in the European arena; while, conversely, conflicts over policy issues already within the competence of the Union are not fought out in its own political arena – as they should be – but in those of the member states. As a consequence, the choices of voters at both levels and along both policy dimensions 'become increasingly irrelevant to the outputs of the system, and the … preferences of citizens constitute virtually no constraint of, or mandate for, the relevant policy-makers. Decisions can be taken by political elites with more or less a free hand' (Mair 2008: 29). The reason for this 'depoliticization and displacement' is to be found not in the qualities of the infrastructure but in the behaviour and choices of the political elites, who deliberately devised the Union as a non-democratic 'problem-solving exercise' in the first place, and who do not wish it to be otherwise: they *want* decision-making at both levels – European and national – 'to evade the … constraint of popular democracy and accountability' (Mair 2008: 49; see also K-D. Wolf 2000). From this vantage point, the far-reaching claims made in academic debate about the impossibility of democracy in Europe resemble nothing more than a discourse designed to prove the political class right: it excuses as inevitable what is in fact the result of deliberate action.

For some time now, international political science has been taking the same line as the political actors, to the extent that the tricky subject of EU democracy has been evaded altogether. More precisely, while articles allegedly dealing with democracy do abound, a closer look at them reveals that, in point of fact, they merely discuss its surrogates at best. Subjects instead taking pride of place include output legitimation, citizen rights, deliberative bodies, and accountability. These elements are apparently thought to compensate – some more, some less – for the lack of democracy; and not just taken together, but singly as well. Scholars describe the EU as a non-majoritarian regulatory agency distinguished by expert decision-making; they deem it effective at producing outputs (desired by whom … ?); they praise it for granting rights to its citizens; they consider it accountable (to whom … ?), inasmuch as its institutions effectively check each other; and they even view it as working in (quasi-)democratic fashion, since its numerous committees are of a highly deliberative character. In short: the European political system is not so bad, after all; it is certainly not as black as it has sometimes been painted. For all we know, moreover, adding more elements of popular democracy may impair its performance rather than improve it.

Unfortunately, however, voters have repeatedly objected to this view of the matter, when asked in referenda to give their consent to quasi-constitutional documents enshrining such arrangements. They feel quite rightly that this wonderful new supra-national world is not theirs, that they do not belong. European integration, as they see it, went awfully wrong somewhere. I might add that, as I see it, the academic debate on Europe's democratic problem went seriously wrong too. The problem was not properly discussed, owing to the fact that, with few exceptions, all of those taking part in the debate had an overly narrow conception of democracy. It is true, no doubt, that a full-fledged representative, majoritarian party democracy of the Westminster type would not solve the problem: the 'European spaceship' would, in that case, remain as far above citizens and as unresponsive to them as the Brussels set-up is at present. There is accordingly little need to prove the impossibility of establishing such a system at the European level. This does *not* prove, however, that there is no *other* way of making the EU more democratic, or that alternative and more adequate institutionalisations of democracy cannot be conceived (see Abromeit 1998: Chapter 5). I shall return to this subject in the last section.

Why is it so difficult to talk about democracy in Europe?

The single-mindedness of political scientists in debating the possibilities and impossibilities of democratising the EU is all the more surprising, in light of the evidence that academic communities in the different member states take widely varying views on democracy: its character as such, its essentials and connotations, its specific value and its limits. For several years (2004–6), a small group of us – political scientists and public lawyers from various European countries – tried to discuss and explore notions and concepts of democracy, under the heading of 'National Traditions of Democratic Thought' (in the context of the CONNEX Research Group 2; see Abromeit 2007 and Curtin and Wille 2008). It was an interesting but futile experience, because we were literally unable to arrive at any common understanding of what democracy is all about. In fact, our notions of democracy varied so widely – both theoretically and normatively – that we could not even agree on an analytical framework for mapping out the differences in systematic fashion. For whenever an idea cropped up, it was a safe bet that one or more of us would object that 'this does not apply to us' (in most cases, by the way, it was the French tradition to which the idea could not be applied).

The problem is that, in trying to compare different democratic traditions, we cannot do without a notion of democracy that is stripped of its varying institutional clothing and laid bare in its core meaning – a core meaning which ought, in my view, to have something to do with its ultimate object and justification (see Abromeit 2002: 113–5). However, we can discuss this question of 'why democracy?' for years on end without reaching a consensus. Is it the 'pursuit of (individual) happiness'? The 'promotion of the general welfare'? The 'rule of reason'? Or is it merely the prevention of tyranny or a fallibilistic reaction to the impossibility of knowing the truth about the nature of the common good? These varied notions are incompatible, at least in part. It thus verges on the miraculous that, all the same, democracy is universally expected to have *something* to do with freedom and participation.

Within any one of the different national cultures such basic notions rarely derive from any consistent theory (whether drawn from native thinkers or borrowed from elsewhere); and even when they do, they have evolved within a specific mixture of older – for instance religious – traditions, historical experiences, social practices, and so on. Often, therefore, national core concepts of democracy are not 'genuinely democratic', but are rather drawn from non-political aspects of social life. A pre-democratic concept of consent, for example, is central to the Dutch democratic tradition. It can be traced back to Protestant and Catholic thinkers whose focus was not on individual self-determination or popular sovereignty, but on 'sovereignty in independent spheres of society' (Michels 2007: 9). Freedom, within this context, means 'freedom in restraint' – the restraint being the continuous necessity to reach consensus within the greater whole – and it is balanced by the principles of subsidiarity and of the plurality and autonomy of groups.

In France, the statist tradition took precedence over the democratic one, due to the lack of democratic and constitutional continuity. A single democratic tradition proper, in the sense of a common national understanding of what democracy really means, apparently does not exist (Xifaras 2006). Instead its place is taken by the doctrine of the 'unity of the republic', as embodied in the state and the law – both of them pre-democratic in their origins and independent of the various institutionalisations of democracy that France has known. Indeed, pre-democratic notions seem to have been formative for democratic thought in many places: in Britain, for example, the doctrine of 'parliamentary sovereignty' arose in medieval times, and is aristocratic rather than democratic in its origins. One of the exceptions is Swiss democracy, firmly rooted as it is in the medieval tradition of the 'Landsgemeinde', whereby 'sovereign' individuals ruled themselves through joint decisions. It bears emphasising, however, that the revival of direct democracy in Switzerland since the late nineteenth century is not explained solely by age-old practice and experience: there is also a 'systemic need' for a corrective to federal asymmetries – in order to build up trust and acceptance between the highly heterogeneous, multiple 'sovereign demoi' of the cantons. As our Swiss colleague expressed it, Switzerland is in fact a dem*oi*cracy, rather than a dem*o*cracy (Cheneval 2006; so much, accordingly, for the argument that the EU cannot be democratised because, instead of one *demos*, it has a multitude of *demoi*!).

These examples indicate why it is so difficult to arrive at an all-European understanding of the essence of democracy. When the core concepts of national democracies often derive from pre-democratic traditions, and democratic and pre-democratic ideas are inextricably mingled, it would appear to be very difficult – maybe next to impossible – to find a core concept common to them all. Our French colleague Xifaras summed up this situation nicely in the words: 'we have to admit that it is not possible to set *a priori* standards of what is democratic and what is not'. It is not to be wondered at, in view of all this, that the debate on European democracy has narrowed down to the demand for an elected parliament and for a modicum of public accountability: these are the lowest common denominator. Any deeper analysis of what democracy really means would have brought all the different notions to the fore – revealing that democracy, as such, is a highly contested concept.

What does accountability have to do with democracy?

Can public accountability and the existence of an elected parliament – to which those who govern must 'give account' – be considered the minimum core meaning of democracy? If so, why? And if not, why not?

For most British political scientists, public accountability (for the following see, in part, Bovens 2007a) is a critical component of democracy – perhaps *the* decisive element. Continentals do not even have a word for what Anglo-Saxons mean by it: an arrangement wherein politicians are answerable to voters, ministers to members of parliament, bureaucracies of various sorts to ministers, office-holders of the most varied kinds (including MPs) to the courts, etc. If this is taken to be the core of democracy, the crucial thing is that there be an intact chain of accountabilities (ending with the one enforced by the electorate), and that the entire process be public. To give a (once notorious) example: the concept behind the 'ministerial control' of nationalised British industries (Abromeit 1986) in bygone days was as follows: management ran the industry, and was held to account by the responsible minister; the latter was held to account by a Select Committee of Parliament, which published its minutes; and Parliament was held to account by the voters. In practice it did not work that way: ministerial control clashed with the 'managerial responsibility', discretion, and secrecy necessary for running a business and competing successfully with private industry. Hence the formal chain was interrupted: a senior official of the ministry was assigned to the industry's board. But rather than serving as part of the public forum and holding management to account, he became an insider. If he was soon 'house-trained' (the expression used at the British Steel Corporation), he would be treated as an equal; otherwise he would not be, and full information would not be provided him. As an insider, moreover, he was pledged to a high degree of secrecy when reporting to the Select Committee on Nationalised Industries, the body tasked with holding him to account. He probably furnished no more information, in fact, than the management itself was willing to give to the press.

It is a typical feature of *public* accountability nearly everywhere, in fact, that information is passed on in a highly selective and restricted manner. Small wonder, then, that the political system in which the concept originated is in fact famous for its culture of secrecy: civil servants are punished if they leak information about their department. In practice, the whole point of being held to account is to avoid being sanctioned; in theory, being sanctioned for bad conduct is the whole point of being held to account. The likelihood of suffering sanction grows with publicity. Accountability can therefore be quite acceptable to office-holders – when it is not public.

This is why, both in theory and in practice, forms of accountability *other* than the public and electoral type have taken precedence over the latter. To return to the case of the nationalised industries: after privatisation they were, if monopolies, assigned a watchdog (OFTEL, OFGAS, etc.) in the shape of a 'quasi-(non-)governmental organisation'. This organisation was staffed with experts from the world of business and finance (from the private sector, at any rate), and its charge was to search for inefficiencies and perhaps unsocial conduct. This is what is now called 'horizontal accountability': one bureaucracy supervises another, and there is no link to politics – let alone voters. The recent literature on accountability abounds with praise for arrangements of this type, such as 'mutual accountability' or even 'accountability networks', i.e. systems of checks and balances working within one policy domain (see, e.g. Scott 2000). If applied to the political sphere these involve a managerialisation of politics, inasmuch as they deal not with mandates or outcomes but with performance, cost-effectiveness, and the like. It is not democracy they enhance but rather – and at best – 'good governance', narrowly understood as efficiency. And even that remains in question, for these forms of accountability shun publicity: outsiders are not apprised of what goes on in the network, and it is the job of the actors themselves to hold each other to account. One is reminded of old-boy networks, wherein birds of a feather flock together.

Yet even in its two most celebrated forms – public accountability and constitutionally entrenched checks and balances – accountability cannot be equated with democracy. Let us begin with checks and balances. When two institutions within a system of government – say, two chambers of parliament – serve to check each other, this may or may not be good for policy outcomes (frequently it is not). But it is hard to see what it has to do with the people, who are not asked to pass a judgement on what is to them, as likely as not, mere bickerings going on above their heads. Judicial review, as a specific element within a system of checks and balances, is often praised as enhancing citizens' rights, and thus as being democratic *per se*. But it is not: the people are not asked in this case either whether – for example – they agree with the conclusion reached by judges that social benefits like child allowances ought (on the principle of equality) to be issued to the better-off as well as to poorer citizens. As to public accountability: it is rarely linked to any mandate given beforehand; nor is it, as an ex-post evaluation of government conduct, to be confused with responsiveness. The criteria for such an evaluation, moreover, are not necessarily those that the people themselves would choose; instead they reflect what politicians consider to be appropriate. This criticism may not apply to a political system in which 'manifesto politics' are a reliable habit. However, it certainly applies to the European political system, in which voters are not given the least chance to issue a mandate; and in which, in any case, they are not sufficiently well-informed to make such an evaluation.

What is democratic, anyway?

This brings us back to the question of what really is democratic. We have seen, after all, that mere accountability is not (or that it only is on very specific conditions). The sheer existence of an elected parliament is not democratic either, for elections may not be 'meaningful'; and parliaments and governments are perfectly capable – even elected ones – of behaving in autocratic fashion. I described above some of the difficulties in establishing an all-European consensus on what democracy really means. Let us try now once again, starting from the assumption that democracy has *something* to do with the people. Indeed, for a political system to be called democratic, it must *somehow* involve the people (and not just a few but rather all of them, equally): it must furnish them some means or other by which they can bring their wishes to bear on political decisions. The means for so doing may vary according to context; indeed they must, if they are to be effective.

They will also vary according to the objects democracy is expected to achieve. In section 2, I have listed the objects likely to be linked with democracy. I shall now briefly discuss them with an eye to which of these objects *necessarily* entails decision-making by the people.

First, preventing tyranny requires oversight and a form of accountability that discourages the abuse of power (Bovens 2007a: 463, calls this 'constitutional accountability'). This can be achieved by dint of institutions checking each other; active participation by citizens is not needed. In fact, some argue that such inter-organ supervision is better suited to the object, inasmuch as the people allow themselves every now and then to be persuaded by charismatic leaders to forgo the necessary checks.

Second, promoting the general welfare, in the shape of a prospering economy and/or widespread social benefits, may necessitate economic freedom, the 'free flow of capital', and the like; but the involvement of the people in political decision-making is not required here either. It is partaking rather than participating that is in question here: everybody getting his due share. Such an objective, it may be, is much likelier to be achieved by a government of experts than by popular democracy. Indeed, the latter may even be a stumbling block in the way of economic growth, as business experts tell us daily (neither voters nor party politicians being fully cognizant, supposedly, of the intricacies of managing the economy, and so being apt to make the wrong decisions).

Third, the fallibilistic approach to democracy aims at the gradual evolution of better political concepts for solving problems and furthering the common good. This calls for a constant readiness to revise political decisions and a willingness to experiment repeatedly with new and alternative programmes. These cannot be expected to originate in the electorate, but the latter may be asked to choose among them. However, the same can also be done – perhaps to better effect? – in deliberative circles comprising experts of various sorts.

Fourth, as for the 'rule of reason', it is more easily achieved if ordinary people are kept out, since they are prone (as theorists of deliberative democracy tell us) to egoistic passions and preferences which blind them to the most reasonable arguments, and which prevent them from appreciating what lies in the ('well-understood') interests of all.

Fifth, all of the above approaches conceptualise democracy as an expedient for reaching some goal lying beyond it. However, the last object we shall explore here – the (individual) 'pursuit of happiness' – is an altogether different case. The goal here is to enable individuals to lead a self-determined life. But of course individuals live in societies, which makes it inevitable that collective decisions affecting all or most of them will be made. Individuals thus face restrictions: they can no longer do as they like. If they are unable to participate in such decisions, therefore, their lives are not self- but rather other-determined. This particular democratic object, then, is the only one that clearly requires some kind of *joint* decision-making – the kind we call democratic. As Alain Touraine (1997: 12) puts it: 'democracy is the politics of the subject'. And as such, it is not an instrument for the achievement of any other goal; it is an end in itself.

We may conclude (assuming the reader concurs with my reasoning so far) that the essence of democracy is the participation – *effective* participation – in collective decisions of all individuals affected by them (Ross 1952; Dahl 1971). It is in connection with effectiveness that the different societal and political contexts come in. Participatory regimes do not all work in the same fashion everywhere; what is sufficient in one country may result in a democratic deficit in another; what is required in one place may be superfluous (just 'keeping the customer satisfied' and busy) elsewhere. The decisive variables are societal heterogeneity and political complexity (for the following, see Abromeit and Stoiber 2007: 50–1).

Electoral democracy – or electoral accountability – can yield a sufficiently effective participatory regime in a society which is fairly homogeneous, and in which the political system has a fairly simple structure. An additional requisite is that party competition be of such a nature as to allow voters to make sensible choices: that is, voters have to be properly informed about what to expect, and they must know how parties conducted themselves in the previous period(s). In fact, 'proper information' is crucial for accountability in all its variants. As we all know, however, party leaders and campaigners are usually not so keen on giving proper information or on publicly committing themselves, preferring to act instead upon hidden agendas; while programmes, when they are presented at all, serve merely as window-dressing. In short (and as mentioned before), electoral accountability requires reliable 'manifesto politics'. If the only choice is between 'the head and the emotions' (as one of the core principles of political advertising has it), then just going to the polls will not offer any effective – or 'meaningful' – participation.

Societal heterogeneity – a high number of cleavages, the existence of distinctive ('structural') minorities, the non-existence of a 'natural' majority, etc. – calls for a different regime. It starts with the need for minority ('proportional') representation and for super-majorities (in parliament), and ends with the need for direct-democratic elements. Mere electoral accountability cannot work properly in such societies: in such a setting, discontented minorities are not in a position to sanction politicians, because – being minorities – they will be outvoted. Hence the need for minority vetoes, which transform the political system into a 'negotiation democracy'. The main feature of such a system is that representatives from various minorities and groups are bound together in complex interactions for negotiating compromises and get integrated eventually into elite cartels. This serves to alienate these representatives from their voters, and to render politics opaque and incomprehensible to the latter: voters cannot tell who is to be held accountable – which party and which politicians – for any given decision. No one has to take responsibility for political decisions. Everyone can put the blame on everybody else, and nobody can be sanctioned for their record in upcoming elections. In such a situation, there is no electoral accountability.

The same can be said of any complex political system (such as a federation, for instance). The typical result is an intricate system of negotiations for overcoming blockades. The same problem of blurred responsibilities arises, leaving voters at a loss as to how to react and how to ensure that their choices are heeded. Even worse in this respect are systems of decision-making, like corporatism, that give a policy role to collective societal actors: there is namely no way to hold private actors (business leaders, for example) accountable. We may therefore venture the following generalisation: whenever a system of collective decision-making features a plurality of veto-players, thus generating elite cartels whose dealings remain opaque to citizens, the mere existence of an elected parliament will not suffice to ensure democracy. Such systems – frequently named consociational – are autocracies in (quasi-) democratic disguise. They can only be made democratic and accountable through direct-democratic means – in particular, through the institution of the direct-democratic veto (see Abromeit 1998; more recently, Magnette and Papadopoulos 2008).

This is not the place to discuss at length the pros and cons of direct democracy. Suffice it to say that direct-democratic instruments are not always effective, any more than other modes of participation are. The decisive factor for their effectiveness is what we elsewhere have called 'dominance structures' (Abromeit and Stoiber 2007: 53ff.): i.e. patterns of strong allegiance that can be mobilised at will by political or societal leaders, and which enable the latter to exercise great influence on the thoughts and preferences of their clients (such influence being the correlate of a high 'partyness of society'; see Katz 1987: 8).

Conclusion

The point I wish to make is that it is difficult – next to impossible, in fact – to make the EU truly democratic by stubbornly following the road to electoral democracy. There are too many obstacles in the way of this path to democratisation – above and beyond the EU's multiple *demoi* and its lack of a collective identity. That the former obstacle can be overcome by broadening the narrow concept of representative democracy is shown by the example of Switzerland. The greater problems are the ones posed by the resulting 'non-majoritarian' and consociational traits of the European political system, which result both from heterogeneity and from the insistence of national governments on keeping their position as strong veto-players intact. This in turn has led the Commission to find ways and means by which to circumvent the stubborn leaders of the member states – e.g. through comitology, as well as by inviting collective societal actors to participate. This has served to make European decision-making even more opaque than the institutional set-up by itself would have made it. Here again the Swiss example points to a solution. The specific obstacles to democratisation we have identified can only be surmounted in one way: if voters are not in a position to contest *politicians*, then they must have a means by which to contest their *policies*, in the shape of a direct-democratic veto. Refraining from re-electing politicians is not the only way of holding them to account; rejecting their decisions is another way.

All of the contextual factors described above indicate that the EU has developed exactly the kind of political system in which the electoral mode of participation is not effective. At the same time, however, it has *not* yet developed the kind of dominance structures that render direct-democratic instruments ineffective (least of all does it exhibit, for example, a high partyness of society). Such instruments offer, it would appear, the only way of making EU decision-making both responsive and accountable to the peoples of Europe – and hence democratic: democratic in the sense of dem*oi*cracy.

Sceptics might argue that methods that work well with the Swiss – united as they are by a long (and peaceful!) history, and not least by the pride the multiple dem*oi* take in making up their democracy – cannot be expected to do so well in a 'young' Union, the multiple dem*oi* of which view each other with distrust as foreigners. Yet the matter of trust and distrust is a tricky one. European integration was and is an elite project, albeit one that long benefited from a 'permissive consensus' (which did not really amount to support) on the part of its peoples. But this consensus has eroded since the 1990s, as referenda on recent treaties – not least the constitutional one – have demonstrated. Now there is distrust everywhere – and not only of 'those bureaucrats in Brussels', but also of (business) elites in the member states. At the present moment, it does not seem unlikely that European citizens feel their trust growing in fellow citizens who unite with them in opposition to decisions taken in Brussels – by representatives who are 'foreign' to them all, in more senses than one. Trust of this kind will grow if such opposition can be made effective and successful: by direct-democratic means. Having a say in European matters will also enhance a sense of – maybe even a pride in – belonging to the European democratic sphere.[1]

Notes

1 I have outlined in detail elsewhere (Abromeit 1998: Chapter 5) how to proceed with introducing direct-democratic elements into the European constitutional system. Direct-democratic vetoes should take precedence over popular initiatives (contrary to what the constitutional convention proposed), and care should be taken that voters from one country not be able to dominate the rest. The guiding principle ought to be the following: whenever the peoples of various countries strongly feel that their preferences have been overruled by some directive or other, they must be ensured a means by which effectively to object.

4 Putting limits on accountability avoidance

Sverker Gustavsson

Political theorists tend to argue one-sidedly in favour of more democratic accountability (Ross 1952; Kielmansegg 1977; Spitz 1984; Abromeit 2002; Lewin 2007). When the EU is in question, however, arguments for less accountability must be considered as well. Otherwise, we will fail to understand that the existing Union is the result of two contrary strivings. On the one hand, the sphere of national decision-making is subject to democratic control. On the other, 'we the people' are bound by a suprastate beyond electoral reach.

As a matter of pure logic, accountability avoidance is the opposite of accountability promotion. In real politics, however, the inconsistency between these two ambitions is overcome on the basis of the notion that 'output' legitimacy can compensate for a lack of 'input' legitimacy. This is another way of describing the everyday distinction between substance and procedure. It is the idea of government 'for' the people – rather than 'of' or 'by' them – that supposedly makes such a double standard acceptable (Scharpf 1999: 6–28; Bartolini 2005: 165–76).

The notion of output legitimacy raises an important problem. According to this idea, an order is accepted on account of 'its capacity to solve problems requiring collective solutions because they could not be solved through individual action, through market exchanges, or through voluntary cooperation in civil society' (Scharpf 1999: 11). Such a notion would seem, on the face of it, to be both reasonable and pragmatically sound. But if output legitimacy is such a good idea, how is it that accountability avoidance has not become the only game in town? Why do limiting procedural arrangements persist – arrangements defended on a basis 'unrelated to any costs and benefits calculations'? (Bartolini 2005: 168).

The answer I offer is close to common sense. Universal suffrage, freedom of speech, and freedom of association were conquered in the aftermath of the French and American revolutions, and they remained contested in wars and political upheavals throughout the twentieth century. Therefore, output legitimacy cannot entirely compensate for the absence of opposition, or the lack of any opportunity to change office-holders and public policies. It is for this reason that accountability avoidance cannot always have the upper hand.

However, history is not the only limiting factor. What happens in the long run is also a matter of choice. If 'we the people' cannot make an effective difference by casting our votes, our belief in the very idea of accountability will be seriously undermined. This makes it difficult to argue that avoiding accountability in the short run is necessary if the maximum degree of accountability is to be rescued in the long run. Nevertheless, that sort of calculus is actually being made, and it is worth taking seriously.

In what follows, I begin by defining accountability and locating it within a wider spectrum of policy options. I then proceed to dissect two salient arguments for not holding power to account. One is the idea of cleavage-management; the other that of the public interest. I conclude by arguing that these two reasons – however effective they may be from the standpoint of output legitimacy – fail to answer the question I have posed. Why are political theorists and politicians so hesitant when it comes to *complete* accountability avoidance?

Broad or narrow use of the key term?

Whether we argue for more accountability or for less, two different approaches to the question of definition present themselves. One is to take the path shown by Robert Keohane in his contribution to this volume, and by Mark Bovens in his much-cited 2007 article. These two authors suggest we broaden the meaning of the term. According to Bovens, for example, we should define accountability as 'a relationship between an actor and a forum, in which the actor has an obligation to explain and to justify his or her conduct, the forum can pose questions and pass judgement, and the actor may face consequences' (Bovens 2007a: 450).

A broad definition of this kind encourages a view of accountability as constituting a very wide category – one that includes not just democratic, fiscal, legal, market, and participatory accountability, but public-reputational accountability as well. We are thereby tempted, both empirically and normatively, to regard the different senses of the concept as comparable and interchangeable alternatives. One positive aspect of this is that the normative issue does not get mixed up with the question of definition so easily. On the other hand, if we choose to stretch (Sartori 1970: 1041) the meaning of the term that far, it becomes difficult to focus on what is controversial and contested. The central matter at stake tends to drown in an all-embracing discussion about legal, economic, and social issues.

The other and – as I see it – more fruitful approach is to use the word in a narrow sense: that of *democratic* accountability. This makes it easier to concentrate on the controversial question: namely, is accountability something to be promoted or something to be avoided? If any conceivable forum or sanctioning mechanism is thought to promote accountability, the conclusion lies close at hand that one type of accountability can substitute for another. There is less risk of that if we stick to a more parsimonious use of the word.

According to my minimalist definition – and in line with the notion of a 'strong' mechanism set out in the introductory chapter – accountability means that 'we the people' are able – on the basis of universal suffrage, freedom of association, and freedom of information – to reject one set of office-holders and public policies in favour of another, and to do so in a way that is genuinely effective.

A broader understanding of democratic accountability – in terms of markets, organisation, administration, public opinion, and the like – tempts me to contextualise my understanding of the concept. It happens easily that the democratic accountability in the sense adumbrated above – whereby 'we the people' are able to govern ourselves, by changing policies and office-holders – becomes merely one among many different possible solutions. The fact that my definition is a contested one is no argument for adopting the broadest possible analytical scheme. Differences should not be glossed over so much that our concepts become useless from the standpoint of highlighting what is contested and controversial. On the contrary, as a rule we should neither shun disagreement nor unnecessarily stretch a concept needed for our analysis. If fruitful controversy is to be advanced, it is best to delimit our key concepts in such a way that they enable us to call in question how other researchers describe, explain, and evaluate the political phenomenon in question.

Democratic accountability is fundamentally controversial. Therefore, the concept should be defined with an eye to what is being contested: namely, whether 'we the people' should be able to change policies and office-holders. In light of this definition, the crucial question is whether the electorate should be *inclusive*, in the sense of universal suffrage; and *effective*, in the sense of actually being able to influence the legal and fiscal order (Ross 1952: 86–90). Using the key term in a broad sense makes it harder to figure out what is really causing the factual and normative disagreement. On the contrary, it encourages us to look in directions which are basically irrelevant.

Five main positions: two purist ones at each extreme, three in-between

From the standpoint of democratic accountability so defined, it is easy to see that there are basically five positions in the debate on whether it should be promoted or avoided.

Within the broader menu of conceivable recommendations, there are two theoretically pure – and in a pragmatic sense extreme – positions. According to both, the basic arrangement in Europe today – monetary union in the absence of fiscal union, and double asymmetry as to both procedure and substance – is empirically and normatively unsustainable. The proponents of these two pure positions are highly critical, accordingly, of the 'balance of terror' (Gustavsson 2008: 328) that characterises the living constitution. The first asymmetry is the procedural democratic deficit: i.e. the fact that the power to legislate is centralised, while electoral accountability is not. The second asymmetry – which is intertwined with the first – relates to political content:

policies for the market and currency are centralised, while those for positive integration are not (Gustavsson 2006: 165–8). 'Positive' policies are those aimed at mitigating the social consequences arising from the free movement of capital, goods, services and labour. The four freedoms form part of the basic treaties; social policies do not. The latter are much more difficult to handle at the European level than are regulatory policies aiming at a 'negative' integration marked by de-regulation and the creation of a single market (Scharpf 1999: 43–83).

To a full-fledged *federalist*, social and fiscal policies should be made suprastatist as well, and the European Parliament should be given the same constitutional status as the German Bundestag. A full-fledged *confederalist* stakes out an equally pure position, but at the other extreme: the suprastatist parts of the living constitution should be re-nationalised, thus making the Union symmetrical through movement in the opposite direction. In other words: full-fledged federalists and full-fledged confederalists are in full agreement that democratic accountability and actual decision-making should take place on the same constitutional tier – either at the national level or at the federal level (Dahl 1982a: 98–100). One might call this 'the either-or criterion'.

As judged by the either-or criterion, however, EU decision-makers are not held to account on the appropriate level. Exponents of the purist critique take aim, from both ends, at defenders of the constitutional status quo in the middle. These defenders make a wide variety of policy recommendations. However, they have one thing in common. In practice, that is, they favour retaining the established asymmetrical solution to the problem of how national self-determination is to be combined with partial federalism (Gustavsson 2008: 326–9). Within this broad centrist camp, three basic alternatives can be fruitfully distinguished as to what should be done with today's living constitution – characterised as it is by double asymmetry, monetary union without fiscal union, and a constitutional balance of terror. In a compacted and stylised way, these three in-between positions may be described as follows:

According to the first, today's living constitution needs to be corrected by a political technique that I would term *marginal majoritarianism*. It must be admitted, according to adherents of this view, that our founding fathers made a historic mistake. But their mistake can be gradually repaired, through deliberate politicisation along lines of left and right (Hix 2008).

According to a second line of thought in the central part of the spectrum, today's living constitution embodies what can best be described as an *end-of-history* notion. Our founding fathers, in the view of proponents of this notion, created something historically marvellous and admirable, and we should try to understand and protect it – against all sorts of politicisation, and in the face of worries about its inherent risks (Majone 2005; Moravcsik 2008).

Finally, according to a third line of thought in the middle portion of the spectrum, today's living EU constitution is best described as an *informal pact of confidence* between the suprastate and its member democracies. Admittedly, our founding fathers made a historic mistake. However, the appropriate response is neither politicisation nor self-congratulatory enthusiasm. Rather, the uneven de-nationalisation that is taking place demands extreme political caution, if devastating outbursts of nationalism are to be avoided. There is no good answer to the question of what justifies the absence of accountability for suprastatist legislation and rule-adjudication. The Union should therefore respect national democracy, in exchange for the loyal support of its member states for suprastatist rule (Scharpf 1994, 1999, 2008, 2009; Bartolini 2005, 2008).

Viewed from any of the other standpoints, it is the end-of-history position that is particularly provocative. Its thrust is that we have reached a constitutional settlement and equilibrium which is sustainable over the long term, which requires no further revision, and which need not even inspire any general precaution. What specific balance between promotion and avoidance makes the proponents of this argument so sure? How do they reason in defence of the position that the combination which is presently established – of a mixed economy and a mixed polity – is the one for the ages?

In my view, the end-of-history argument for avoiding accountability boils down to two key contentions. These ideas are historically interrelated, yet analytically distinguishable. One is that we should avoid accountability because cleavage-management is facilitated thereby. The other is that we should avoid it because policies in the public interest are promoted thereby. How can we fruitfully interpret these two reasons? And how can we take them into proper consideration, even while seeking actually to promote accountability?

Facilitating cleavage-management

The most prominent proponent of the *cleavage-management* argument is Arend Lijphart. His studies of power-sharing and majority rule throughout the world and at different times have convinced him that majority rule is 'a flawed paradigm' (Lijphart 2007: 111). This is not the place to assess his general argument. The interesting thing here is what he has to say about accountability avoidance as a method for managing cleavages within this particular Union.

In his globe-spanning exposition of 'patterns of democracy', Lijphart presents the EU – together with Switzerland and Belgium – as the most prominent example of a consensus-oriented political system. 'Instead of concentrating power in the hands of the majority, the consensus model tries to share, disperse, and restrain power in a variety of ways' (Lijphart 1999: 34). In practice, he avers, there are at least ten such methods, including executive power-sharing in broad coalition cabinets, interest-group corporatism, federal and decentralised government, strong bicameralism, constitutional rigidity, judicial review, and central-bank independence. According to Lijphart, majority rule is incompatible with the needs of deeply divided, plural societies – and the EU 'is clearly such a plural society' (Lijphart 1999: 46). All of his criteria are met by the way the Union is organised. It is easy to predict, he further argues, that the Union will eventually become a state. However, from the standpoint of accountability avoidance, that will not make much difference. 'If and when the EU develops into a sovereign European state, its institutions are likely to change … but it is not likely to stray far from the consensus model' (Lijphart 1999: 47).

In an analysis of Canada and the United States in the early 1990s, Lijphart and his co-authors, Ronald Rogowski and Kent Weaver, elaborate in a most illuminating way on accountability avoidance as a solution to the problem of deep-seated cleavages. Their argument applies not just to the EU, but to every conceivable system. They take their point of departure in the idea that cleavage-management is the fundamental purpose of political institutions (Weaver 1992: 9–15; Lijphart *et al.* 1993: 303–6).

Basically, there are five ways of managing cleavages, Kent Weaver claims in his chapter on Canada. *Majoritarianism* is functional for avoiding stalemate, and it gives politicians 'incentives to make appeals to voters across cleavage lines in order to build a majority or plurality of support' (Weaver 1992: 11). *Consociational* mechanisms, on the other hand, 'involve broad consultation and bargaining among elites representing the most important groups in a society, with the groups choosing their own representatives.' When policy changes need to be adopted quickly, they facilitate the reaching of broad agreements (Weaver 1992: 11–12). The *limited-government* mechanisms, meanwhile, includes all sorts of minority-rights legislation, as well as permanent delegation to lower levels of the political system (and higher ones, I would add, in the case of the EU). It strengthens the position of the minority in question by 'complicating the sequence of decision-making or by barring some issues from the agenda altogether' (Weaver 1992: 13). *Devolutionary* mechanisms represent a fourth method for taking an issue off the political agenda. They do so by granting decision-making autonomy to legally identified groups along territorial or cultural lines. *Arbitral* mechanisms, finally, place 'decisionmaking authority in the hands of officials who are not directly accountable to voters and who are only weakly accountable and thus need not be concerned about maintaining the political support of majorities.' By definition, such mechanisms offer an institutionalised opportunity 'to resist decisions demanded by political majorities that would oppress minority rights, especially if those institutions enjoy widespread legitimacy' (Weaver 1992: 15).

After analysing the mixture of majoritarian and non-majoritarian techniques of cleavage-management used in the United States, Lijphart and his co-authors pull the threads together. They conclude that the American form of power-sharing is less effective than another blend of methods would be. One reason for this is that the U.S. political system, due to the bipartisan character of its electoral structure, is in fact much more majoritarian than it might seem on the surface. Another reason is that the four non-majoritarian mechanisms tend to hamper the redress of political grievances. In a contradictory way, this makes the promotion of social peace less efficient. Mechanisms 'that require consensus or near-consensus may actually inhibit effective cleavage management by allowing "minorities of the majority" to block such redress'. As a result, the redress of legitimate grievances becomes so difficult in practice that the use of these non-majoritarian techniques tends more often to deepen than to overcome cleavages (Lijphart *et al.* 1993: 315).

Lijphart is known as a principled defender of the consensus model. Here, however, he admits that there are limits to accountability avoidance. Sometimes, if politicians shut their eyes and ears in an effort to protect minorities, the effect is actually to make cleavages still deeper. If cleavage-management is the goal, they must instead be able to act in order to meet new historical needs, thereby contributing to a self-reinforcing trust in politics and political institutions. After all, democratic accountability does not serve only to deepen cleavages. Majority rule, for example, cannot work unless forces seeking a majority try to form coalitions across cleavages. The fruitful contrast, argues Lijphart in his latest book, is therefore between 'bare-majority and broad-majority models of democracy' (Lijphart 2007: 12).

When push comes to shove, then, Lijphart is reluctant to go the whole hog. That is an interesting fact, in light of my general argument. For even where pure cleavage-management is concerned, accountability avoidance proves unsuitable for the purpose: that of maximising consensus. If the avoidance of disagreement and opposition is stressed too heavily, *more* rather than *less* conflict can easily result. In addition, I would argue that Lijphart is mistaken to put Belgium, Switzerland, and the EU together in the same consensus category. This is misleading, as I see it. In Belgium and Switzerland, namely, the composition of the broad majority can vary, according to the results of general elections. In the EU, by contrast, the very point is that *no* joint election is effective when it comes to determining the composition of the Commission, the Council, and the ECB.

Promoting the public interest

Let us turn now to the second main reason for accountability avoidance cited by adherents of the end-of-history position. This will give us a basis for comparison. The key notion for this argument is not cleavage-management but the *public interest*. The idea is that policies should be in the 'real' and 'long-term' interest of those affected. Voters do not always have the capacity to judge what is best for them. Therefore, a broad and ill-informed popular majority should not be allowed – at least not in any effective way – to affect the functioning of the executive, the legislative, the judicial, or the monetary authority.

The main champions of the public-interest argument are Giandomenico Majone and Andrew Moravcsik. In order to clarify their way of justifying accountability avoidance, I shall concentrate on two of their statements. First,

I consider what the latter writes, together with Andrea Sangiovanni, in a *Festschrift* dedicated to Fritz Scharpf. In this meditation on the 'reformability' of modern democracies, Moravcsik and his co-author portray accountability avoidance as a technique that has been established in order to compensate for an inherent social democratic bias in the political systems of the Union's member states (Moravcsik and Sangiovanni 2003: 134–46). The second statement to which I wish to call the reader's attention is Majone's claim that market integration, market-preserving public policies, and participatory democracy form 'an impossible trinity' (Majone 2005: 181–201).

Moravcsik and Sangiovanni take their point of departure in what I characterised at the beginning of this chapter as a specific combination of double asymmetry, monetary union without fiscal union, and an informal constitutional balance of terror. Whether we like it or not, the two combined asymmetries are fundamental to the really existing Union. As the informal-pact-of-confidence theorists Scharpf and Bartolini see it, these asymmetries are best addressed through a twofold approach. At an empirical level, accordingly, they claim that double asymmetry undermines the problem-solving capacity of both the Union and its member states. Normatively, they argue for expanding the space for political action in fiscal and social affairs, at both European and national levels. In other words, they recommend a double strategy. On the one hand, we should try to constitutionalise social rights at the European level. On the other, we should try to reinforce the informal pact according to which the suprastate respects the policies of its member states in exchange for their loyalty to the Union as a historical project.

One interesting feature in this context is the sharp disagreement between end-of-history theorists and their informal-pact-of-confidence counterparts regarding the presumed 'neutrality' of double asymmetry, from a substantive point of view. Double asymmetry, according to the former, is indeed biased against social democracy, and in favour of market-liberal solutions. This is according to design. For double asymmetry 'is not a policy designed to be neutral, but a policy designed to counteract pre-existing biases in national policy'. The problem, as Moravcsik and Sangiovanni see it, is that 'European social welfare systems entrench powerful special interests at the expense of the longer-term interests of a more diffuse citizenry'. From that perspective the function of the EU, is to provide 'a forum to offset the national under-representation of diffuse interests'. Hence, they conclude, 'a neo-liberal EU may in fact be output *legitimate*' (Moravcsik and Sangiovanni 2003: 134).

There is an elementary distinction, however, which is conspicuous by its absence in this polemical passage. It is one thing whether or not the EU, in its present-day form, contains a bias against social democracy and for market liberalism. It is another thing whether or not we as observers like or dislike that bias. Both questions, certainly, are interesting in this context. But both would benefit from being analysed and answered separately.

As to the normative aspect, informal-pact-of-confidence theorists take it for granted that procedures need to be neutral; if they are not, they will not be open, ready, or useful for continuous problem-solving. Democracy should be defined procedurally, and the formal treaties should lack policy content. Double asymmetry is thus something to be disliked, according to these theorists. What the public interest requires is not a theoretical given. It is rather something to be decided continually in practice, by the people and their representatives. By contrast, the underlying idea of the end-of-history theorists is that we can and should distinguish between justifiable and unjustifiable preferences. The very point of double asymmetry, as they see it, is that it gives a better 'balance' between those interpretations of the public interest which are analytically justifiable and those which are not.

When push comes to shove, it all boils down to the question of who is to decide upon the justifiability of preferences. Is that the task of the voters? Or is an expert solution to this problem available – a solution that can be constitutionalised? At the end of their chapter, Moravcsik and Sangiovanni suggest that Scharpf would be better advised – in his efforts to defend social democracy against market liberalism – to argue for 'his' policy content on the basis of pure normative theory, and to claim it is 'his' notion that ought to be constitutionalised. In their view, the force of Scharpf's argument lies more in his commitment to social democracy, and less in his insistence on the possibility of effective electoral support for a policy content which is social democratic rather than neo-liberal (Moravcsik and Sangiovanni 2002: 142–6).

In his book from 2005, Majone takes the public-interest argument yet one step further than Moravcsik and Sangiovanni. He does so by actively addressing the question of why accountability should be avoided. He argues, namely, that the EU is a market-preserving federal arrangement based on transnational constitutionalism. The specific combination of double asymmetry, a living constitution, and a vertical balance of terror has a beneficial effect. The straitjacket imposed by these three elements makes the policies of member states better than they would be if full-fledged democratic accountability obtained (whether at European or national level, as called for by the pure theories of democratic federalism and democratic confederalism respectively). We should in fact be grateful, Majone avers, that our Union is as intelligently organised as it is.

As Majone sees it, the transnational constitutional straitjacket offers a way out of that 'eclipse of constitutionalism' which, by historical accident, came to dominate twentieth-century Europe. The economic role of the state increased immensely during that period, on account of the need to tax, spend, and borrow to finance two world wars as well as far-reaching welfare provisions. It was more or less inevitable, against that background, that an old constitutional truth would be rediscovered: that 'discretionary powers can be abused and the prevention of such abuse is, to a large extent, a matter of institutional and constitutional design' (Majone 2005: 197).

The point Majone wants to make is that there are two forms of constitutionalism: one national, the other transnational. National constitutionalism means that the parliament of a sovereign country binds itself for the future by writing certain legislative competences and aspects of its legal structure into a constitution. Laws found therein are more difficult to change than are other laws, but they can still be altered. In a transnational constitutional arrangement, however, the parliaments in question bind themselves much more effectively. That is because they decide to *share* their legislative competences with their counterparts from the other member states, thus binding themselves by treaty rather than by their own constitutional rules. Alterations thus become impossible, unless all member states agree to them. According to Majone, embedding one's own national problem-solving capacity in a transnational constitutional structure is a more effective way of promoting the public interest than is national constitutionalism. In the latter case, namely, the nationally defined people and its representatives can alter the constitution relatively freely – without being hampered by any transnational obligations enjoining them to follow the common rules of a larger union.

For Majone, 'the contribution of transnational constitutionalism to the idea and practice of democracy consists … in affirming the values of the liberal nation-state by policing its boundaries against abuse'. The main lesson of European integration is that 'supranational rules can be reasonably effective even without the traditional state monopoly of coercive power' (Majone 2005: 199). The Union lacks, namely, any military, fiscal, or monetary resources of its own. Its impact rather reflects the normative obligations undertaken by its member states – to accept the straitjacket of double asymmetry, monetary union without fiscal union, and a constitutional balance of terror.

In its fundamental features, this theory of how to promote the public interest through accountability avoidance echoes the argument made by Joseph Weiler, in his much-cited book on trans-European constitutionalism. The last resort, for both Majone and Weiler, is a voluntarily enforced 'policing' of the boundaries of the nation-state against abuse. Boundaries, in this view, are not just 'frontiers in the legal-geographical sense of separating one nation-state from another'. There is also a second type of boundary, which 'delimits the nation from the state'; as well as a third, which delimits 'the internal consciousness … of those making up the nation'. This is another way of saying that European nation-states have a record of external war, oppression of civil society, and intolerance against all kinds of minorities that do not belong. But we do not need, in order to 'police' these three borders *between* and *within* member-states, to create a 'Jacobean-type centralized Europe'. It is quite enough to place 'the hitherto warring Member States within a political union of federal governance' (Weiler 1999: 340–1).

The reference to a 'Jacobean-type centralized Europe' helps us understand Majone's notion of a market-preserving federalism based on transnational constitutionalism. At the end, he locates his theory within the notion of a third stage: 'from democracy in the national state to democracy in the transnational state' (Dahl 1989: 320). The three-stage historical trajectory – from city-state through nation-state to transnational state – will not consist of any mechanical extrapolation of national principles and institutions to areas and levels of governance where democracy as we know it cannot flourish. 'Rather, an essential feature of the transformed democracy will be its ability to extend the scope of democratic accountability to areas that representative institutions had previously abandoned to executive prerogative' (Majone 2005: 201). Along with other end-of-history theorists, Majone wants to 'seize the EU opportunity to establish a superior-order economic constitution capable of weakening "rent-seeking" activities at the national level from the outside' (Bartolini 2008: 7).

As the end-of-history theorists see it, the 'public interest' is better served by a market-preserving and asymmetrical order than by one in which a parliamentary majority is held to account in symmetrical fashion – whether at the national *or* the European level. As democracy undergoes its third transformation, a market-preserving federalism based on transnational constitutionalism serves as a necessary straitjacket. The substantive policies thereby promoted accord with the precepts of neo-liberalism, which seems to be synonymous with the 'public interest' in today's end-of-history discourse.

Opposition: classical, of principle, or waning?

For the sake of discussion, I shall refrain from disputing the cleavage-management and public-interest arguments for accountability avoidance. The question that then becomes interesting is why these two arguments do not seem to trump all other considerations. How is it that advocates of accountability avoidance appear, notwithstanding everything, to be somewhat hesitant to give output legitimacy the ultimate upper hand? What would be, from their point of view, a reasonable counter-argument in favour of at least a minimum of majority rule?

When answering that question, I think, we should take the broader historical context into consideration. According to our present Western self-understanding, the two world wars and the Cold War were fought precisely on the grounds that universal suffrage, freedom of expression, and freedom of association were worth all the enormous sacrifice. Rolling back these conquests is not, accordingly, a serious alternative for proponents of accountability avoidance. They too, after all, view themselves as historically rooted in the Western context.

The meaning of this caveat becomes clear when we recall the Chinese and Russian reluctance to move beyond liberalising the economy to liberalising the polity as well (Gat 2007). Where the EU is concerned, after all, the end-of-history position does not issue in any suggestion to disfranchise parts of the electorate, or to re-introduce public censorship, or to legalise union-busting. Universal suffrage, freedom of expression, and freedom of association are considered to have been conquered once and for all.

Within this particular self-understanding, which derives from the upheavals and world wars of the twentieth century, the notion of *legitimate opposition* stands out as crucial:

> Political opposition gives voice. By losing opposition, we lose voice, and by losing voice we lose control of our own political systems. It is not at all clear how that control might be regained, either in Europe or at home, or how we might eventually restore meaning to [Robert] Dahl's third great milestone on the road to building democratic institutions.
>
> (Mair 2007: 17)

In other words: if we take the right to vote, the right to express ourselves, and the right to unionise for granted, then we also think we have the right to disagree without being considered disloyal. From the standpoint of input legitimacy, even an end-of-history theorist might argue – quite correctly, I would say – that the practical implication of these three freedoms cannot be ignored. Taken together, namely, these three freedoms imply an elementary principle of political liberalism: that 'we the people' must be able – *effectively* – to replace current office-holders and public policies with others.

In my view, the most fruitful analysis of the problem of legitimate opposition is not a futuristic one, like the one Robert Dahl presented in the first issue of *Government and Opposition* in 1965. In that issue, let us recall, he expressed a hope that 'new forms of structural opposition' would arise as 'a product of long evolution and hard struggle, welfare-oriented, centralised, bureaucratic, tamed and controlled by competition among highly organised élites, and, in the perspectives of the ordinary citizen, somewhat remote, distant and impersonal even in small countries like Norway and Sweden' (Dahl 1965: 21). New forms may arise, undoubtedly. In my view, however, we should instead take our point of departure in a distinction between three different attitudes towards opposition – attitudes which have been present in Europe since the days of the French Revolution. Paradoxical as it may seem, a historical perspective may be more fruitful than a futuristic one for clarifying the problems posed by marginal majoritarianism, the end-of-history argument, and the idea of an informal pact of confidence.

The historical perspective I have in mind is the one taken by Otto Kirchheimer, a German political scientist who experienced Weimar. According to Kirchheimer, there are basically three ways of thinking about political disagreement, each corresponding to a particular form taken by political opposition. The first type of opposition is the *classical* form originating in eighteenth-century England, in which government and opposition hold certain critical ideas in common, and in which the latter is considered legitimate within the living constitution. The second is opposition *of principle*, which is 'bent not only on wrenching power from the government of today but on ending once and for all the system on which that government rests' (Kirchheimer 1957: 127). In such a system, the opposition is illegitimate and unconstitutional. The third type of opposition is the *waning* kind, in which co-government or cartel arrangements prevail. Throughout the history of the European state system since the French Revolution, Kirchheimer claimed, legitimate opposition in the British sense has been the exception that proves the rule, rather than the empirically predominant way in which disagreement has been handled. It has been much more common to allow opposition to wane, or to let it become opposition of principle. Sometimes, in fact, these two approaches have been applied simultaneously, and in such a way that they reinforce each other.

It would be misleading to say that Kirchheimer's threefold classification of approaches to opposition solves the problem of what should ultimately limit accountability avoidance. It does us a service, however, in clarifying what is at stake in the debate among the five main positions in the debate on the future of the living EU constitution. Federalists and confederalists take it for granted that opposition should be of the legitimate kind. They are accordingly negative to all three of the half-way solutions that lie between their own pure and in a certain sense extreme positions. The idea of legitimate opposition also animates one of the three positions in the middle part of the spectrum: that of marginal majoritarianism. Proponents of this position argue that a more visible left-right confrontation in all parts of the EU system will impel the living constitution to develop, in a dynamic way, into an all-embracing European system with a governing majority and a legitimate minority in opposition.

In sum, I would say that three of the five positions incorporate the unproblematic idea of legitimate opposition. The two remaining positions, both of which fall in the middle of the spectrum, remain to be characterised. We can do this with the help of Kirchheimer's theory of how disagreement is handled under modern conditions. According to the first of the two positions, European constitutional history has found its balance – a balance both inherently reasonable and sustainable over the long term. According to the second, an informal pact of mutual confidence between the Union and its member states is the only feasible way to handle the mistake made by our founding fathers.

The end-of-history position set out by Lijphart, Majone, and Moravcsik incorporates Kirchheimer's notion of waning opposition. These authors adduce, as a matter of fact, two diametrically opposed arguments in favour of their view that the EU must not, for the sake of its long-term sustainability, let loose the forces of majority rule, opposition, and disagreement. The theory behind the cleavage-management argument is that deep-seated social and cultural differences require us to maintain accountability avoidance. By contrast, the theory behind the public-interest argument presumes that fundamental unanimity prevails. Double asymmetry, monetary union without fiscal union, and a constitutional balance of terror lie in our true and long-term interest, regardless of our subjective notions on the subject. As so often in the history of political ideas, two contrary notions – in this case, that basic cleavages obtain and that unanimity is complete – work in parallel. For notwithstanding their mutually contradictory character, they both serve as arguments for accountability avoidance.

According to the second of the two remaining positions, an informal pact of mutual confidence is needed. This viewpoint, associated with Scharpf and Bartolini, has a more complicated character. Nevertheless – and precisely because of its complexity – we can make sense of it with the help of Kirchheimer's theory of opposition as legitimate, of principle, or waning.

Within the living constitution of a member state, left and right compete for power and opposition tends to be legitimate. In practice, both sides benefit from an element of mutual trust. And within the historically given constitution and the historically given borders, this mutual trust is self-reinforcing. But, Bartolini and Scharpf caution us, a politicisation of the vertical dimension will not work in that way. As soon as European issues get politicised, a constitutional question will explode in the face of the political elite. What the formerly apathetic 'we the people' will be asking is why, and on what basis, people living in other countries are entitled to legislate on 'our' behalf.

Politicians will find it hard to give a good answer to that question. It is for this reason that European legislation and European adjudication should remain apolitical. Within each member state, 'we the people' are willing to accept majority rule, because the minority wielded political influence previously, and it can imagine becoming a majority after the next election. Vertically, however, citizens cannot be active in the preparation of legislation. Since the most important legislative issues – particularly the trumping principle of free movement – are constitutional ones, citizens will not so readily regard majority decisions as legitimate. Opposition will then develop all too easily into disagreement at the level of constitutional principle.

This is why Scharpf and Bartolini are so convinced that all the other policy options in the debate, except confederalism, will all too easily provoke outbreaks of devastating nationalism in the electorate. Such tendencies will arise, they believe, if the suprastate makes the mistake of legislating and adjudicating in a way detrimental to feelings of national self-respect. When opposition is waning, and all conceivable disagreement is regarded as opposition of principle, there is no room for legitimate opposition. We should therefore let ourselves be guided, according to Scharpf and Bartolini, by their notion of a mutually reinforcing informal pact of confidence. Loyalty from below for the suprastate can only be purchased at a price: 'we the people' in the member states must be respected (Scharpf 1994: 219–27; Bartolini 2008: 17–19).

Conclusion

As I pointed out initially, the problem of putting limits on democratic accountability avoidance is not just historical in character. It is also a matter of choice. But my own conclusion remains to be stated. Why do I take a negative view of accountability avoidance? And why do I nonetheless prefer the informal-pact-of-confidence strategy to its four alternatives?

On the general question of avoidance or promotion, I take the side of those who stress the importance of legitimising opposition and holding power to account. Politics shorn of disagreement will undermine our belief in democracy, which is a system for choosing between different policies and office-holders. From this point of view, the two positions at the extremes of the spectrum – full-fledged federalism and full-fledged confederalism – are both unproblematic. By definition, their proponents solve the problem through symmetry. In the first case, power and accountability are both situated at the European level; in the second, both are lodged at the national level.

One could say, however, that the 'purists' are only successful because the situation addressed by their arguments is not the one found 'on the open sea', but rather the one that obtains in various 'dry docks' (Gustavsson 1998a, 1998b, 2003, 2006). Nothing unforeseen can happen, because the ideal union is being modelled from scratch, and according to principles that are theoretically sound by definition. The problem in the real world is of a different kind. Politicians have no choice but to rebuild our ship on the open sea. Our founding fathers made their mistake long ago. Their followers have refrained for generations from adopting a stringently federal or confederal point of view. On account of this lack of clear principles, the Union is marked today by the above-mentioned combination of double asymmetry, monetary union without fiscal union, and a constitutional balance of terror. This particular status quo is viewed positively by end-of-history theorists, and regarded as a potential powder-keg by informal-pact-of-confidence theorists.

As for what specifically we should do, my own definite preference – given that I take my point of departure in the really existing Union – is for the informal-pact-of-confidence approach. For one thing, I think the approach taken by the end-of-history theorists is too cynical, and will have the effect of undermining popular belief in democracy. For another, I believe the adherents of marginal majoritarianism underestimate the potential negative consequences of 'dynamically' mixing up the politicisation of left-right issues within the member states on the one hand, and the constitutional issue of why the Union should be entitled to legislate and adjudicate in controversial matters on the other. Only the proponents of the informal-pact-of-confidence position are sufficiently sensitive, I would say, to the obvious risk of letting aggressive nationalism loose in Europe. They are realists who do *not* – and I consider this the heart of the matter – lose sight of the element of deliberate choice. Their specific combination of realism and normative sensitivity is exemplary.

The Union's institutional set-up today – with its mixture of double asymmetry, monetary union without fiscal union, and a constitutional balance of terror – does not fill the heart of an informal-pact-of-confidence theorist with joy. However, I see no feasible alternative in the short term. There is nothing else immediately at hand which is better. My argument here is familiar from the field of environmental policy. That is, I plead the precautionary principle. We should not just consider what would be ideal; the worst-case scenario has to be kept in mind as well. 'Constitutionalism' and 'legitimacy' must indeed be taken seriously (Bartolini 2008). But 'acountability' deserves serious consideration too. It belongs, namely, to the same category of potentially explosive ideas. That in itself is a strong argument for caution.

> As long as the demos could effectively retrieve any matter for decision by itself, the criterion would be met.
>
> (Dahl [1979] 1998: 114)

As long as the democratic state is more powerful than any other organisation in society – such that it can hold public or private actors effectively to account for the policies they promulgate – there is no democratic problem arising in connection with the use of non-democratic procedures of decision-making within public or private administration.

The above argument develops a classical position in moral philosophy: namely that, while there are certainly laws and political procedures which should be observed, we cannot and must not alienate our capacity to make moral decisions (see Kuflik 1984 for a brief survey). Somewhat more recently, in what appears to be another development of the classical position, Henry Richardson (2002: 225) has sought to specify such norms of public reasoning as he believes can prevent arbitrary domination by politically independent agencies – though he urges as well that 'the existence of the agency and the general definition of its mission be subject to recurrent legislative review, revision, and rejection or endorsement'. Differing accounts of normative democratic theory converge, then, on one critical point: that it must be possible to retrieve the authority exercised by agencies which do not apply democratic procedures, and to transfer it to those which do.

Turning now to the application of this argument to the international context, I will use as my main example the European Union, the notorious democratic deficit of which has spurred a large literature and a deep concern with constitutional structures. As we shall see when we look at some more general arguments, however, this problem is far from being uniquely European. It was the German Constitutional Court, in the *Brunner* case, which supplied what is still probably the most famous defence of the Union's constitutional structure in respect of democracy and delegation. In its verdict, the Court recognised that the 'Maastricht Treaty ... confers further ... powers on European organs – which at Treaty level are not yet supported by a corresponding strengthening ... of the democratic bases'. According to the Court, however, the ratification of the Treaty still did not violate the right to democracy stipulated in the German Basic Law. This was because 'Germany is one of the 'Masters of the Treaties' ... which could ultimately ... revoke ... [its] adherence [to the Union Treaty.]' (as translated in Winkelmann 1994: 781, 798).

The bottom line of the argument, of course, is that authority has been delegated rather than alienated to the EU. More recently, this assumption has been taken for granted in academic efforts to rehabilitate the democratic reputation of the EU (Majone 1998; Moravcsik 2004). Moreover, scholars taking a principal-agent approach for other normative purposes than those of Majone and Moravcsik proceed on this assumption as well (e.g. Pollack 2003; Tallberg 2007). Certain authors, furthermore, argue that the delegation of authority to the EU – or to any other international body – does not differ significantly from the delegation of authority currently found in domestic politics. Moravcsik (2004: 356) makes normative use of such a claim to similarity: 'EU officials (or insulated national representatives) enjoy the greatest autonomy in precisely those areas – central banking, constitutional adjudication, criminal and civil prosecution, technical administration and economic diplomacy – in which many advanced industrial democracies, including most Member States of the EU, insulate from direct political contestation [*sic*].' In a similar vein, Kahler (2004: 135) suggests that the standard appropriate to an international agency of political economy is not that of a representative democratic institution, but rather that of a national regulatory agency or a central bank. It is thus no more difficult, according to these authors, to justify an international regulatory agency by reference to the notion of delegation than it is so to justify a national one.

Delegation and international politics

Earlier democratic theory appears to have ignored the fact that two fundamentally different relationships are involved when democratic states transfer authority, revocably or not, to national and international institutions respectively. In the first case, a single principal authorises an agent to act while exercising sole control over said agent: hence the agent is accountable to a single principal. In the second case, a number of principals must apply collective procedures – which typically require a degree of unanimity – to exercise control over their common agent: hence the agent is accountable either to a collective principal or to multiple ones.

When examining the implications hereof, we should recall that this difference does not coincide altogether with that between national and international politics. There are national cases of the second kind, as when individual citizens empower a common state; and there are international cases of the first kind, as when various institutions of the European Union delegate the implementation of directives to local authorities. However, such cases need not concern us here. States are the only relevant actors whose political procedures measure up to present-day standards of democracy. Instances where the delegator is an international agency are therefore of little normative relevance, since international agencies will in any case not be able to furnish the requisite democratic justification. Furthermore, when democratic legitimacy is claimed for international organisations today on the grounds that an equivalent delegation is currently accepted within national politics, the fitting analogy is not with upward delegation at the national level, as when individuals allocate powers to a common state; but with downward delegation at the national level, as when a government or parliament creates a central bank or a regulatory agency. In order to scrutinise this argument, therefore, we must focus on the relationship between transferring authority upwards (from states to international institutions) and transferring authority downwards (from states to national institutions).

To illustrate the main contrast, let us begin with an example taken from the national context (whence the theory of delegation emerged, after all). Consider the transfer by a democratic state of the authority to make decisions about medical treatment. If the recipient of this transfer is a state-run national hospital, the democratic state will have several effective instruments at its disposal to control the manner in which said authority is exercised. By their own decision, for example, the supreme political bodies of the state can decide to limit the hospital's budget or expand it, to install certain officials or remove them, and to furnish new facilities or close old ones. They can allow for certain medical treatments; they can require specific forms of organisation; and so on. The point is: when a state grants authority to a national hospital, it can control the policy undertaken by enacting laws *at any level of detail*. For this reason, we can say that authority in this case has been delegated rather than alienated, and that the agent is accountable to the principal. Such a transfer meets the basic criterion for democratic legitimacy cited above.

Now let us consider an international version of this case. Here, the recipient of the transferred authority is a state-run international hospital – i.e. a hospital constituted by an international treaty ratified in national parliaments. Each signatory state claims a substantial, and perhaps even equal, degree of control over its operations. In such a case, some of the control instruments possessed by each democratic state can only be used at a significantly higher cost in comparison with the national case; and most of the control instruments cannot be used at all. No single state, however unified and centralist, is able by its own decision to expand the hospital's budget, or to limit it, or the like. This is because, according to international law and the principle and reality of sovereignty, such decisions must be taken by agreement among all the states involved. In contrast to the case with the national hospital, no single state is able here to determine the medical policy *at any level of detail*. The only thing an individual democratic state can do by its own decision here – depending on how the international treaty is formulated and how powerful the state is – is to withdraw from the international hospital altogether. But that, of course, is a most limited method of control, as compared to the panoply of instruments available to the democratic state in the case of a national hospital. If the state withdraws altogether, certain forms of medical treatment will become unavailable to its citizens; alternatively, the state will have to build a new hospital on its own, thus consuming resources that could otherwise have been used for medical treatment. Either way, the state in question faces significant limits on the control it can exercise over medical policy – and hence on the extent to which it can hold the agent to account.

Clearly, the democratic justification applying at the national level – that the democratic state is able to wield certain instruments of policy control – is to some degree absent on the international plane. So while the national case is one of delegation, this does not mean the same is true at the international level.[2]

In order to provide a more determinate assessment of the democratic legitimacy of international organisations, it may be instructive to clarify two further points: (i) what we mean by authority; and (ii) what we mean by recovering authority. In regard to the first, we shall consider two possibilities: (i.i) that authority is a juridically specified decisional competence, and one independent of the actual content of any given decision (because the holder of such competence will be limited by factors beyond the juridical competence itself) as well as of the particular people and territory involved (because a juridical competence is typically specified with regard to particular functions rather than the particular people or territory to which it applies): e.g. the competence to decide on trade relationships or monetary policy; and (i.ii) that authority is a power over an actual set of decisional alternatives, and one determined by the concrete content of said alternatives: e.g. the power to decide that peoples with rich natural resources shall be allowed to trade with peoples possessing advanced technical skills, or that the effective rate of interest among major trading partners is to be set at 4 rather than 2 per cent. As for the second point (what we mean by retrieving authority), we shall distinguish two interpretations: (ii.i) that retrieving authority entails redistributing the power to make decisions from an institution which is less procedurally democratic to one which is more so: as when, for example, a policy developed by civil servants is revised by a democratically elected parliament; and (ii.ii) that retrieving authority means influencing the policy of a procedurally less democratic institution in the direction of the norms laid down by a procedurally more democratic institution: as when, for example, a democratically elected parliament enacts new laws so as to influence the decisions made in turn by courts or private companies.[3] The section that follows takes the first interpretation of the meaning of authority as a given (i.i), while considering both interpretations of what it means to recover authority.

Recovering juridical competence

What prospects does a democratic state have for *taking back* a juridical competence from an international organisation? Provided the competence is defined not in terms of the territory or people concerned but in policy terms (e.g. agriculture or taxation), then the probability is high that the competence can in fact be effectively retrieved. The state can ultimately secede from the international organisation in question, and then proceed to introduce new national legislation in the area in question (although seceding from an organisation like the EU may be enormously costly).[4] The principal difference between the national and international cases lies rather in the fact that, in the case of the latter, a state may be left with no other option than to retrieve the entirety of the competence in question, even as it wishes to retrieve only a portion of it. Let us see why.

A proposal at the international level must be agreed to by all states – or at least by a sufficiently strong state or group of states – in order to be adopted.

Within democratic states, by contrast, public policy is enacted through majority rule in the supreme political body, or else by a directly elected president. Exceptions can be found, but generally this is the case. Hence, a state seeking to recover only the competences of its own choosing from an international organisation can easily be blocked by another state; the only change it is guaranteed to achieve is outright secession. Moreover, this limit on the capacity of states to control international institutions has been codified in international law. According to paragraph 60 of the Vienna Convention of 1969, if a state breaks an international treaty unilaterally (as it may be forced to do if it seeks to recover only the competences of its own choosing), then the other parties to the treaty are no longer bound to observe said treaty – at least in respect of their policies towards the treaty-breaking state (viz., the other states are given full freedom to determine how much can in fact be retrieved).

Let us turn now to the second interpretation (ii.ii) of what it means to recover authority (i.e. the ability to influence decisions made by another agent effectively). One critical difference between the national and international cases must be borne in mind here: they represent two different principal/agent structures. The international situation is one in which several principals control a single agent; at the national level, by contrast, a single principal controls one or more agents. Only in the former case are there transaction costs for sharing information and coordinating policies between different principals. The degree to which policy outcomes at the international level can be controlled is accordingly limited, as we saw in the example of the hospital above. Some international institutions (e.g. the European Council) may help principals to coordinate their policies; however, it remains substantially more difficult to coordinate policies among several governments – all of which claim to represent a sovereign state – than it is within a single government. Moreover, the single national principal has a wider set of alternative alliances among the plurality of potential agents; indeed, it can even create new agents by its own decision. Internationally, by contrast, the creation of every new agent must be agreed to by all the other states. And as in any power struggle, having a wide range of alternative alliances is an asset.

On both interpretations of what it means to recover authority, then, the conclusion is the same: the fact that delegation exists on the national level cannot be taken to imply that it does internationally.

Retrieving power over a set of alternatives

We may now turn to the second interpretation of authority, according to which it represents power over a specific set of alternatives (i.ii), rather than a juridically specified competence (i.i). A decisional alternative may involve, for example, setting conditions for trade among particular peoples differing in respect of natural resources and technological development, or choosing whether to undertake expansionary or contractionary monetary action among major trading partners. A juridically specified competence, by contrast, need not involve any requirements as to the actual content of decisions; it is not necessarily violated, therefore, if certain policy options are absent in practice.

The decisional alternatives available to international organisations do not typically exist within individual member states. For example, no state is able, by its very nature, to provide for as ramified a division of labour as the World Trade Organisation can do. No national central bank can manipulate the demand of European consumers to the degree that the monetary institutions of the European Union can. Hence the authority of these organisations – interpreted here as their power over concrete decisional alternatives – cannot in truth be retrieved by procedurally democratic states.

This argument can be easily generalised to all decisions affecting more than one country. If a decisional alternative effectuated by an international organisation among its members were to be recovered by a specific state, then this state would have to occupy the territory of all the other members of the organisation in question; otherwise, it would not gain the power over decisional alternatives that the international organisation had in fact had. Of course, the state in question might retrieve the authority which the international organisation had in some sense exercised *over its own population only*, but that would be something different – a far cry from the authority wielded by the international organisation: namely, the power to decide policy *in or among all of its member states*. Yet even were someone to defend the peculiar view that the occupation of other countries is an element of democratic politics, it would not solve the problem identified here: in the strange instance at hand, after all, the power over decisional alternatives would be restored to the people of a single state only, which would render the people in all the other countries completely alienated from the power exercised over them. The conclusion is simple: the power over concrete decisional alternatives wielded by an international organisation can never be retrieved by procedurally democratic states.

The reality that internationally taken decisions have effect in more than one country is perhaps most evident in relation to the European Union: the doctrines of legal supremacy and direct effect have been operating in that body for several decades. Yet to a relevant extent, the same can be said of all the major international organisations, such as the International Monetary Fund, the United Nations, and the World Trade Organisation. Only for the most powerful states (or the most rogue-ish ones) is a persistent refusal to comply with important decisions a real option. Even such states, moreover, may find that an act of dissent serves to reduce their assets if they wish to propose binding agreements in the future.

Here it may be objected that the only power which cannot be restored to a given democratic state is the power to affect individuals living in a territory controlled by another state – and, of course, the alienation of that specific power from democratic procedures should not be interpreted as a democratic problem. One can only agree with the latter part of this objection: the democratically relevant capacity on the part of a collective actor is the capacity to affect the individuals who constitute the collective itself, not individuals in general. However, a real democratic problem – in the view of Dahl and of Richardson, among others – arises when an international organisation develops a policy that *only* exists because of the international organisation. Such a policy will indeed affect people who are themselves unable to retrieve the authority and to subject its exercise to democratic control. This problem would seem to arise in the case of all policies made possible by the efficiency gains deriving from scale, and all policies whose efficiency in one country depends on what happens in other ones. Put more precisely, the actions that cannot be justified by traditional theories of democratic delegation are those that can be undertaken *only* through a transfer of authority to a procedurally non-democratic international agency. The fact that such a power could never exist at the level of the nation-state does not diminish the normative difficulty of this condition. For the criterion of democracy, as specified by Dahl and by Richardson, is not that only such powers as can be exercised within nation-states must be democratically controlled; rather, *all* significant powers must be democratically controlled.

The myth of international delegation

We have seen that the possibilities for delegating or alienating authority vary as between the national and the international level. Although the potential for normatively justifying independent agencies depends on how we interpret *authority* – or the *retrieval* of authority, more precisely – the international context is, on all interpretations, imbued with difficulties which do not exist at the national level (which is where, after all, the normative theory of delegation first developed and gained acceptance). In sum, the suggestion that politically insulated international agencies are democratically legitimate because equivalent claims are commonly accepted for national agencies must be rejected as severely misleading.

Moreover, the authors who have done the most to develop the notion of democratically acceptable delegation, Dahl and Richardson, are themselves hesitant to suggest that the relevant principles are generally observed even in national politics. Against the background of the far greater difficulty – even the structural impossibility, under some interpretations – of recalling the authority allocated to *international* agencies, the only fair conclusion would seem to be that the conditions under which insulated agencies can be legitimised in terms of recoverable authority are absent in cases where states transfer authority to international organisations.

As we have just seen, furthermore, international organisations appear most illegitimate from a democratic standpoint if we define authority in terms of the power over alternatives, rather than as a juridically specified competence. Nevertheless, the power-oriented interpretation is the more appropriate of the two: democracy is commonly acknowledged to be a question of the power rather than the law of the people. This should strengthen the case for rejecting the view that the politics of international organisations originates in a delegation of authority from the state level, and is democratically justified to the extent that the states involved are democratic. This view is incorrect: it wrongly assumes that the authority conferred on international agencies can be retrieved by democratic states, or effectively influenced through democratic procedures.

But let us now shift analytical perspective, from a critique of the theory of power as being delegated in international politics to a description of the meaning taken on by the term 'delegation' within that theory. After all, it is not unlikely that my critical conclusions will only be expected by authors like Andrew Moravcsik, Giandomenico Majone, Miles Kahler, and Robert Keohane, but that they will continue none the less to speak of international powers as being delegated. The meaning of the term 'delegation' will then have undergone some change, as compared with a usage according to which a power is delegated only if it can be recovered by the delegator. Let us assess the significance of this conceptual change by exploring its implications for another central concept in democratic theory, namely accountability.

Implications for accountability

Delegation, as opposed to alienation and as traditionally defined, involves accountability: for A to be able to hold B to account, A must have at least some power to affect B's behaviour. According to Keohane (chapter 2 in this volume: 13), an 'accountability relationship' presupposes that the principal is able to 'impose costs on the agent'. This is the case when A has delegated power to B in the traditional sense. The ultimate power over choices made by B will then remain with A. But if the relationship is different – such that A has alienated power to B or B has delegated power to A – then there is no authority on the basis of which A can seek to change B's behaviour. Moreover, since the concept of accountability presupposes that the power whose exercise is held to account has been delegated rather than alienated to an agent, a change in the meaning of 'delegated' will yield consequences for the meaning of 'accountability'. It behoves us, therefore, to explore three overlapping changes in the concept of accountability – changes which tend in general to weaken the concept, and all of which derive from the shifts that take place in the concept when it is applied to the transfer of international powers.

Individualisation of accountability. To begin with, the new concept of 'delegation' serves to individualise 'accountability'. Consider a case where several states seek to hold their common international agency to account. Any state can impose whatever sanction it likes on its own representative in the collective international institution, but the responsible *group* of representatives will be held to account by no one. This reveals a dramatic difference in comparison with accountability as we are familiar with that concept from national politics and democratic theory. When a national parliament holds a government to account, it is not restricted to sanctioning only individual members of said government; nor is its ability to vote the government out of office conditioned on any agreement with another institution independent of itself. Yet these are precisely the constraints that (necessarily) apply within international institutions when the principal seeks to hold its agent to account. In addition, the individualisation of accountability which takes place when international powers are described as being 'delegated' has the consequence not only that parliaments lose some of their ability to control the making of executive, legislative, and judicial decisions; it also means that the political role played by the general public is diminished. Since the mass media pay more attention to the actions and powers of national politicians than to those of their counterparts from other countries, the individuals within the international institution – rather than the whole of it – become the focus of attention for the general public too. Thus, the individualisation of accountability implied by a changing concept of delegation has consequences for the relationship between vitally important political institutions, as well as for the capacity of the people to act in concert. In sum, the kind of accountability that remains under the new conditions of 'delegation' is one in which individuals, not responsible groups, are held to account.

It may be objected at this point that the new meaning of 'accountability' extracted here is no different from that which applies in any multi-constituency national electoral system: just as the composition of the national parliament in such a system cannot be determined by any single constituency, so the composition of an international institution cannot be determined by any single state.

However, the individualisation of the concept of accountability which takes place here – as a consequence of using the word 'delegated' in reference to international powers – is much more radical than anything with which we are familiar from national politics. The members of a national representative institution are not only individuals; they are also members of political parties which are common to many or even all of the constituencies of the state. These political parties forge common positions from the aims of varied constituencies, and they present a limited number of decisional alternatives to voters in general elections. This has the effect of making the entity which is held to account into a more collective one. When national citizens hold their political representatives to account, they hold those bearing political responsibility – the governing party or parties – to account at the same time. By contrast, when national parliaments hold their representatives in intergovernmental institutions to account (said representatives being, it bears recalling, members of a national government), there is no equivalent act of choosing between the group bearing political responsibility and its alternatives. Representatives in intergovernmental institutions are elected by parliaments (as a function of the election of governments) on the basis of whichever political parties predominate in those bodies. In such elections, parliamentarians are *not* presented with the option of voting for or against the entire group of people responsible for the decisions and non-decisions of the international institution. For parliamentarians to be presented with such an option, there must in the first place be a limited number of political parties which include all of the potential members of all of the national governments within the international organisation. The emergence of international parties of that kind may not be completely unrealistic; moreover, a certain similarity among party systems in different countries may obtain in Europe already today (see, for example, Mair and Thomassen 2008). In addition, however, such international parties (or structural similarities among party systems in different countries) would need to serve as effectively as national parties do in (i) developing comprehensive political programmes, (ii) communicating policy positions to the public, and (iii) achieving internal cohesiveness. Under these conditions, the accountability of international powerholders would indeed be no less collective in character than the accountability of national parliamentarians within a multi-constituency electoral system. But the problem, of course, is that international parties (or the structural similarities of party systems in different countries) do not perform these functions to an extent even approaching that which national parties do. In sum, national parliamentarians have no opportunity to choose between alternative governments constitutive of alternative international coalitions, with programmes ready to be enacted upon international electoral victory.

The kind of accountability implied by the changing concept of delegation is therefore not comparable to that ordinarily seen in the election of parliaments in national politics. It resembles, rather, the kind of accountability that would characterise national politics if there were no political parties forging common positions from the aims of varied constituencies. And that would indeed, as compared to anything with which we are familiar from national democracies, represent a dramatic individualisation of accountability.

De-politicisation of accountability. In addition, the new way in which 'delegation' is understood serves to de-politicise 'accountability'. Consider once again the relationship between a group of states on the one hand, and their common agency on the other. All states may withdraw their own representatives from the common agency; however, to change any more fundamental aspect of the institution – its voting rules or its policy aims, for example – they must first arrive at a common position. This means that the usual contention between ideologically opposed parties with which accountability is associated in national parliaments must give way to a more *sotto voce* style of politics, developed so as to maximise the chance for unanimity. The sole alternative for the principals – at least in regard to any of the more fundamental political issues, which can only be decided on the basis of consensus – is to renounce their own powers and confer them on the people who (in the past) created the institution in question. The self-interest of principals in protecting their own powers reduces the extent to which they can disagree among themselves.

Objections could be raised here too. One might argue, for example, that the intensity of debate is low because the political issues in question are uncontroversial. One might furthermore contend that the policy changes which are prevented by the requirement of unanimity are typically those which do not benefit all states within the international organisation. Requiring agreement among states before their common international institution can be significantly changed is not so much, on this view, an institutional bias against political contestation in general, as a bias in favour of efficiency-enhancing, pareto-optimal policies that no state has any strong reason to contest; furthermore, the promulgation of such policies is precisely the purpose for which international institutions have typically been established (Majone 1996b). Hence it may appear that 'accountability' takes on a de-politicised form in intergovernmental institutions not because of any institutionalised bias against contestation, but on account of a limited *need* to engage in public debate.

However, the view that 'accountability' is being de-politicised for universally good reasons is not uncontroversial, at least not outside fairly narrow neo-liberal circles. Why should we expect efficiency-enhancing and pareto-optimal policies to be uncontroversial? Why should we even expect them to be less controversial than redistributive ones? Consider an international policy from which state A gains 10 units, while state B gains 100. The policy in question is indeed efficiency-enhancing, but it is not necessarily less contentious than a redistributive policy in which 10 units are transferred from state A to state B (cf. Karlsson 2001: 146–7). Whether the latter situation will be more contentious than the former depends on the initial absolute positions of A and B, as well as on the use A expects B to make of its relative gain in the future. If an efficiency enhancing policy implies, say, that A gains 10 units from 20 to 30 while B gains 100 units from 90 to 190 (and perhaps even that A will be increasingly dominated by B in future negotiations as a result of B's greater gain), this policy may well threaten A's interest in a fair political outcome to a greater extent than a redistributive policy in which A transfers 10 out of 1,000 units to B possessing 100 units to begin with. Surely, in this case it would be in the interest of A to have the possibility of joining combat in the making of efficiency enhancing policies, without fear that such contestation will undermine the possibility to reach a decision together with B and thereby reduce the influence of both A and B over future institutional changes. Hence the problems arising in connection with the de-politicisation of accountability should not be neglected on the grounds that the policy issues are uncontroversial and in need of little debate. The source of the silence, namely, lies elsewhere: in the determination shared by all states to protect their joint power over institutional change.

De-radicalisation of accountability. Finally, the new concept of 'delegation' entails an ideological de-radicalisation of 'accountability'. In whatever broad or narrow sense political decision-making is ever believed to result in some kind of change, it becomes *less* likely to do so when multiple principals hold a single agent to account than when a single principal holds a single agent to account. The more numerous the actors that must embrace a proposal for it to be adopted (i.e. the greater the number of veto players), the lower the likelihood that a decision will be made (e.g. Tsebelis 2002: 2–3). Conversely, any given change in policy or institutional set-up is more likely to occur if but a single principal needs agree to it than if an entire collection of principals operating independently of each other must approve it. In sum, an arrangement in which multiple principals hold a single agent accountable is less likely to yield changes in its status quo than is one in which a single unified principal holds a single agent accountable.

The most serious objection to this reasoning would be that it neglects the problem of implementation. If decisions are not implemented by authorities under the direct control of the decision-making institution itself, but rather by authorities under the control of the distinct components making up the decision-making institution, then deviating minorities within the institution will have both the interest and the ability to obstruct the process of implementation. So, when decisions are made within an international institution, but implemented by authorities under the control of individual states, a consensual process need *not* be less effective than majority rule in promoting change – if by change we mean change which is actually implemented. In fact, it can be suggested even that a decision-making structure based on unanimity may be more effective than one based on majority rule, inasmuch as it forces members of the majority to heed the demands put by minorities and to adapt to them (so that, in the end, everyone is reasonably satisfied and ready to act in common). Unanimity rather than majority rule would then stand out as the more radical procedure.

However, this argument is based on exceptions that might possibly arise, rather than on any general tendency characterising the behaviour of self-interested political actors. If a status-quo-friendly minority is protected by the requirement of unanimity, there is little incentive for the members of the said minority to change position; at the same time, a change-friendly majority will be effectively constrained. By contrast, if a status-quo-friendly minority is *not* protected by the unanimity requirement, but instead must abide by the will of the majority (at any rate when it comes to the making of decisions), said minority may perhaps succeed in obstructing the *implementation* of majority-approved decisions; however, the larger number of states – the majority – will be free to implement the change in question. In other words, a political system will indeed become less prone to change as the number of veto players taking part in its decision-making increases. Accordingly, the type of 'accountability' that can exist in an international system is intrinsically less radical in character than that found when a single principal – one internally unified by majority rule – holds a single agent to account.

Conclusion

Viewed as a description of European politics, my propositions on the weakening of 'accountability' do not appear especially controversial. For example, the picture I have painted is similar to the portrayal of the European Union as partly based on the fiduciary principle, according to which regulators can 'pursue the statutory objectives of the agency, even when those objectives, because of changed economic or political conditions, no longer enjoy popular support' (Majone 2005: 67). However, my aim is not to refine empirical characterisations of existing governance arrangements, but to bring the normative implications of some changing concepts into the light. Should we strive for an individualised, de-politicised, and de-radicalised kind of accountability? Or should we instead develop our common institutions in the other direction, towards collective, politicised, and radical decision-making? This question deserves a more direct treatment than is possible when relegated to the barely conscious production of theoretical implications of a particular conceptual change. Whenever international powers are being named 'delegated' in a discussion of accountability we should therefore require an explanation of why an individualised, a de-politicised, and a de-radicalised kind of accountability is an unproblematic implication or even a good thing.

While existing research contributions are largely unsatisfactory in this regard, there is an urgent political need actually to remedy the situation. The creation of a political union at the European level has for a long time pushed politics towards a weaker kind of accountability. Scholars ought not to obscure this reality by conflating different concepts of delegation. Instead they should clarify the implications of different political alternatives so as to facilitate an enlightened and ultimately democratic political choice.

Notes

1 Contributions featuring normative analysis on the basis of this position include Majone 1998; Pollack 2003; Moravcsik 2004; Kahler 2004; and Keohane in this volume. The most influential example, politically speaking, is probably still the Maastricht verdict of the German Constitutional Court in 1993 (see Winkelmann 1994). I present an argument in this chapter which appeared in part in an earlier publication (Agné 2007).

2 It bears recalling here that some variation may be found as between national cases. As compared with a unitary state, for example, a federal state would appear to find it harder to keep ultimate control over such authority as it has delegated to its regional sub-units. The experience of federal states, accordingly, ought to be closer than that of unitary states to the international pattern. However, the major difference still remains. Sovereign states, whether federal or unitary, retain ultimate control over their territory – by force if necessary (a prerogative lacked by the regional sub-units of federal states). Hence the latter have far fewer opportunities when confronting their states over questions of authority than states enjoy when so confronting international organisations. Yet more important, however, is the fact that transfers of authority from federal to regional level within democratic states

require far less in the way of democratic justification, inasmuch as the regional sub-units – in contrast to international organisations – qualify as relatively democratic, due to their internal political procedures.

3 Dahl comes close to interpretation ii.i. in his article 'Procedural Democracy' and to interpretation ii.ii in his more exploratory book *Dilemmas of Pluralist Democracy*. See Dahl (1982b and [1979] 1998).

4 Many analysts regard the EU, of course, as something much stronger than a mere international organisation. On such an interpretation, however, the ultimate claim being made here – that the EU's authority cannot be democratically justified by reference to the recoverability of authority – is actually strengthened.

6 EU treaty reform and accountability

Christer Karlsson

This chapter examines whether European Union (EU) citizens have a meaningful influence over the most fundamental decision taken in the Union, namely those that lay down the rules of the game. EU treaties are of crucial importance, for they define the competencies of the Union, the powers afforded to different actors and institutions, and the various procedures for making decisions. Are there any effective mechanisms for holding treaty reformers accountable?

Some scholars argue that concerns over limited opportunities for citizens to hold treaty reformers accountable are largely unfounded, since the power to revise the treaties is in the hands of member-state representatives, and the requirement of unanimity obtains. Government representatives negotiate, and changes to the treaties are ratified by national parliamentarians – and the latter are indeed subject to strong accountability mechanisms within their own state. Risse and Kleine argue, for example, that 'EU treaty-making faces fewer problems of input legitimacy and accountability than everyday decision-making', because '[m]ember states remain the "masters of the treaties" as a result of which national procedures including referendums for ratification of international treaties apply' (Risse and Kleine 2007: 73).

The negotiations for the Amsterdam and Nice treaties were generally perceived as inefficient, with 'leftovers' that had to be passed on to subsequent intergovernmental conferences (IGCs). During the debate following the Nice summit, demands were raised for a more open, effective, and reflective process of treaty reform. In response to these demands, the European Council decided that the next IGC would be prepared by a Convention modelled on the EU Charter Convention that had worked in parallel with the 2000 IGC. The main novelty was the broader composition of this body, which included not just representatives of member-state governments and the Commission, but also members of the European Parliament (EP) and of national parliaments.

Scholars have praised the European Convention for being more open, more deliberative, and more responsive than IGCs have been; as a result, they contend, the legitimacy of the EU's treaty-reform process has been strengthened (Shaw 2003; Pollak and Slominski 2004; Fossum and Menéndez 2005). Some observers have argued explicitly that the convention method has improved accountability in the treaty-reform process (Risse and Kleine 2007: 75, 77).

In this chapter, I investigate the question of accountability in the treaty-reform process, through a comparison of the IGC method with the convention method. In the course of this examination, it becomes clear that EU citizens have only limited opportunities to hold treaty reformers accountable, and that the convention method improves only marginally on this state of affairs. The basic problem remains: namely, that there are no electoral contests over European issues. Neither national elections nor EP elections are fought on issues relating to the future design of European integration, and EU citizens are never presented with alternative views on the issues decided at IGCs. National governments have no explicit mandates in this area, and there is no clear opposition to which the public can turn if it feels discontent with the new deals negotiated and adopted by governments on their behalf. In practice, EU citizens have no effective means for sanctioning those responsible for deciding on new treaties, even if formal mechanisms do exist for holding treaty reformers to account.

This chapter proceeds in five steps. I begin with a brief discussion on delegation and accountability, thereby laying the foundation for the examination to follow. I then describe the main characteristics of the treaty-reform process, and the formal differences between the IGC method and the convention method. In subsequent sections, I examine the question of accountability in relation to these two methods. I conclude by discussing my main findings and making some suggestions as to how accountability in the treaty-reform process can be strengthened.

Delegation and accountability

Representative government is based on the principle of delegation. For delegation to be meaningful, the person or institution represented (the principal) must be able to control the actions of the representative (the agent), at least in some minimal way (Strøm *et al.* 2004). Sometimes, it is true, the very point of delegation is to ensure that the principal cannot affect the agent – as when we decide to delegate powers to independent agencies or courts. However, if we restrict our discussion to those instances of delegation where the agent is a representative, we find there is a need for mechanisms of accountability.

By accountability (cf. the introductory chapter of this volume and Bovens 2007a), I mean two things: first, that the principal has the right to monitor and evaluate the actions of the agent; and second, that the principal has the right to impose sanctions on the agent. The primary purpose of imposing sanctions is not to punish agents, but rather to furnish them with incentives to act in accordance with the standards defining their responsibilities. This presupposes, in turn, that there is some sort of agreed-upon deal on the powers that agents are to have (cf. the contribution by Robert Keohane in this volume).

There are a variety of mechanisms for accountability. They can be located on a continuum from weak to strong. Towards one end of the continuum we find mechanisms for ensuring access to information, for posing questions, and for receiving explanations. Towards the other we find mechanisms for passing judgement and imposing sanctions.

In some contexts, weak mechanisms are sufficient to ensure that the representative performs properly. Weak mechanisms are also important in that they may be necessary for an effective use of stronger mechanisms, such as sanctions. However, in the absence of strong mechanisms allowing the principal to impose sanctions on the agent, the incentive for the representative to act in the best interests of the principal diminishes, and the risk of 'agency-shirking' increases. So while weak mechanisms for accountability – public access to documents, for example – are important, and in many cases sufficient to guarantee that representatives are loyal to their brief, strong mechanisms are crucially important, as the measure of last resort.

Two methods for EU treaty reform

Intergovernmental conferences have been the prevailing institutional tool for revising EU treaties for more than five decades, and their procedures have changed little. In recent years, however, the IGC institution has come under criticism. An 'anti-IGC coalition' (Magnette and Nicolaidis 2004: 383) started gaining support in 2001, as the upcoming revision of the treaties was being prepared by the Belgian presidency. Demands for a revised treaty-reform process were fuelled by failures at the summits in Amsterdam in 1996 and Nice in 2000. In both of these cases, negotiations resulted in deadlocks that were impossible to break. Both meetings, moreover, produced 'leftovers': important issues left unresolved.

As a response to the criticism of the Amsterdam and Nice negotiations, the Laeken European Council of December 2001 decided that the upcoming IGC would be prepared by a Convention. But said Convention would not replace the IGC; it would only be a preparatory body. Final decision-making power would remain with the IGC. The decision to create a European Convention does not, accordingly, imply a complete overturning of the treaty-reform process.

The treaty-reform process can be divided into three different phases. The first is that of preparation. This may also involve pre-negotiations, in which preliminary deals are sometimes struck. The second phase is that of negotiation and final decision-making. This is where the actual content of a treaty revision is agreed upon by representatives of the member states. The final phase is that of ratification. This is where the revised treaty is approved or rejected by national parliaments, and (in some member states) by the electorate as well, through referendum.

The main difference between the IGC method and the convention method lies in the design of the preparatory phase. The mandate of the Convention is to 'pave the way for the next Intergovernmental Conference as broadly and openly as possible' (European Council 2001). Key issues relating to the EU's future development are to be discussed at its proceedings, and possible responses to these challenges identified. The Convention is then to prepare a final document that may serve as 'a starting point for discussions in the Intergovernmental Conference' (European Council 2001).

The future standing of the convention method is currently uncertain. However, should the Lisbon Treaty be ratified by all the member states, there would appear to be a future for it. Article 48 of the consolidated version of the Treaty on European Union (*Official Journal* 2008/ C 115/01) states that, once the European Council has decided – in accordance with an 'ordinary revision procedure' – to examine a proposal for amendment of the treaties, 'the President of the European Council shall convene a Convention'. The Convention is then required to examine these proposals, and to 'adopt by consensus a recommendation to a conference of representatives of the governments of the Member States'.

The role of the Convention as a preparatory body is once again underlined, even if the term 'recommendation' could be taken to suggest that the formal mandate of future conventions will be somewhat stronger than that of the European Convention charged with preparing the 2003–4 IGC. On the other hand, the member states have included a safeguard, by requiring the Convention to make its recommendations by consensus. In theory, this means any single member state can prevent the Convention from issuing a recommendation to the IGC.

Should the Lisbon Treaty fail to be ratified, future amendments of the treaties will be undertaken in accordance with the IGC method, as laid down in article 48 of the Treaty on European Union (as long, that is, as the European Council does not decide otherwise and convene a Convention anyway). For the time being, then, we have two contending methods for deciding on future treaty reforms, and we cannot be altogether certain which one will be applied.

The main difference between the two methods lies in how the stage of preparation for an IGC is designed. Focusing first on the IGC method, we can identify two different ways in which the preparatory phase has been organised.

In the preparations for the 1990–1 IGC, the Delors Committee played an important role in setting the agenda for negotiations. Led by Jacques Delors, this Committee included two commissioners, three independent experts, and the central-bank governors from all of the member states. The Delors Report delivered to the European Council in June 1989 set out a plan for the implementation of Economic and Monetary Union (EMU), which was adopted with only minor changes by the IGC. It is fair to argue, then, that the Commission played a very important role in preparing the negotiations that eventually led to the signing of the Maastricht Treaty.

The preparations for the 1996 IGC were very different, inasmuch as the Commission's influence over the process was only marginal. At a meeting in Corfu in 1994, the European Council had decided to set up a 'Reflection Group', the task of which would be to prepare the upcoming IGC and to bring order to the agenda. This group of 'wise men' was chaired by Carlos Westendorp, Spanish minister of European affairs; and it included one commissioner, two representatives from the EP, and 15 national representatives – ministers, diplomats, and ambassadors – all of whom were linked to their respective home governments (Svensson 2000: 48–50). The final report of the Westendorp Group was rather vague. It simply reflected prevailing divisions among the member states on controversial issues, like whether the powers of the EP should be increased or the use of QMV extended.

Despite these differences, there is one important common denominator to the preparatory work carried out under the IGC method: member-state governments are in charge (even if they sometimes choose to give an important role in the process to expert actors and the Commission). By contrast, applying the convention method means that preparations are entrusted to a body composed of a broader range of actors, in which government representatives must share power with delegates representing not just the Commission, but the European Parliament and national parliaments as well.

Aside from the chairman, Valéry Giscard d'Estaing, and vice-chairmen Giuliano Amato and Jean-Luc Dehaene, who were all appointed by the European Council, the European Convention was composed of 102 delegates. The Commission had two representatives, the European Parliament had 16, the governments of member states and candidate states had one representative each (28 *in toto*), and the national parliaments of the member states and candidate states had two representatives each (56 *in toto*). So, national parliaments and the EP were not only represented; their delegates had a clear majority, with 72 of the 105 seats at the Convention.

As the main difference between the two competing methods lies in the preparatory phase, it is there we must search most intensely for possible improvements in accountability. The other phases of treaty reform (negotiation and decision-making at the IGC; ratification in the member states) do not differ as between the IGC and convention methods – a fact which might lead us to conclude that no difference in opportunities for accountability can be expected either. After all, what is really important during the treaty-reform process is: first, the final deal negotiated and decided upon at the IGC, and second, the decision to ratify the new treaty. However, while these are indeed the two main decisions for which EU citizens must be able to hold their representatives to account, this does not mean that what happens in the preparatory phase is irrelevant from the standpoint of accountability. There are at least two different reasons for this.

First, while it is analytically prudent to distinguish between three different phases of the treaty-reform process, these are of course closely linked in practice. For example, the preparatory phase often includes pre-negotiations, and proposals made at this stage sometimes survive the IGC without any changes being made in them. The 1990–1 IGC on Economic and Monetary Union, for instance, made only a few amendments to the final report delivered by the Delors Committee (Beach 2003). The draft Constitution delivered by the European Convention to the European Council in 2003 also survived the 2003–4 IGC without any major changes being made in it. In practice, then, there is not always a sharp boundary between the first two phases of the treaty-reform process, and the actual content of treaty amendments is sometimes set already in the 'preparatory phase'.

Second, we should acknowledge the possibility that the effective use of accountability mechanisms in the later stages of the process can be affected indirectly by differences in the design of the preparatory phase. For example, having an IGC prepared by a Convention may lead to a more open process, making it easier to monitor and evaluate the actions of representatives. The information so acquired may be an important prerequisite for putting strong accountability mechanisms to effective use. Thus, introducing weak mechanisms for accountability during the early stages of the process may facilitate the effective use of strong mechanisms later on.

The IGC method: indirect and direct accountability

What mechanisms for accountability are at the disposal of European citizens when the IGC method for treaty reform is being used?

National governments have usually controlled the preparatory work done prior to IGCs, as well as the negotiations and the actual decision-making. The Commission has also played an important role at times. To understand the prospects for holding treaty reformers to account, we should accordingly focus on the mechanisms available through indirect channels: in particular, those that work through the electoral contests that decide the fate of national governments.

In addition, there are two mechanisms for direct accountability in the ratification stage: one via the national parliament of each member state; and one by means of referendum, wherein the people have their say on treaty amendments directly.

I shall first examine the mechanisms for indirect accountability that are afforded via national governments. I shall then consider the two mechanisms for direct accountability which are available during ratification.

Indirect accountability

According to Andrew Moravscik, talk of a democratic deficit is exaggerated in the main, and there is no reason to be concerned over the prospects for holding EU decision-makers accountable (Moravscik 2002: 611–2). As long as democratically elected governments dominate the governance structure of the EU, citizens will have sufficient opportunities to hold decision-makers accountable. If Moravscik is correct in this, then decisions on treaty reform should be the least of our concerns when we examine the question of accountability in the Union. For national governments are truly in charge of the process, and citizens have every opportunity to hold them accountable in national elections.

The basic flaw in this analysis is that it does not take into account how national elections actually work, or what real opportunities they afford citizens to hold EU decision-makers to account. Moravscik's conclusion is based on a theoretical understanding of how national elections *could* serve as an accountability mechanism, rather than on an empirical assessment of what opportunities they *actually* offer citizens for holding their national governments to account in this area.

Moravscik's idea here is that indirect accountability can be secured through the chain of delegation that runs from national citizens via national governments to the European Council, where final decisions on treaty amendments are taken. The problem, however, is that national elections are not fought out on issues relating to the future institutionalisation of the EU. In fact, European issues of all types – whether about the future design of EU institutions, the scope of competencies the EU is to have, or the content of the policy agenda – are largely absent from the debates preceding national elections. Political parties and their leaders have by and large chosen to exclude European issues from national elections (Hix 2008: 70). An analysis of national parties' election manifestos, for example, shows that less than 2 per cent of the content is dedicated to EU policy issues (Klingeman *et al.* 2006; Hix 2008: 78).

The absence of European issues at national elections means that voters are not presented with clear alternatives, and that no strong opposition is formed. What we have is a situation defined, as Peter Mair puts it, by a 'remarkable under-politicization of the Europeanization dimension' (Mair 2008: 30). In the absence of national debates and electoral contests over European issues, and about matters like the future construction of the Union, no real mandate is given to national governments on how to act prior to or during IGCs. And in the absence of an explicit mandate and a clear opposition that gives voice to alternatives, the real opportunities for holding governments accountable are greatly undermined. In practice, voters have nowhere to turn if they are dissatisfied with the record of those currently in office.

What we have, then, is something resembling an illusion of accountability. The formal mechanisms are in place, and citizens are able *in theory* to mandate their representatives on issues like the Union's constitutional structure, and to hold them to account if they do not perform as promised. If citizens were able to do this *in fact*, national governments would have a real incentive to take their preferences into serious account. To date, however, national elections have been contests in which European issues and concerns over the future design of the European integration project are more or less absent. Thus we have a situation where, 'despite the seeming availability of channels of access, the scope for meaningful input and hence for effective electoral accountability is exceptionally limited' (Mair 2008: 29). The indirect accountability exercised by EU citizens via their elected national officials is therefore ineffective for ensuring that their preferences are taken into account when the future of the EU is decided.

Direct accountability

What mechanisms for direct accountability are available during the ratification process? Might they provide EU citizens with a reasonable opportunity to hold treaty reformers accountable?

National parliaments are the key actors in the ratification process. The national parliament of every member state must ratify any new treaty before it can come into force. A referendum, moreover, is sometimes held prior to the parliamentary decision. There are accordingly two institutional mechanisms for holding a national government to account for its decisions on a new treaty: first, the vote taken by representatives in the national parliament; second, the choice made by voters in a popular referendum.

National parliaments are directly elected by the voters. In theory, therefore, the accountability they afford should be stronger than the indirect accountability supplied via national governments. All things being equal, the longer the chain of delegation, the more difficult it is to maintain effective accountability. In this case, however, direct accountability via national parliaments proves as hard to achieve as indirect accountability via national governments, since both rely on national elections to furnish a real contest on European issues. Thus, the 'under-politisation' of European issues undermines the effectiveness of this accountability mechanism as well, since national elections do not result in a national parliamentary majority with a mandate in this area, nor in a minority that gives voice to alternatives.

Do referendums offer a more promising tool for EU citizens to hold treaty reformers to account? It is a matter of constant debate whether referendums work well with representative-democratic institutions. Critics tend to argue that the former are dubious instruments for ascertaining the public will; that they give citizens more responsibility than they can handle; and that they undermine representative government and the role of parties and elected representatives (cf. Budge 2006).

Still, referendums are held in most representative democracies, and are considered a legitimate institutional supplement to representative decision-making. From an accountability point of view, referendums can be problematic, inasmuch as they can be strategically used by governments that seek to evade responsibility for unpopular decisions and that wish to avoid being held to account (cf. Setälä 2006: 712). Under some circumstances, however, a referendum can be an effective mechanism for accountability, since it enables citizens to overturn a decision made by their representatives. Accountability, it bears recalling, requires that citizens be able to monitor and evaluate the actions taken by their representatives – and to impose sanctions on them as well, should they feel they are not being adequately represented. Imposing sanctions does not necessarily mean throwing someone out of office; it can also mean overturning a decision, or changing the competencies accorded to representatives.

In order to assess referendums as an accountability mechanism, we need to make two important distinctions. First, there is a crucial difference between *mandatory* and *optional* referendums. In terms of accountability, it makes a big difference whether a referendum is mandatory under a state's constitution, or whether it merely represents an option which the government or parliamentary majority can decide to use. In the latter case, of course, the referendum will be much weaker as an accountability mechanism, since the representative institutions (meaning the government, in practice) are able to control its use.

Second, there is an important distinction to be made between *advisory* and *binding* referendums. If the representative institutions can choose to ignore the outcome of a referendum, then the function of the said referendum as an accountability mechanism is of course weakened. This difference is less crucial than that between mandatory and optional referendums, since the outcome of advisory referendums is usually respected by governments and parliaments. Still, there are no guarantees that the result of an advisory referendum will guide the actions taken by representatives.

We may conclude, then, that only mandatory referendums provide citizens with a strong mechanism for holding representatives accountable. Optional referendums, when controlled by the representative institutions, tend to become a strategic instrument serving government interests, rather than a control mechanism strengthening democratic accountability. Governments may use referendums to avoid internal division, to boost their popularity, or to increase their chances of winning an election. Only rarely do they call a referendum in order to give citizens the opportunity to hold their representatives accountable for decisions taken.

Where the ratification of EU treaties is concerned, it is only in Ireland that the constitution requires that a mandatory referendum be held. The Irish constitution needs to be amended, namely, whenever a new EU treaty comes into force; and all such amendments require direct approval by the Irish voters. The Danish constitution requires that a new treaty implying the transfer of new competencies from the member states to the EU be decided by a 5/6 majority in parliament, or by a simple parliamentary majority in combination with a binding referendum.

In all of the other member states, referendums on EU treaties are optional, which means that the government has the power – assuming it has the backing of parliament – to decide whether the people are to be given the opportunity to challenge the deal negotiated by governments in the course of an IGC. Governments are only likely to hold a referendum if they are under heavy pressure from public opinion and their opposition, such that they believe their chances of winning the next general election will be severely impaired if they refuse to hold a referendum. Tony Blair, for example, only agreed to hold a referendum on the Constitutional Treaty when he realised that a continued refusal to do so would seriously damage the prospects of the Labour Party in the 2004 EP election and the 2005 general election. By giving in to demands for a referendum, he deprived the opposition of one of its main weapons.

Referendums on new treaties, then, are mandatory only in Ireland. In every other member state, it is the government – or president, in the case of France – that holds the power to decide whether the voters can challenge an agreement to amend the treaties. Optional referendums, it bears stressing, are not strong mechanisms for ensuring accountability; rather, they are instruments that governments can use at will when they deem their purposes to be served thereby.

The convention method: improving accountability?

Will the convention method improve accountability, as some scholars (e.g. Risse and Kleine 2007: 75) have argued? The main difference between the IGC method and the convention method is the inclusion in the latter case of the EP and of national parliaments, all of which are directly elected by EU citizens. This does not mean, however, that the convention method furnishes EU citizens with a strong mechanism for accountability, whereby those in charge of EU treaty reform can be effectively sanctioned for their actions. There are two fundamental reasons for this.

First, while the convention method affords directly elected representatives an increased influence over the treaty-reform process, their role is restricted to the preparatory phase. Final decisions on treaty amendments during an IGC are still the prerogative of national governments.

Second, EP elections are not fought out over European issues any more than national elections are. The ability of citizens to hold MEPs accountable through EP elections is greatly limited by the fact that these are second-order national contests fought on national rather than European issues (Reif and Schmitt 1980). The absence of a real electoral contest over European issues thus undermines the ability of citizens to hold MEPs accountable for their actions, just as it makes it difficult in practice to hold national governments to account indirectly.

However, while the convention method does not afford EU citizens strong mechanisms for accountability, we ought not to rule out the possibility that it has some positive effects in this area. The possibility of sanctioning one's representatives is of crucial importance, but weak mechanisms for accountability also matter. To be able to hold one's representatives accountable, one must be able to monitor and evaluate their actions, and to examine the reasons for their decisions (Majone 1998: 20–2). Transparency is of vital importance here. If decision-makers are forced to take a position and to defend it in public, they are more likely to act in accordance with generally accepted principles and beliefs. Making discussions on treaty reform public is thus one way of ensuring that representatives take the views of the public into serious consideration.

Without any doubt, the convention method has increased the transparency of the preparatory phase of treaty reform. Compared with preparations that take place under the IGC method, the Convention was extremely open. The publication of various types of document on its website – speeches, background notes of the Secretariat and Praesidium, contributions of Convention delegates, reports from the working groups, draft articles, amendment proposals, and at last the final proposal – ensured public access to important information. In theory citizens could get, first-hand, a rough idea of how the proceedings were developing. In practice, of course, the great number of written documents and the complexity of the issues made it difficult for ordinary citizens to penetrate the material. Still, the easy access to relevant information clearly worked to enhance media coverage – thus improving the opportunity for citizens to follow the Convention's preparations indirectly.

The Convention clearly contributed to a more open process of treaty reform; and openness is a necessary albeit insufficient condition for accountability (cf. Manin *et al.* 1999: 24). Nevertheless, three factors combined to limit the importance of the Convention as a public forum in which citizens could acquaint themselves with different ideas on how to reform the EU.

The pursuit of a single proposal

From the outset, the mandate of the Convention was rather ambiguous. According to the Laeken Declaration, it would 'be the task of the Convention to consider the key issues arising for the Union's future development and try to identify the various possible responses' (European Council 2001: 4). This was basically the mandate of an agenda-setter. As for the final document the Convention was supposed to deliver, the Laeken Declaration explained that it could include 'different options, indicating the degree of support which they received, or recommendations if consensus is achieved' (European Council 2001: 4).

By enabling it to make *recommendations*, the European Council had opened the door for the Convention to be something more than just an agenda-setter. Chairman Giscard d'Estaing realised this at an early stage, and argued in his introductory speech that the Convention should aim at reaching 'a broad consensus on a single proposal' (European Convention 2002), in order to ensure that the IGC would not ignore or by-pass its ideas. This strategy was certainly successful in terms of maximising the Convention's influence over the IGC proceedings, but there was an obvious downside to it: making consensus on a single proposal an overarching goal for the Convention had the effect of rendering alternative options on how to solve various problems less visible to the public. If the final document had instead offered a variety of options, it would have given EU citizens a better understanding of the possible range of solutions. It would also have forced advocates of both the main option and its alternatives to argue explicitly on behalf of their preferred solution.

The consensus method

Making the search for a broad consensus an overriding concern also affected the internal decision-making procedures of the Convention. A crucial choice was made early on: all decisions at the Convention were to be taken without voting. Instead, the Praesidium relied on a 'consensus method' that involved both arguing and bargaining (Karlsson 2008). The mandate given at Laeken had not ruled out the use of voting as a mechanism for decision-making at the Convention. Its exclusion was rather a strategic choice on the part of the Praesidium, which believed that the introduction of voting would make it next to impossible to reach broad consensus on the final report.

The consensus method applied at the Convention gave the Praesidium the power to define – on the basis of working-group reports, written contributions, plenary debates, and amendment proposals – the precise meaning of consensus on different issues. It was the chairperson – usually Giscard d'Estaing himself – who summarised plenary debates, decided on which issues a consensus had been reached, and how the said consensus was to be understood. Likewise, the Praesidium summarised the content of amendment proposals, defining what it took to be the middle ground. The consensus-finding process involved a balancing act on part of the Praesidium: on the one hand, it wanted to make an impact on the final draft treaty and to promote its pet solutions. On the other, it could not ignore the opinions expressed by Convention delegates. The power to interpret the situation – to decide on which issues a consensus had been reached – could not be excessively abused without jeopardising broad support for the final document.

The Praesidium managed in the end to find (at least on paper) a broad consensus on a single proposal: a draft treaty on a Constitution for Europe. In this respect the consensus method was a success; from an accountability perspective, however, it had some obvious drawbacks. Since the final document was framed as a single proposal, the draft treaty was less informative than it would have been had it consisted of various options. The latter approach would have given members of the public an opportunity to acquaint themselves with opposing positions and arguments. Furthermore, the consensus method made it more difficult to discern differences of opinion among the actors. A broad consensus was reached, but that did not mean all of the delegates who signed the draft treaty were satisfied with its contents. As many delegates emphasised, consensus rather meant that one was able to accept the package *in toto*. When all was said and done, most delegates preferred to make the compromises needed in order to maximise the influence of the final report. Only a small group of eight delegates, led by the Danish MEP and

Eurosceptic Jens-Peter Bonde, refused to support the final report in the end (Norman 2003: 297–9).

There is no doubt the consensus method was an important tool for reaching a broad consensus. Its use also helped, however, to give the public a false impression of unity among the delegates to the Convention. In the absence of voting mechanisms, it fell much on the Chairman – often Giscard himself – to interpret the meaning of the consensus on various issues. Ultimately, the delegates had no effective way of giving voice to conflicting views; they could only choose to accept the Praesidium's final proposal or to reject it. If they refused to sign on to it, moreover, they would jeopardise the ability of the Convention to influence the IGC. Convention delegates thus developed a common interest in downplaying differences of opinion and supporting a package deal, rather than in giving open voice to their real preferences and building an opposition to the majority view championed by the Praesidium. In this sense, the operating procedures helped to obfuscate rather than clarify differences of opinions among delegates to the Convention. This did not contribute, certainly, to improving the accountability in the treaty reform process.

The unclear boundary between the IGC and the Convention

The decision to give priority to the search for consensus also affected the boundary between the Convention and the IGC. Looking back at the process, it is difficult to tell in practice where the Convention ended and the IGC began. The Laeken Declaration had clearly envisaged a two-stage process, but the boundary between the Convention and the IGC was undermined by the fact that national positioning started already during the Convention – as soon as the member states recognised that the Convention was aiming at a broad consensus behind a single proposal.

During the first stage of the proceedings – the listening phase – the Convention succeeded in avoiding national positioning. However, as the listening phase ended and work got under way, some of the member states showed clear signs of wanting to make their presence more visible. In the autumn of 2002, for instance, Germany and France decided to upgrade their presence at the Convention by appointing Joschka Fischer and Dominique de Villepin as delegates. On the one hand, Convention delegates welcomed the presence of Fischer and de Villepin, as it raised the status of the proceedings. On the other, they soon came to realise it signalled a shift in the process, in which the big member states would seek to make their presence felt – as a response to the fact that the Convention was clearly becoming more important than anyone had predicted at the outset (Norman 2003: 155–61). This pattern became still more obvious in January 2003, when France and Germany delivered a joint declaration on how work at the Convention ought to proceed. This was clearly perceived by many delegates as introducing elements of an IGC. This impression was reinforced by the fact that the Praesidium allowed contributions to be made in the name of member states (European Convention 2003).

Furthermore, it became clear during the final phase of the proceedings that many member-state delegates were in fact negotiating on their own government's behalf. In effect, then, the IGC had already begun before the Convention had ended. The Laeken Declaration had called upon the Convention to explore different methods for making the division of competence more transparent. It may therefore seem ironic that the Convention ended up causing problems in this very field, by making it more difficult for citizens to ascertain which actors were responsible for what in the treaty-amending process. If members of the public are to be capable, namely, of holding decision-makers to account, they must know who in fact is responsible for the different decisions.

Conclusion

Andrew Moravscik argues we should not be concerned about a possible deficit of accountability at the European level, as long as democratically elected governments control the governance structure of the EU (Moravscik 2002: 612). When it comes to treaty reform, in fact, we should not have anything at all to worry about in terms of accountability, since national governments and parliaments have the power to veto any decision to amend the treaties. According to this view, national elections furnish citizens of the Union with strong mechanisms for holding treaty reformers to account.

I have argued in this chapter that this line of reasoning is flawed, because it does not take into account what real opportunities EU citizens have to hold treaty reformers to account through such formal mechanisms. National elections, to begin with, are not fought on European issues – especially not those European issues upon which IGCs are empowered to decide; accordingly, national governments have no explicit mandate in this area. EU citizens are never presented with alternative views on the issues decided at IGCs, and there is no clear opposition to which they can turn should they feel discontent with the actions of their governments and parliaments. Although strong accountability mechanisms are available – in theory – at the national level, EU citizens have no effective means in practice with which to sanction those responsible for treaty reforms. As it turns out, the availability of formal mechanisms merely creates an illusion of accountability.

Referendums could be viewed as a mechanism for correcting this unsatisfactory state of affairs – a mechanism through which the people can sanction their representatives by overriding the deals struck at IGCs. In almost all of the member states, however, referendums in connection with the ratification of new treaties are optional (which means they are controlled, in practice, by the government).

The arrangements spawned at Laeken – whereby preparations for the 2003–4 IGC would be the responsibility of a Convention – do strengthen accountability to a degree, by introducing weak mechanisms in the preparatory stage of the treaty-reform process. The proceedings of the Convention were no doubt more open than previous IGC preparations. Plenary-debate minutes were made public and available for scrutiny, as were working-group reports, contributions from individual delegates, draft articles by the Praesidium, and proposals for amending the treaties. Even in the absence of strong mechanisms for holding treaty reformers to account, the enhanced transparency brought to IGC preparations by the convention method does have some positive implications for accountability. Increased transparency does indeed strengthen the ability of EU citizens to monitor and evaluate the work of their representatives, and to initiate a public debate that can affect the level of support for the government and even its chances of success in the next general election. Decision-makers who must act in public are less likely to deviate from generally accepted principles and beliefs.

Article 48 of the consolidated version of the Treaty on European Union (TEU) suggests that the convention method is here to stay. However, if this new method for treaty reform is to reach its full potential in terms of improving accountability, it is important that future conventions be forums in which various opinions are publicly stated, debated, and justified, rather than institutions in which all concerned parties strive to reach consensus at all costs.

According to the consolidated version of the TEU (*Official Journal* 2008/C 115/01), a Convention shall 'examine the proposals for amendments and shall adopt by consensus a recommendation' to an IGC, which then has the power to determine 'by common accord the amendments to be made to the Treaties'. This differs from the mandate laid down in the Laeken Declaration, which stated that the task of the Convention is to 'draw up a final document which may comprise either different options, indicating the degree of support which they received, or recommendations if consensus is achieved' (European Council 2001).

This means, as a matter of fact, that future Conventions are required to reach consensus – they do not have the option that the European Convention had: namely, to deliver a final report consisting of different options on how to amend the treaties. This is bad news for accountability, for two reasons.

First, the consensus requirement means the Convention will lose much of its potential to serve as a forum in which citizens have the opportunity to acquaint themselves with alternative options, and in which opposition to majority standpoints can be formed and made public. As we saw in the case of the European Convention, the quest for consensus threatens to result in a process in which a small group of leading actors assumes responsibility for interpreting the meaning of the prevailing consensus; in which differences of opinions are downplayed for the sake of displaying unity; and in which the boundary between Convention and IGC is blurred, due to the fact that member states feel a need to control what happens (since recommendations issued by a unified Convention can only be altered marginally by an IGC).

Second, the actors that in theory could challenge the deals struck at IGCs and take the lead in initiating public debate and forming opposition – i.e. national parliaments and the EP – will now be standing behind the recommendations guiding final decision-making in the IGC. If all concerned parties are included in decision-making and required to take part in forming a consensus, there will be no one left to formulate alternatives and give voice to opposition.

It is impossible, of course, to determine with any degree of certainty from the new article 48 how future conventions will work. However, the consensus requirement does raise legitimate concerns about how much the convention method helps to improve accountability. Future conventions operating under this requirement are likely to become 'quasi-IGCs', in which member-state governments dominate and the supreme object is to negotiate an outcome acceptable to all. This is far from the ideal of a deliberative forum, where alternative options are openly discussed and opposition is given a voice – thus strengthening accountability.

7 Delegation to the permanent representation and mechanisms of accountability

Thomas Larue

The core subject of this chapter is national delegation: more precisely, the pattern displayed by different EU member states when the national administration delegates powers to its permanent representation (PR) in Brussels. The link between the two levels is important to study, as it constitutes a critical case of delegation. This delegation goes beyond that expressed by the English term *delegated legislation*, or the German concept of *Rechtsverordungen*, or what is referred to as rule-making in American administrative law, i.e. the 'exercise of lawmaking power delegated by the legislature to administrative agencies to create supplementary norms that fill in the details of the generally worded provisions of statutes' (Shapiro 2002: 14). Indeed, bureaucrats serving at the permanent representation are delegated the power to shape the very statutes (and thus the core norms) of EU legislation; and since EU law has supremacy over national law, it follows that EU law-making is even more salient than 'the creation of supplementary norms'. In the case of Sweden, Jonas Tallberg (2001: 55) points to the permanent representation as a potential source of challenges to the government's autonomy in the making of EU policy: 'The government's control over its own EU policy could also be challenged by those who represent the member state in Brussels – the national permanent representation'. Neil Nugent (1999: 475) argues it is important to increase our understanding of the ways in which member states partake in EU decision-making processes (and ultimately determine the outcome of European integration) ' ... because there are significant variations in the ways in which governments attempt to control, and do control, their input into the Council via their representatives'. Not only, Nugent (1999: 477) argues, do governments have their own ways of coordinating their EU policies; it is also the case that the coordination and control of EU policies has become more and more complicated. This greater difficulty in managing EU issues is caused not only by the escalating numbers of decisions taken by the EU, but also by the sheer increase in the pace at which policy is shaped in Brussels. This also affects the scope of EU coordinating efforts at the domestic level, since an increasing number of ministries are involved.

My aim in this chapter is to describe, analyse, and compare the delegation and accountability designs characterising different national governments and ve PRs in Brussels. The primary focus is on questions linked to ns of *accountability established between the principals and the* s specific act of delegation. These accountability mechanisms the hazards of delegation. If we are to gain a deeper under- e process of delegation to national bureaucrats at the European ential to describe and assess these mechanisms. They involve n, institutional checks, screening and selection mechanisms, and monitoring and reporting requirements. To what extent are such mechanisms present in the case at hand? In what way do different accountability and delegation designs contribute to the efficient functioning of delegation between national capitals on the one hand and Brussels on the other? How do existing accountability mechanisms and patterns of delegation to the EU appear from a democratic perspective?

This chapter is based heavily on an earlier research project (Larue 2006), which was an explorative and descriptive (Yin 2003) comparative case study of two EU member states: France and Sweden. While that study did not draw on the traditional comparative method (cf. Ragin 1987), it can still be used in order to distil general inferences into the workings of accountability. For further details on methodological aspects and case selection, the reader is referred to my thesis (Larue 2006: 63–85).

Theoretical basis of delegation designs

Based on the writings of Kiewiet and McCubbins, and following the previously mentioned description of control mechanisms used by principals to design the institutional incentives of a specific delegation, a model (similar to previous operationalisations of Kiewiet and McCubbins's four control mechanisms, cf. Depauw 2003) specifies variables, for both the principals and the agents. The analytical variables are four control mechanisms described by Kiewiet and McCubbins (1991: 27–34): *contract design*, *screening and selection mechanisms*, *monitoring and reporting requirements*, and *institutional checks*. While the original study on which this chapter is based had a slightly more comprehensive analytical model (see Larue 2006: 51–61), I choose here to concentrate on the four main analytical variables below.

Variable 1: Contract design lays down the terms, limits, goals, and sanctions (available to the principal in case of negligent or derelict behaviour on the part of the agent) of the relationship between the principal and the agent. This encompasses the contract terms of the national bureaucrats' employment at the permanent representation (PR) – such as the nature of the contract (incentive or risk-sharing based contracts, cf. Shavell 1979), the level of salaries and other remunerations compared to other similar employment within each respective member state, and the longevity of the contracts, i.e. how long do PR civil servants stay in Brussels (*turnover rate*)? Are these formalised into guidelines and, if so, are these in turn followed or partly/totally ignored?

Variable 2: Screening and selection mechanisms refer to the procedures used by a principal when he/she chooses an agent. This variable focuses on the ways principals structure selection processes of national bureaucrats: for example, through candidate screening (i.e. whether candidates are vetted in competition or appointed directly by superiors without due nomination processes), agent selection, use of signalling (cf. Spence 1974 or Balla and Wright 2001 on third-party signalling) or other information in screening and selection processes, and initiation of contact (i.e. whether the agent contacted the principal or vice-versa).

Variable 3: Monitoring and reporting mechanisms installed by the principal will be measured by the following criteria, among others: frequency and nature of reporting, frequency and nature (fire alarms or police patrols, cf. McCubbins and Schwartz 1984) of monitoring, and changes in administrative processes. It should be mentioned that some fire alarms (third-party monitoring and reporting mechanisms) are not included in this study; these include, for example, the scrutiny offered by the press. The data measured through this variable include main systems and institutions which have been set up by the principals.

Variable 4: Institutional checks represent one of the most potent systems for curbing agency loss. Technically, institutional checks ' … require that when authority has been delegated to an agent, there is at least one other agent with the authority to veto or block the actions of that agent' (Kiewiet and McCubbins 1991: 34; Ferejohn 1999: 132; Huber and Shipan 2000: 28). Actual cases of institutional check in this study will fall within a slightly broader definition. The reasons for using a broader definition are twofold. First, it is not just agents who can act as institutional checks. Second, a more stringent definition would overly constrain the identification of functions of institutional checks. By broadening the definition, we can characterise ministers at the Council level and national parliament and their EU committees as institutional checks.

Depending on the nature of these institutional mechanisms, we can assess in what way they influence the delegation between principal and agent. Thus, by assessing the degree and nature of asymmetrical information and the different institutional mechanisms set up by respective principals, we can measure and describe the propensity for agency loss, although not the *exact* level of agency loss. It is the environment and incentives together that shape the behaviour of individuals, whose actions (and thus underlying preferences) shape the level of any possible agency loss. The exact level of agency loss can only be specified when the preference of the principal and the agent's action on a particular policy (as well as the policy outcome) are known. This short study investigates a broader picture rather than individual policy fields or policy decisions; consequently, the findings will discuss the general propensity (or lack thereof) for agency loss within the scope of each member state's national delegation and accountability design. To sum up, the four analytical variables enumerated here will give me a good picture of the general institutional *delegation and accountability design*. In other words, this model will help us understand the extent to which there are institutional safeguards against two of the most common problems of delegation: first, *moral hazard*, or the extent to which the agent(s) behave in ways inimical to the interests of the principal (also called hidden actions: e.g. Holmstrom 1979); and second, *adverse selection*, or the extent to which agent(s) harbour attributes (or even preferences) unknown to the principal (also referred to as hidden information, cf. Arrow 1985).

Each of these variables will be assessed for each country according to a five-level scale, ranging from very weak (−−) to very strong (++), depending on their presence and efficiency. The efficiency is based on the analytical variables' ability to structure an effective delegation and to diminish the propensity to agency loss (and problems of hidden actions and information). The assessment of the variables will be based on the yardstick of an ideal type of delegation and accountability design given above, and on an analysis performed in a larger study (Larue 2006). When assessing each variable's values, both formal and informal processes and structures are reviewed.

Main empirical findings

Below, the *mechanisms of accountability established between the principals and the agents* for this specific act of national delegation within the framework of EU legislative politics are presented. As stated previously, these accountability mechanisms help alleviate the hazards of delegation, and are thus critical to describe and assess if we are to gain a deeper understanding of the way in which delegation to national bureaucrats at the European level works. To what extent are these mechanisms (i.e. contract design, screening and selection, monitoring and reporting requirements, and institutional checks) present? How do different delegation and accountability designs contribute to the efficient functioning of delegation between member-state capitals and Brussels?

Contract design

The first mechanism is *contract design*. The purely formal design of the agent's contract does not differ significantly as between the permanent representation of France and that of Sweden. Both countries have similar methods (in reference to their own system) of establishing the contract that governs their bureaucrats in Brussels. Given that each national system has its own regulations and contract conditions applying to civil servants who are stationed abroad, the contract conditions for the employees of the permanent representations are still quite similar. The only marginal difference is in the tenure of the envoys' posting. In Sweden, the general rule is that civil servants serve as attachés for a period of around two or three years. In France it is generally four years, although some ministries have started talking about a three-year-long appointment to the permanent representation. Both Swedish and French agents at the permanent representation are dependent on how their principals design their contract in their daily work, but the fundamental basis of the delegation between Brussels and the national capital is not primarily based on that specific contract design. In addition, the demands coupled to *participation constraint* (cf. Aghion and Tirole 1997) are met.

Both French and Swedish civil servants make active and arduous efforts to secure employment at their permanent representation. The design of both countries' contract with its bureaucrats is limited to a *risk-sharing* agreement. The only additional incentive incorporated into the contract is the positive benefit that being posted at the PR in Brussels may have on the bureaucrat's career. The last element is noteworthy; many interviewees mentioned it in their discussions. Most interviewees voiced a concern over the lack of interest accorded the specific knowledge they had acquired in Brussels. While strongest amongst the PR officials, this concern also appears in interviews with domestic actors. A comparison between Sweden and France does not reveal any significant differences. To sum up, neither the nature nor the extent of present French or Swedish contract design indicates that efficient *ex ante* influence over the agent can be executed through this control mechanism. The contract design of Brussels-based national representatives appears to be weak.

Screening and selection

The second mechanism is *screening and selection.* In both Sweden and France, the responsible ministry *de facto* appoints the bureaucrat, from within its own ranks, to a specific position in the permanent representation. This is true of the standard positions, such as that of counsellor or deputy counsellor at the permanent representation. For senior positions within both Swedish and French permanent representations, the screening and selection mechanisms preceding the appointments are somewhat different. They are not formalised in any way, for example. When asked about their promotion to their position, almost all of the permanent representatives and deputy permanent representatives responded that they were asked to take the post. None actually passed through the usual screening and selection process of job applications commonly used when filling executive vacancies. One could argue that there is little need for such measures, and that the principal can be said to have had the opportunity of testing and screening the candidate's skills and talents on previous occasions. Here the pattern of recruitment to high-level posts at the permanent representations (evidently the two posts of COREPER I and II ambassadors are implied) is remarkably similar between the two countries. In both, the government tends to appoint senior civil servants with a very long experience of both bilateral and multilateral diplomacy, as well as of European diplomacy. However, certain interesting differences appear. In the Swedish case, screening and selection mechanisms of the highest representatives are something of a puzzle, since governments at first appointed persons with a political affiliation opposite to their own. This ended with the nomination of Sweden's third permanent representative in 1999. Choosing an agent with potentially contrary preferences is indeed a risky business for any principal. Yet this is what happened in Sweden during the first years of its membership. If one looks at the French case, the behaviour of French executive is more congruent with the basic assumptions of principal-agent theory: all of the French permanent representatives and the heads of the SGAE (the French interministerial committee for coordination of EU affairs, previously abbreviated SGCI) have been chosen according to political affiliation.

Turning our attention to the general provisions for screening and selection mechanisms of regular personnel at the permanent representations, we find both similarities and differences as between the two cases. First, both national systems use similar screening and selection techniques. The choice and preparation of choosing an appropriate agent to a position in Brussels is taken back home by the responsible ministry. Judging from the interviews, the procedure followed is more or less clear. Usually, agents are approached by their superiors and offered the job; in some cases, however, the candidate applies to the position and has to compete with others to obtain it. In the Swedish case, the results from a questionnaire (Larue 2006) confirm this conclusion: 35 per cent state that they were offered the position at the PR in Brussels. In contrast, French PR officials were customarily (in 75 per cent of cases) offered the position by their own administrative services or by their superior. It appears that French officials are more often offered positions within the PR. This would reflect the administrative culture within Paris, whereby posts are assigned to specific *corps* or ministries. This is not done, however, without some type of screening and selection process. Many interviewees stated that their principals contacted them prior to offering them a position in Brussels. In one case, in fact, the agent was actually persuaded to accept a senior position at the permanent representation (cf. Larue 2006: 176). To sum up, the screening and selection mechanisms used in this specific act of delegation do not differ from other selection procedures used in domestic appointments. The level of efficiency displayed by the existing mechanisms could be rated as barely adequate, mainly because they do not offer the possibility of a coherent selection process by the permanent representation's leadership (although both the French and the Swedish COREPER II ambassadors can formally refuse to employ a civil servant, the existing systems do not allow this to happen without significant internal administrative costs).

Monitoring and reporting requirements

The third mechanism we identified consists of the so-called *monitoring and reporting requirements*. In the Swedish case, the monitoring and reporting requirements installed by the principals seem most adequate. The reporting activities are concentrated on the bureaucratic agents themselves. Though the chances for hidden actions are theoretically high, both formal and informal practices assure that monitoring and reporting requirements are high. Any possible deficiency in formal monitoring is balanced by informal channels for discussion between officials in Stockholm and their 'mirror' officials at the permanent representation in Brussels. Given that relations between these two, for the most part, seem to be very intense, we can conclude that efficient control is exerted through these channels. However, while these informal channels seem to offer the possibility of containing agency loss, they cannot *guarantee* it. In other words, even though informal channels for discussion between bureaucrats in Stockholm and Brussels seem to offer the possibility of containing agency loss, the mechanisms represented in informal discussions are of little value when it comes to assuring, formally speaking, a good delegation.

A particularly interesting factor with regard to the Swedish system is the innovation of the Monday notes [*måndagsnoterna*], which were introduced after the Swedish presidency in the first half of 2001. They have succeeded insofar as they are now an integrated routine part of Swedish coordination of EU legislation. Other monitoring and reporting requirements are also useful, but they all more or less involve the principals themselves. While this reduces cost-efficiency in the principals' monitoring of agents, it nevertheless provides them with an important contact with Brussels-based agents. Such a requirement is the weekly meetings on Fridays between the top strata of Brussels and of Stockholm in EU affairs.

Perhaps even more important, although it is difficult to make exact comparisons with the previously mentioned meeting, are the monthly breakfast meetings (Larue 2006: 208) that the head of the permanent representation has with the highest EU troika: the prime minister, the foreign minister, and the state secretary for EU affairs. At first, the different structures and the slightly different monitoring and reporting requirements mechanisms that apply to issues belonging to the CFSP (Common Foreign and Security Policy) field might appear to be a weakness in the system. This is because they open up the possibility of having an instruction that is contradictory to more general policy standpoints and/or views within the rest of the governmental organisation. On the other hand, some evidence suggests that the monitoring structures in place in fact guarantee an *additional* level of control. Every single instruction sent down to the Swedish PSC ambassador and to the officials taking part in meetings in PSC or subordinate working groups is checked by EUKORR (a small unit within the Swedish Ministry of Foreign Affairs with formal coordination responsibility for CFSP issues). A certain quality of coordination and coherence is thus maintained. In a certain sense, EUKORR acts as a form of permanent *police patrol*, at least on CFSP issues.

It remains to see what will happen with the coordination and the drafting of instructions in the aftermath of the 2005 reform, in which the UD-EU unit at the Swedish Ministry of Foreign Affairs was reformed into the SB-EU at the Prime Minister's Office (for more details on this reform, see Persson 2007b).

The monitoring and reporting requirements installed by the principals in Paris are adequate and well-ingrained. They are very impressive at a formal level, but less so in the real day-to-day and informal handling of EU dossiers. It seems there is a certain discrepancy between the formal rules and informal praxis. While the SGAE seems to be handling its task of controlling and coordinating EU issues relatively well, it is constantly under pressure. Furthermore, even though the reporting requirements can be seen as rather strong and well-developed, this must be weighed against the rather important rise of informal contacts between Paris (the ministries) and Brussels (the PR). One clear drawback is also that the system installed for the coordination of EU issues falling under the scope of the first and third pillar is not applied to the CFSP proposals (as is the case in Sweden). This opens up for misunderstanding and confusion about issues belonging to the second pillar, which are coordinated by a ministry that lacks a tradition of working with other ministries. This could prove to be serious for the long-term ambitions of French foreign policy, as it will undoubtedly lead to friction between the Foreign Ministry and the Ministry of Defence and, in some cases, between the Ministry of Interior and the Ministry of Justice. In theoretical terms, it is also dangerous because it enhances the risk of slippage by either the Ministry of Foreign Affairs or the agents in Brussels, because the number of police patrols is reduced to at best one or two (i.e. another ministry besides the Foreign Ministry). A general assessment of combined informal and formal monitoring and reporting requirements points to strong mechanisms in the Swedish case and adequate ones in the French case.

Institutional checks

This brings us to the fourth mechanism, *institutional checks.* These are the most potent and crucial tools available to the principal for preventing agency loss (but also the most costly). They are defined as the institutions, in a given case of delegation give to a specific agent, with the ' … authority to veto or block the actions of that agent' (Kiewiet and McCubbins 1991: 34). In both the French and the Swedish case, institutional checks are essentially absent. In fact, it may be that the most efficient and real institutional check in place is the ministers themselves, when they meet at the level of the Council. In purely formal terms, the ministers gathered at a Council meeting have the ability to annul the decisions taken by their PR civil servants at working-group or committee level. One important drawback with this institutional check is that it means the principals (i.e. the ministers) must themselves assume the costs of actually checking their agents. However, this does not constitute a real institutional check, as defined by our stringent criteria. This is because the ministers are not agents; in which case, the above-mentioned 'control mechanism' is more like a police patrol. In fact, following a strict theoretical definition of what constitutes an institutional check, no such mechanism exists.

Summary analysis

The following scale was used in order to assess the degree of presence and impact on the delegation link between member-state capitals and their respective permanent representation: (−−) very weak, (−) weak, (±) adequate, (+) strong, and (++) very strong.

In summary the results show that when it comes to *contract design* both countries have weak (−) mechanisms. In the case of *screening and selections mechanisms*, these are adequate (±) in both countries. Sweden has very strong (++) *reporting and monitoring mechanisms* even if these are strong (+) in France as well. As for *institutional checks* both countries have very weak (−−) mechanisms.

What shall we conclude from this brief summary? Moreover, what kind of general conclusions can we draw from this study? With regard to contract design, it is clear that the principals in this case have not chosen to emphasise this aspect of the delegation. Contracts lack specific incentives and motivating factors. Both the formal and informal benefits of being employed at the permanent representations are low. Thus, both French and Swedish contract designs are barely adequate, because they do not solve problems of adverse selection in any efficient or genuine way. Consequently, they may be appropriately labelled as weak. The screening and selection mechanisms do not stand out as being especially effective either. They meet 'normal standards' for assuring a certain degree of expertise amongst Brussels-based bureaucrats. However, there are no common standards or guidelines as to which screening and selection mechanisms and processes are to apply. Each ministry is left to its own devices. The level of influence exerted by the PR leadership in filling counsellor positions is often limited. The competition between agents is in real terms very low (while there may be some type of *formal* competition, the real and *informal* decision is characterised by a total lack of competition). The reporting and monitoring requirements imposed on the agents are adequate for their tasks. Standard operating procedures are unambiguous, and they are normally followed by civil servants in Brussels. They allow the principals to receive information and to evaluate the work done by the agents. Unfortunately, most of the monitoring devices installed are of a *police-patrol* nature. This makes the costs of monitoring the agents higher than the frequency and intensity of *fire alarms* oversights.

Formal institutional checks are totally absent from the delegation and accountability design of both France and Sweden. If institutional checks exist, they appear in the shape of actors or processes external to the national chain of delegation, such as intra-institutional checks at various levels in the Council, or inter-institutional checks at the European level (e.g. between the European Parliament and the Council of Ministers). So what should we conclude at a general level about the nature of national delegation in EU affairs? One conclusion would be that the delegation is designed in a very open-ended way, and that control mechanisms are weak. The level of control mechanisms in place is low. In the few instances that control mechanisms are actually installed, they are seldom of such a character as to bestow on principals the ability to control their agents effectively. Thus, it seems that the national agents based in Brussels are left largely to their own devices. The mechanisms in place do allow principals to force agents to pay some attention to their wishes when acting in Brussels. But while principals thus possess formal and direct action-forcing leverage, it is rarely used. Why?

First, the level of information asymmetry is too high. Full knowledge about the desires of the other member countries on any specific issue or legislative proposal, or about the nature of the deal-breaker limits of other member states on sensitive issues, is restricted to the agents in Brussels (and sometimes also to individual counsellors at ministries and national agencies, when they partake in working groups).

Second, the fact that the agents are embedded in multilateral negotiations makes it harder for their principals to force them to obey. In many cases, forcing the hand of the agent – whether through direct instructions or through the delegation and accountability design – is simply counterproductive, and the outcome of the delegation is not altered (majority rule allows a number of member states to vote through legislation).

Third, the political will to assume responsibility is often lacking. This is shown by the design of the delegation between Paris and Stockholm on the one hand, and Brussels on the other. Both France and Sweden have established – albeit to varying degrees and in differing manners – a delegation and accountability design that leaves the government free to shift the blame.

Looking at the Swedish case, it seems the evidence points to a weak policy-framing ability at the domestic level. The main problem lies in the inability of political actors (especially politicians) within the chancery to exert influence over the day-to-day handling of EU proposals. Most chancery interviewees describe the handling and coordination of EU issues as a chore for the ministerial officials. In turn, the bureaucrats within the ministries view the role of political leadership provided by ministers and the government as subordinate to other bureaucratic values (cf. Jacobsson and Sundström 1999: 109). The lack of political initiative can no longer be excused on the grounds that Swedish political actors are unacquainted with the European system, as could be argued during the first years of membership. The influence of Brussels-based agents on policy-framing in Stockholm is unmistakably important. Yet another observation that can be made in the Swedish case is that priorities among preferences have only recently been dictated by the principal. Earlier on, instructions to the permanent representation did not include specific prioritisations among issues (something that has now been incorporated, although not to an ideal extent). Even today, Brussels-based agents have to make important decisions as to how to prioritise among Stockholm-based preferences on EU proposals. In France, on the other hand, the policy-framing process is a more complicated affair. This is largely due to the influence of the *cabinets*, which play a vital role in French politics and in the coordination of political preferences in Paris. While policy-framing in

French politics is also under the domination or heavy influence of bureaucrats, the influence of politicised bureaucrats (especially *cabinet* members) allows us to conclude that EU proposals are reasonably well-anchored at the political level. Setting priorities for the articulation of policies is left to bureaucrats and Brussels-based agents.

In France, this is done by letting the PR handle the negotiations and giving Brussels-based bureaucrats a rather wide leeway, as well as some influence on how French EU policy is framed. In Sweden, this is done by not automatically coordinating *all* of the issues handled (i.e. legislation handled in working groups) by the Swedish permanent representation. The general opinion in each country serves to mitigate these factors, as governments in Sweden are more often criticised for their European policy than are French governments. This study shows that the national bureaucratic agents in Brussels are left largely to their own judgment as to how to argue and act in many situations. Some of the evidence disclosed in this chapter may thus point to trust rather than control as a core element when a member state's capital delegates responsibility to its civil servants in Brussels. This distinction in the logic of delegation has been made by Majone (2001), who argues that one negative consequence of studies that use agency theory (as this chapter does) is that they tend to overlook the fiduciary relations between actors involved in European integration (i.e. member states and EU institutions). Despite some initial doubts on my part, some of the evidence I have seen would appear to support Majone's arguments on trust as a basis for efficient delegation. I concede that initial trust can be one of the basic foundations for delegation, but it also bears noting that 'fiduciary delegation' is primarily encountered in specific situations, e.g. when the principal wishes to solve the problem of credible commitment (cf. Miller 2005: 219). Solving this problem is desirable when a principal wishes to delegate power and responsibilities even while being (for example) uncertain as to whether his/her short-term preferences are aligned with his/her long-term ones. In other words, the awareness of this problem has impelled principals to initiate a pattern of delegation where the agent only acts when his/her interests conflict with those of the principal, and where the agent is assured a degree of autonomy. However, the logic behind using delegation in order to solve problems of credible commitment only applies if one accepts the idea that fiduciary principal-agent relationships only work when the principal's overarching preference is to have an agent over whom he/she has little or no control. Assuming otherwise – i.e. that a principal would choose an agent who will unfailingly disagree with his/her employer – is simply to throw the baby out while keeping the bath water.

Conclusion

What general insights into the workings of accountability in national delegation have we reached? National idiosyncrasies remain important in every study which aims at describing and explaining the management of EU affairs, whether it is the domestic coordination of core executives (cf. Fink-Hafner 2007) or coordination at European level (cf. Kassim *et al.* 2001). Still, a couple of general conclusions suggest themselves in light of the evidence presented above.

First, the delegation and accountability design does account, to some degree, for the way in which delegation is established. Indeed, both countries have a fairly weak delegation and accountability design, and both display a slightly sub-optimal delegation in terms of democratic efficiency. Yet the structure of delegation implies that the system established between capitals and member-state PRs also relies on efficient negotiations to improve policy results, and to raise the level of influence for both countries (this is perhaps clearest in the case of Sweden, cf. Naurin 2007, Naurin and Lindahl 2007). I still maintain, however, that the search for an efficient delegation structure can and should be applied as well to the democratic values embodied in existing national chains of delegation. We should endeavour to analyse and assess the democratic aspects of delegation, rather than just focusing on efficiency in terms of negotiations or the capacity to network. In other words, how effective are delegation mechanisms in conveying domestically shaped preferences? And to what extent do they allow citizens, parties, and elected representatives to shape these same preferences? We should start viewing both law-making (cf. Johannesson 2005) and the political system (cf. Blomgren and Bergman 2005) as increasingly intertwined at the European and national level. This will make the analysis of delegation between member states' political institutions and domestic national policy-making processes on the one hand, and European decision-making institutions and processes on the other, even more important in future. The newly negotiated treaty reforms –with the increased role they assign to national parliaments in the EU policy-making process –points to the need for further research on this matter, as does the increasing level of 'national EU-parliamentarism' (cf. Hegeland 2006).

A second inference is that formal and informal mechanisms of accountability sometimes differ greatly, and that national bureaucratic agents in Brussels are left largely, as an informal matter, to their own judgement as to how to argue and act in many situations. This serves to underline that agents in Brussels are influential policy-makers who work in a law-making environment where there is little room for error. The ability of national parliaments to stop package deals from being voted through the Council once they have been agreed upon is limited. Bureaucrats bind their governments to specific standpoints in negotiations. But if national parliaments have a hard time reversing or stopping package deals, that is nothing compared with the political costs incurred when a minister reverses earlier positions taken by civil servants negotiating in Brussels. The widespread proliferation of informal procedures may lie at the heart of implicit delegation problems (cf. Eberlein and Grande 2005). Informal processes obfuscate chains of delegation, and render the task of holding agents accountable more onerous. Strengthening delegation and accountability designs could improve delegation substantially, as could reforming formal institutional and procedural practices so as to close the gap between formal and informal processes.

Third, and in reference to the third question presented in the introduction to this chapter, it could be said that, with the appearance of the EU and its system of law-making, democracy – and most clearly representative democracy – faces a new and dangerous challenge. We can argue about the risks and virtues of delegating power to bureaucrats, but most people would agree that at least some degree of delegation in the processes of self-government is beneficial. If principals, wherever they are positioned along the national chain of delegation (voters, members of parliament, or ministers), are not satisfied with the outcome of the delegation, they can alter it at some reasonable cost. For example, they vote in the next elections, or pass a vote of no confidence, or introduce new legislation, or appoint a new agency, or issue new guidelines to existing agencies, or even change budget allocations. However, in the case of law-making at the level of the EU (or, metaphorically speaking, at the 'European link' along the chain of delegation), back-pedalling is extremely costly, if not downright impossible. In the words of one high-level official, the EU is an organisation where national representatives must be constantly ready to nail their colours to the mast.

Revoking a national standpoint in COREPER negotiations, or in a working group, entails a severe loss of credibility. And such credibility is regarded by national governments as an essential currency. Abolishing or dramatically changing a directive or regulation central to Europe's internal market, for example, would encounter great resistance, not least from the Commission. Rescinding its membership in the Union, or in any basic way altering the nature of delegation between itself and the EU, remains a Herculean task for any single member state. These institutional realities promote a type of governance in which accountability is not feasible. It is important to stress this, because an argument often made on behalf of the Union's democratic character – amongst others by Germany's *Bundesverfassungsgericht* in its famous Maastricht verdict – is that a member state's delegation to the EU is revocable. Can democracy, and more specifically representative democracy in Europe, really thrive in an environment where accountability is a *de jure* possibility but a *de facto* chimera? We would do well to concede that national bureaucrats stationed in Brussels are a crucial cornerstone of our democracies, and that holding them accountable is not to be considered a hindrance to efficient modern governance, but rather a crucial enhancement to modern democracy.

8 European intelligence cooperation and accountability

Thorsten Wetzling

Intelligence has once again become a thriving business across Europe. National and European decision-makers value the clandestine and highly versatile *modi operandi* of modern security and intelligence services in the fight against international terrorism, organised crime, and the proliferation of weapons of mass destruction.[1] Contemporary agencies operate, however, in a remarkably different context from that which applied during the heyday of cloak-and-dagger operations in the Cold War. It can briefly be characterised as follows: First, European intelligence agencies all now serve and defend open societies. As a consequence, the direction of intelligence activities has become subject to increasing democratisation across the continent. Second, in accordance with the mantra that 'networked threats require a networked response' (Slaughter 2004b: 160), European nations have intensified their cooperation in intelligence matters. Cooperation can thus now take a variety of forms, and it is being practised at a range of levels. This can be seen in the proliferation of bilateral joint ventures, in the increasing resort to multilateral arrangements, and in the coordination of intelligence capabilities at the level of the European Union (Müller-Wille 2004; Daun and Jäger 2005; Wetzling 2008). Third, intelligence has been subject to a growing privatisation (see Shorrock 2008); it is no longer, consequently, a *domaine réservé* for the public services.

However, while progress has no doubt been made at the domestic level in democratising the direction of intelligence activities, it would be premature to assume that the entire spectrum of European intelligence activity today stands under sufficient democratic control. Indeed, the fact that a growing number of previously national intelligence competences are now being coordinated and practised outside national confines would appear to be a mixed blessing for citizens: in addition, namely, to the enhanced security it potentially provides, it poses major challenges to democratic governance. One particularly important challenge will be to establish and maintain mechanisms of public accountability for the conduct of European intelligence cooperation. So far, national and European politicians have been slow to apprehend and respond to the 'transnationalisation of bureaucracies of surveillance' (Bigo 2008: 11). Yet it is critical – and well past time – to shed more light on European intelligence cooperation, and on its compatibility with this quintessential norm of democratic rule.

In keeping with the general theme of this book, this chapter places special emphasis on accountability for European Union (EU) intelligence bodies. What is the effect on accountability when intelligence moves to the European level? A reasonable assumption from the outset might be that accountability in intelligence matters is least likely to be found in Brussels. In support of this assumption, one might point out that, notwithstanding all the progress that has been made, intelligence still figures as one of the very least transparent fields – possibly *the* least – of domestic government activity in most EU states. Furthermore, in light of the EU's democratic deficit in far less secretive policy fields, there would seem to be little basis for properly accountable intelligence relationships at the supranational level. Alternatively, however, one might proceed on the opposite assumption: that the level of accountability achieved in this area is higher at the EU level than at the national level, at least in most cases. In support of this rather unconventional assumption, one could adduce the growing efforts at collaboration between national parliaments and the European Parliament (EP) – efforts that serve, very likely, to enhance accountability.

Before we can apply this 'least-likely test' for accountability in the European Union, however, we will need to consider a few empirical and theoretical questions more closely. In the first two sections, accordingly, I review the patterns by which intelligence cooperation currently unfolds in Europe. I introduce the main players and their arenas; I describe the nature of the activities concerned; and I sketch the depth of cooperation achieved. The purpose of the third section is to examine the extremely popular (but also highly contingent) concept of accountability in greater detail. In the fourth section, I turn my attention to the question of intelligence accountability within the framework of the EU. In the same section, I also review certain *accountability pathways* between the European Parliament (EP) and the European Council (EC), as these emerged during a recent EP investigation into the possible involvement or complicity of EU member states in the 'illegal deprivation of [the] liberty of individuals, including abduction, rendition, transfer, detention or torture either by act or omission' (European Parliament 2006). Finally, I explore the significance of my findings from the standpoint of a more holistic discussion of accountability within the area of intelligence cooperation.

The actors in European intelligence cooperation

Writing on such a delicate topic requires one to introduce a few important caveats. First, I will limit my attentions in what follows to intelligence cooperation within the field of *counter-terrorism*. Second, I adopt a narrow understanding of *European* intelligence cooperation: that is, I consider cooperation among European partners only. Third, I omit private actors from my account. (Intelligence privatisation is indeed advancing at the domestic level; to my knowledge, however, the outsourcing of intelligence to private actors has not yet been coordinated at the European level.) Lastly, I make no claim that my brief description is an exhaustive one; a number of the actors, after all, are unknown or are not officially recognised.

The creation of an autonomous EU intelligence structure is a recent development. The Treaty of Maastricht (1991), for example, did not even mention intelligence. It was not until the incorporation and subsequent extension of the military and intelligence structures of the Western European Union (WEU) that the EU began, in 2002, to operate as a limited intelligence provider in its own right.

Today, the *Situation Centre* (SITCEN) is an institution where information from all accessible sources comes together, and is integrated into an all-source intelligence report. The core of SITCEN is its analysis department, which employs a dozen seconded national-intelligence agents appointed by the EU's High Representative for the Common and Security Policy. Since 2004, SITCEN's strategic assessments can also refer to contexts *within* the European Union.

Another important player in the EU intelligence architecture is the *Satellite Centre* (SATCEN), which is mainly tasked with imagery surveillance on targets deemed necessary for purposes of European Security and Defence Policy (ESDP). It operates as an early warning unit. SATCEN still needs to purchase imagery material from external (military and commercial) partners; it does not yet possess its own satellite equipment. It answers to the High Representative, who receives requests for imagery intelligence from Union-level institutions and member states alike.

In addition, the *Intelligence Division* (INTDIV) within the EU Military Staff exchanges and analyses military intelligence pertinent to the ESDP. Military-intelligence staffers from all member states work at INTDIV. Their efforts are bent at gaining a coherent picture of the military capacities of actors involved in conflicts where the EU is present, or plans to be (Daun 2005).

Lastly, *EUROPOL* works as a clearing house for the exchange of information between member states. It collates and analyses information and intelligence on terrorism and other forms of international crime. As Müller-Wille points out, however:

> Europol is more than an intelligence broker. By compiling and analysing the information from several states, Europol is expected to detect patterns, spot linkages between different criminal activities and draw conclusions that can be decisive in the fight against crime. In this sense, the output is hoped to represent more than the sum of the input.
>
> (Müller-Wille 2004: 26)

At the multilateral level beyond the EU, one finds intelligence structures yet more arcane. A prominent example is the *Club of Bern* (CdB), a partnership of the security services of the 27 EU member states, plus Switzerland and Norway. It has brought together the heads of European security and intelligence services on an annual basis since 1971. More recently, the G-6 (the UK, France, Italy, Germany, Spain, and Poland) have jointly organised the exchange of information and of liaison officers (Daun and Jäger 2005: 77). The Treaty of Prüm was recently signed by some of its members, together with the three Benelux states and Austria. The hope is that this treaty will play 'a pioneering role in establishing the highest possible standard of cooperation especially by means of exchange of information, particularly in combating terrorism' (Council of the European Union 2005: 3). Indeed, the measures of security cooperation it contains (DNA and fingerprint data-sharing, common rules on flight security, etc.) go much further then what the 27 member states of the EU have hitherto agreed upon. Finally, there is the *Bureau de Liaison* (also known as the BDL network), an encrypted information-technology tool which assists in the transmission of information among member states' law-enforcement bodies, their security and intelligence services, and EUROPOL (Commission of the European Communities 2005: 3).

Looking at this patchwork of multilateral and EU-level intelligence formations, it becomes clear that contemporary European intelligence cooperation is no longer confined to *ad hoc* intelligence-sharing amongst national intelligence services. This remains a quintessential feature, but a wide range of actors has now become indispensable in the larger European counter-terrorism effort.

The processes of European intelligence cooperation

Yet what is the nature of these concerted activities? We must know this if we are to grasp the breadth of potential accountability obligations. Unfortunately, however, information of this kind is very difficult to come by. The following account is based on a thorough review of publicly available sources on the (1) planning and direction, (2) collection, (3) processing, and (4) analysis, production, and dissemination of intelligence.

First, when states decide to cooperate more regularly, they must undertake careful prior *planning* efforts with respect to security standards, procedural rules on security clearance, and means and methods of secure communication. In most multilateral forums, the so-called *third-party rule* is applied, and its observance is strictly monitored. Further precautionary measures may include the establishment of 'a system of security classification and code-words and the installation of joint communication channels as well as the exchange of special liaison officers to the embassies in the capitals of the cooperating countries' (Richelson and Ball 1985: 43). Once such precautionary measures are installed, monitored, and updated, national intelligence services may submit *finished* intelligence reports to one another, and plan further cooperative activities on the basis of shared conclusions. At the multilateral level, for example, the CdB engages in 'a continuous exchange of information between the Club partners to counter upcoming threats, but also to define and to analyze more long-term developments, which could be detrimental to the national and international security' (Bergenstrand 2004: 3–4). However, if and when intelligence planning goes beyond the multilateral level and reaches supranational dimensions, is a contested matter. Many doubt that EU member states are prepared to pool national intelligence competences, thus making possible a genuinely integrated Common European Intelligence Policy under the sole authority of the EU. It is also known that the governments of Britain, France, and Germany rejected a proposal put by Austria and Belgium to create a European CIA. However, while seemingly insurmountable obstacles stand in the way of a full-fledged EU intelligence capacity, one can nonetheless cite imagery and human intelligence as two striking examples where the EU seems to have gotten its foot in the door. For purposes of EU-level planning, moreover, a framework of important goals and targets is formulated by the EU's High Representative for Foreign and Security Policy and the EU's Political and Security Committee. SITCEN then selects priority objectives, which are summarised in the so-called Watchlist (Daun 2005: 141–3). For the most part, however, the EU must rely on intelligence supplied by its member states.

Second, when looking at intelligence collection, we must distinguish between *raw* and *processed* information-sharing. The latter is obviously much preferred, since it allows national services to keep sources, methods, and technological equipment confidential. A recent example of an *ad hoc* multilateral effort at intelligence collection can be seen in the activities at *Alliance Base*, where a team of multinational intelligence agents launched a joint campaign aimed at the pursuit, arrest, and interrogation of suspected terrorists (Priest 2005). Yet concerted intelligence collection extends to the EU level as well. Several law-enforcement databases have been developed, and a current issue in European politics is whether intelligence and security services should be granted access to such information, including the right to add, change, or modify existing entries. Anna Daun maintains that, for all objectives on the Watchlist, SITCEN gathers information and intelligence from all sources available to it, as per Union-level practice in the area of intelligence collection. This includes, in addition to open-source intelligence and intelligence provided by member states, information provided by the EU's own institutions. For instance, the EU Commission has hundreds of delegations in foreign countries, which can be contacted if necessary. The same holds true for the increasing number of personnel involved in current European Security and Defence Policy (ESDP) operations, SATCEN, and the EU Monitoring Missions. When they send codified information to SITCEN, this might be regarded as EU-led human intelligence collection.

Third, very little is known about the concerted *processing* of intelligence. Secrecy requirements prevent the public from gaining knowledge of the content of shared material among liaison partners. That said, cooperation is known to include not just the sharing of processed intelligence and the joint feeding of databases, but joint efforts at decryption as well. At the EU level, SITCEN agents work with the human intelligence collected, and produce so-called all-source intelligence reports.

When it comes, finally, to the *analysis, production*, and *dissemination* of intelligence at the EU level, both EUROPOL and SITCEN representatives take part in EU groups for the coordination of counter-terrorism efforts (Bergenstrand 2004; Daun and Jäger 2005). EUROPOL produces the so-called Analytical Work Files on terrorist threat scenarios, offering processed information from which member states can benefit (Bergenstrand 2004: 7). In addition, SITCEN regularly produces, in cooperation with national security and intelligence services, intelligence conclusions which are widely disseminated in Brussels and in the capitals of the member states. These reports are classified and disseminated among key decision-makers in the pursuit of ESDP/CFSP. Much at the multilateral level is shrouded in secrecy, but intelligence reports from the CdB are regularly submitted to decision-makers at both national and Union levels.

Summarising the above, we can say that European cooperation in matters of counter-terrorism intelligence does not tend to follow the functionalist logic which some see at work in other fields of European integration. More concretely, it is rarely the case that cooperative action in one area leads seamlessly to a further (and more intense) liaison in another. Regardless of which level we consider, it holds true that, 'no matter how dedicated to the general cause, [intelligence agencies] have a natural tendency to mask [their] intelligence capabilities and to retain control of what tasks [they] perform and how [their] products are disseminated' (Coosemans 2004: 14). Thus, even in counter-terrorism – where one should think that cooperation with foreign services poses comparatively fewer counter-intelligence risks – most services are very keen to guard their position in the hierarchy of European intelligence powers, and they carefully weigh the potential advantages and disadvantages of each proposed cooperative endeavour before committing themselves to it. The decisive criteria appear to be the possibility of excluding others from shared information, and the level of trust felt among cooperative partners. As a result, bilateral cooperation remains the deepest and most commonly practised form of intelligence liaison, followed by cooperation within the framework of sometimes quite arcane multilateral institutions. In the EU, where exclusion is not practicable, intelligence cooperation thus remains underdeveloped. What is more (and this should be borne in mind when discussing accountability for intelligence activities), intelligence agents at the EU level are strictly desk-bound. Not possessing operative powers, they pose much less of a risk to civil and human rights than do their colleagues at national, bilateral, and multilateral levels.

Intelligence accountability: a brief conceptual excursion

Modern democracies operate through several modes of power delegation from the people via their elected representatives to the executive, and still further to the bureaucratic agents who implement government policies. When an agent acts on behalf of a principal anywhere along this chain of delegation, the principal in question is in danger of experiencing *agency loss*.[2] Requiring the agent to give an account of his actions is a common means of reducing this inherent risk. In theory, each link in the chain of power delegation should be accompanied by an obligation in the reverse direction to provide an account of one's actions. On paper, this sounds convincing and straightforward. However, while few argue publicly against this ideal-type, it actually poses several challenges:

First, one must grapple with the fact of 'shifting manifestations of the concept depending on the issue being examined' (Justice and Dubnick 2004: 17). In political practice, accountability is often 'used as an ideograph, as a rhetorical tool to convey an image of good governance and to rally supporters' (Bovens 2007a: 4). Scholars, too, write about and define accountability in a variety of ways. As a result, there is little agreement on the term, let alone conceptual work done on its core ontological foundation. Some clarity is gained by breaking the concept down into more tangible parts: 'A relationship qualifies as a case of accountability when there is a relationship between an actor and a forum in which the actor is obliged to explain and justify his conduct and the forum can pose questions, pass judgement and the actor may face consequences' (Bovens 2007a: 450). Richard Mulgan adds three further criteria for identifying accountability relationships: 'Public accountability is *external*, in that the account is given to an outside authority; it *involves social interaction and exchange*, with one side seeking answers or rectification, while the other responds and accepts sanctions; and it *implies rights of authority*, where those calling for an account assert rights of superiority over those who are accountable' (Mulgan 2000: 555).

The second challenge is to agree on the standards according to which accountability performance is to be assessed. Should the aim be to enhance social learning (e.g. to increase the effectiveness of the executive branch), to furnish democratic means for monitoring and overseeing government conduct, or to prevent and rectify government abuses (Bovens *et al.* 2008: 230)?

Given the notorious penchant for secrecy in the intelligence domain, there is no need to dwell further on these conceptual challenges. Instead, let us ask ourselves how Bovens' definition would fare when projected onto the *dark side of government*. If we focus on executive-legislative relationships (the most conspicuous level for public accountability), we find that parliamentary accountability in the intelligence area exists when a government is obliged to explain and justify its conduct; and when the parliament (or other relevant oversight body) is able to pose questions and pass judgement, and intelligence actors may face consequences. Numerous wrangles can be recalled or envisaged in domestic politics about access to government information. Moreover, the independence of account-holders can be severely limited when it comes to their appointment and reporting obligations.

Now let us leave the national level, and consider what accountability might look like at the international level. It is striking how most political scientists switch from government to governance modes of thinking when they turn from the former to the latter. And, indeed, *accountability for government* is remarkably different from *accountability for governance*. The latter is very popular; although, it poses pressing and unresolved questions for many policy fields in Europe. However, as we saw in the previous section, intelligence cooperation does not fit neatly into the governance category. This is mainly due to the fact that one defining criterion of *governance* is missing in this domain: namely, 'a wide variety of actors such as public-private partnerships, voluntary associations, private businesses, [and] political institutions existing at different levels of government' (Peters and Pierre 2006: 37). That said, we should not assume that accountability problems are necessarily less acute in an international context where public executives remain firmly ensconced in the driver's seat. This brings us to our two miniature case studies.

EU intelligence accountability: two miniature case studies

What is the state of the art for EU intelligence accountability? I introduced two different possible assumptions in the introduction: that the record on accountability at Union level is better than at national level, or that it is worse. In this section, I seek to ascertain which assumption comes closer to political reality. My first step is to examine the accountability regulations applying to the EU's own intelligence bodies. My second is to broaden the focus: to an examination of selected accountability pathways experienced by the EP's Temporary Commission on the alleged use of European countries by the CIA for the transport and illegal detention of prisoners (TDIP).

Those interested in EU regulations on intelligence accountability may recall that, in 2001, the European Parliament issued the following policy recommendation: 'The Council and the Member States are strongly urged to establish as a matter of priority a system for the democratic monitoring and control of the *autonomous European intelligence capability* and *other joint and coordinated intelligence activities at European level*' (European Parliament 2001: 85, emphasis added). This would appear to mean that the past had looked rather grim in the area of EU intelligence accountability. But what is the situation today? Has progress been made in establishing a proper accountability regime?

Unfortunately, not much has changed. For example, it remains a highly deplorable fact that, to this day, there is no official legal document outlining the mandate of both SITCEN and INTDIV (Statewatch 2005). Given that 'legislation is the legal embodiment of the democratic will' (Born and Leigh 2005: 17), the total absence of any role for the European parliament (or any national parliament for that matter) in deciding the rules of a public institution is a remarkable flaw. The significance of this democratic deficiency should not be downplayed, as the former EU Counter-Terrorism Coordinator, Gijs de Vries, may have tried to do when he gave the rather succinct assurance that 'the European Parliament can have a dialogue with the Council of Ministers on the work of SITCEN' (*Euractiv* 2005). In view of the fact that the Council is still not obliged to inform the EP on intelligence matters, one cannot but sharply question the value of such a 'dialogue'. Certainly, one rudimentary requirement implied by most definitions of accountability is not met in this situation: such definitions namely imply, notwithstanding their ontological differences, that those to whom an accounting is owed enjoy rights of superiority over those giving the accounting (Mulgan 2000: 555). This sets the Union level clearly apart from the national level, wherein the obligations of governments to inform their respective parliaments are at any rate codified. Obviously, as alluded to earlier, the value of this obligation can be badly undermined in domestic political practice – as when the government (i.e. the ruling party or bloc) single-handedly determines, as a *de facto* matter, which files can be shared with parliament and which are too sensitive. The EU, however, fails to achieve even this kind of elementary accountability. Rather than a facultative option for a dialogue of limited material value, the European Parliament needs codified and regularly practised rights of oversight with respect to EU intelligence bodies. The legality and propriety of the latter's actions must be scrutinised; their budget must be inspected. At the moment, the EP neither hosts an intelligence-oversight committee nor any other body for quality-control in this area. Consequently, there is no continuous accountability relationship between the main legislative and executive bodies of the EU with respect to any of the major decisions made by EU intelligence agencies. Accordingly, the least-likely assumption has proven to be right: EU intelligence agencies are subject to weaker accountability provisions than are their national counterparts. In fact, EU intelligence agencies are not accountable at all.

That said, it is worth recalling that the EU's intelligence structures focus exclusively on strategic EU decision-making in foreign and security matters; moreover, the international collaboration they involve takes the form of 'analytical cooperation and not operational cooperation' (*Euractiv* 2005). Thus, EU intelligence bodies do not possess any of the special powers that one associates with national intelligence services. Far less in the way of potential civil-rights infringements need accordingly be feared. What is more, since EU intelligence units depend largely on information provided by national intelligence services, they bear less responsibility for actions taken on the basis of flawed intelligence.

Let us now leave for a while the question of accountability for EU intelligence bodies, and consider another interesting development where EU institutions have been directly involved in an accountability process connected with intelligence cooperation. For my second miniature case study, I refer to

Art. 7(1) of the Treaty Establishing the European Union (TEU), according to which EU institutions may be tasked to hold member states to account for the compatibility of their activities with Art. 6(1) of the TEU. Interestingly, the European Parliament recently engaged in such a proceeding by establishing the Temporary Commission on the alleged use of European countries by the CIA for the transport and illegal detention of prisoners (TDIP). The TDIP's remit was *inter alia* to 'collect and analyse information to find out whether […] Member States […] have been involved or complicit in illegal deprivation of liberty of individuals, including abduction, rendition, transfer, detention or torture either by act or omission'. In theory, any finding of involvement or complicity by EU member states in US-run rendition and secret detention would have demonstrated a blatant disregard for the 'principles of liberty, democracy, respect for human rights and fundamental freedoms, and the rule of law' (TEU 2002: Art. 6). Council 'recommendations' would potentially have followed.

At least two aspects of accountability arise in connection with this particular provision: First, and more evidently, the member states are formally requested to provide information to the EP – a request which must be considered in light of the 'recommendations' (sanctions) upon which the Council may decide in case of a breach of Art. 6(1) TEU. On paper, then, the EP engaged in an accountability relationship with the governments of the member states. It should be noted for the record, however, that the 'majority of the governments that were invited, who are effectively the most competent on the matter, have refused to cooperate with our commission, even though they were held to answer the (European) Parliament's requests' (TDIP 2006: 2). The second aspect of accountability relates to the interaction between the EP and the Council during the TDIP investigation. The relationship between these two bodies is quite revealing for purposes of our analysis. Art. 10 of the Treaty Establishing the European Community (TEC) enjoins all European institutions to cooperate loyally with one another. The Council thus had a responsibility, when so requested, to cooperate with the TDIP, so that the latter could carry out its work as effectively as possible. This responsibility included giving an account of its activities to the TDIP.

A recent letter from the President of the TDIP to the President of the EP highlights the most blatant accountability flaws experienced during this investigation. It points, for example, to the numerous difficulties the committee members met – and not just from member states, but from fellow EU bodies as well. Notably, the Finnish Presidency of the Council 'did not deem it useful to appear before the committee' (TDIP 2006: 1); and while 'the European Union Coordinator for the fight against terrorism expressed hesitation before agreeing to participate in our meeting […] the Director for the European Police Office (Europol) simply refused to appear' (TDIP 2006: 1). 'In addition', the TDIP President complains, 'the Council has gone so far as to conceal or truncate the truth to the EP'. The TDIP President substantiates this claim by comparing information he had received from indirect sources[3] to the information he had received from the Presidency of the European Council. 'I had unfortunately to observe, by comparing these different documents, that what I had been given to by Mr. Winkler [Austrian Secretary of State] was only a partial summary of the discussions that took place and not a detailed account of them, with some elements passing completely under silence. In truth, it has been a matter of an amputation of essential parts of the minutes of the meeting in question' (TDIP 2006: 3). Unfortunately, no sanctions (aside from the publication of this letter) followed upon this uncooperative behaviour towards the EP on the part of the Council.

In this regard we should also note the confidential request put by the Council to see the shared (albeit amputated) information 'on explicit request from the American government' (TDIP 2006: 2). The TDIP President complained, quite rightly, that the Temporary Commission had found that its 'access to an *internal* Council document [was] limited', which raised an important question of principle: '[can] documents produced by an institution of the Union … be subjected to control by a third party, which thus meddles in matters pertaining to its own internal organisation and, in the event, to the relationship between its institutions?' (TDIP 2006: 3).

Taking all of the above into consideration, it is clear that the Council – and a significant number of EU member states as well – practically *stone-walled* the TDIP investigation. The flaws from an accountability standpoint were numerous: relevant persons failed to appear at committee hearings, information was withheld or its existence denied, etc. Committees of inquiry in national parliaments often possess powers of subpoena; the TDIP does not. It was accordingly forced in its final report to conclude: 'in view of the powers […] at its disposal, […], the […] Committee was not put in a position fully to investigate all the cases of abuses and violations falling within its remit and […] its conclusions are therefore not exhaustive' (European Parliament 2007: 30).

The overall conclusion we must draw from both miniature case studies is that, unfortunately, intelligence accountability is virtually absent at the level of the European Union.

Accountability for European intelligence cooperation: a fairy tale?

Until recently, virtually none of the efforts made in either national or international parliaments to ensure accountability has borne on international intelligence cooperation. Loch Johnson, a prominent scholar on intelligence oversight, claimed just a few years that no parliaments (the US Congress included) have looked closely at liaison relationships. This has now happily changed: various national and international accountability forums have recently been mandated to investigate matters directly pertinent to international intelligence cooperation. Thus, the ambit of national and international *efforts to ensure accountability* in the intelligence area has grown considerably. And whenever new practices emerge, the task of political scientists is to explain the political behaviour in question as accurately as possible. We saw above that intelligence accountability in the European Union is either absent (as regards genuine EU intelligence) or severely hampered (as in the case of the TDIP investigation) by non-cooperation on the part of member states and the EU Council. The pressing question for the last section of this chapter is whether national efforts (or other international ones) have been equally marred, and whether they have ever led in actual practice to accountability for European intelligence cooperation.

Let us begin with the domestic level. There is no room here, obviously, to review different national records of accountability with respect to European intelligence cooperation. In what follows, therefore, I restrict my attentions to a single aspect of a prominent example: the Bundestag's First Committee of Inquiry, which was set up in March 2006 to clarify what political directions had been given to German intelligence services in the field of international counter-terrorism.

While its mandate was very promising, a closer look at the committee's performance reveals numerous constraints on its efforts to ensure proper public accountability. A great many external and self-imposed constraints hampered the ongoing Bundestag investigation. Take just the following three examples:

First, the government exercised what may be termed *slow-rolling*. A recent complaint lodged by the qualified minority of the Inquiry Committee to Germany's constitutional court is replete with examples of how the government responded to requests for additional information in a very belated fashion. Given that the Committee of Inquiry is obliged to produce its final report before the end of the current legislative period, slow-rolling infringes on the committee's right to conduct a parliamentary investigation.

Second, the government *stone-walled* the Bundestag investigation. On numerous occasions, moreover, the government has *de facto* remained the final arbiter when it comes to deciding what information is to be made available to parliament. In the course of the inquiry, the government repeatedly rejected numerous requests by the committee to submit specific files. It dismissed most of these requests on general legal grounds (especially the state secret waiver), which it interpreted as meaning that it was entitled to keep the requested information to itself. But how can parliament discharge its oversight responsibilities meaningfully if it lacks full and timely knowledge of the acts committed by the agents to which it has delegated its power? In cases where the executive has withheld crucial information from the accountability forum, said executive should be required, at the very least, to present a detailed justification as to why it is entitled to withhold sensitive information from parliament. No such detailed arguments were presented to the Committee, even upon explicit request.

Third, partisanship within the oversight body served to constrain the effective exercise of public accountability. The Council of Europe's rendition rapporteur, Dick Marty, described the proceedings in the Committee of Inquiry quite tellingly in this respect.

> While the representatives of government parties, especially the Christian Democrats, who were in the opposition at the material time, take an active and open attitude during the examination of witnesses, government discipline comes fully into play when the facts are being assessed, with the representatives of government parties never having voted for a motion to take evidence tabled by minority representatives or having tabled such a motion themselves
>
> (PACE 2007: 60)

The constraining effect on accountability weighs heavily when face-saving considerations trump concerted efforts by parliamentarians to hold members of the executive to account. As this amounts to common practice, in the Bundestag at least, the model of accountability featured in democratic theory seems incompatible with daily parliamentary practice in respect to intelligence oversight. In terms of Mulgan's criteria for accountability, it is questionable whether public accountability remains *external* in the face of often quite cosy relationships between parliamentarians and the government.

In sum, this national forum for intelligence accountability was initially very promising, but in the end it proved severely flawed. Let us turn therefore to the fate of the rendition investigation conducted by the Parliamentary Assembly of the Council of Europe. One noteworthy feature in this case is that the fate of the investigation is quite well-known. Endowed with just a fraction of the investigative powers that some national parliaments have now acquired, it nonetheless managed to produce a widely read and impressively detailed (if predictably controversial) account of rendition practices. The report revealed several incidents which one can scarcely imagine could have occurred without the support of EU member states. All of the claims made in this report, however, have been quickly dismissed by national governments as mere speculation. Claims of this kind, it is argued, were insufficiently corroborated by hard data (to which Marty and his team were denied access). Like the TDIP inquiry conducted by the European Parliament, then, the investigation by the Council of Europe was prevented from establishing an independent account.

Clearly, this leads to a very worrisome conclusion. A serious accountability gap exists in this area: as a *de facto* matter, concerted intelligence activities escape the remit of national accountability forums, whilst not being absorbed by existing European accountability forums either. Accountability for international intelligence cooperation is therefore nowhere to be found. That said, the most pressing accountability gap that needs closing relates to European intelligence cooperation in bilateral or multilateral settings. Yet given the numerous calls for an extension of genuine EU intelligence powers, the fact that EU-level intelligence is not held to account is surely intolerable, too.

Conclusion

Contemporary political *theory* may have difficulties developing a convincing model for political accountability in governance situations. However, as this chapter has demonstrated, this should not be conflated with the difficulties experienced *in practice* during recent efforts to ensure accountability for European intelligence cooperation. At least for the foreseeable future, concerted European intelligence activities will remain government-driven and government-exercised. One is therefore better advised to adopt the *government* model for analysing accountability in this area. *Turning from governance to government* does not mean, however, that a more convincing model for accountability necessarily appears. It clearly does not, at least in the case of European intelligence cooperation. An examination of the accountability provisions made for intelligence institutions under the EU umbrella turns up major structural flaws. The European Parliament lacks an independent oversight body, and the Council has no obligation to inform the EP on intelligence matters. On a more general level, moreover, it is clear that accountability for intelligence cooperation has been instituted neither at the national level nor in the Council of Europe. It is true that, at the former level, accountability structures are much better established; there are numerous loopholes, however, and many are the practical obstacles that continue to block the path towards truth and transparency.

Structures for intelligence accountability are virtually absent, then, at the level of the EU. As I have pointed out, however, the most worrisome grey zones and accountability gaps for intelligence government are found at the national, bilateral, and multilateral levels. Our civil and human rights are most at risk there. The most urgent task for European and national politicians, therefore, is to modify national oversight regimes so as to give national parliamentarians more enforceable rights to review prevailing practices in the area of international intelligence cooperation.

Scholars, finally, can play an important role in this too. It is not clear to me why, when we study the problem of how to render accountability compatible with political practice, we should put the analytical focus on re-designing accountability regimes so as to make them more amenable to an international context. Rather than watering down such regimes in an effort to make them fit an international context, we ought first of all to raise awareness, so that the international context can eventually be re-designed in accordance with key accountability standards. Second, given the confusion surrounding the concept's core meaning, we may also want to treat the promises of accountability as 'hypotheses rather than self-evident truths' (Dubnick and Justice 2004: 3). This too may help advance efforts to secure accountability – which is still severely circumscribed as yet – in the area of international intelligence cooperation.

Notes

1 No single authoritative definition of intelligence exists. However, I consider the following working definition sufficient for purposes of this chapter: 'Intelligence is

the process by which specific types of information important to national security are requested, collected, analysed, and provided to policymakers; the products of that process; the safeguarding of these processes and this information by counter-intelligence activities; and the carrying out of operations as requested by lawful authorities' (Lowenthal 2002: 8).

2 Lupia defines agency loss as follows: 'the difference between the actual consequence of delegation and what the consequence would have been had the agent been perfect' (Lupia 2003: 35) (a perfect agent having done what the principal would have done had he had unlimited information and the resources to do the job himself).

3 This information concerned the minutes of meetings between Council working parties and the legal services of the American Department of State concerning the practices of the fight against terrorism.

9 Executive power and accountability in the European Union

Jonas Tallberg

One of the defining characteristics of the EU is the delegation of executive power to supranational actors, notably the European Commission.[1] Breaking with the general pattern in international cooperation, the member states of the EU in the 1950s chose to confer extensive executive responsibilities on a supranational secretariat, the Commission. Over the years, these powers have been a contributing factor in the deepening of European integration, due to the policy entrepreneurship in which the Commission has engaged. These powers have also been the subject of a long-standing debate in integration studies on the relative autonomy of the Commission from the member states.

Since the mid-1990s, however, we have witnessed the emergence of a distinct field of research on executive politics, in which the focus is on issues of delegation, agency, and accountability. This field has developed in parallel with an increasing tendency to conceptualise the EU as a political system, rather than as a case of regional integration. Political developments in Europe have furthermore been such as to make the study of executive politics increasingly central to a general understanding of EU politics. In prior years, for instance, the Commission had been the sole supranational body invested with executive powers. In the mid-1990s, however, the member states began establishing a growing number of European regulatory agencies. On 1 January 1999, moreover, they conferred exclusive authority over monetary policy on the European Central Bank (ECB). The political debate about democracy and legitimacy in the EU also grew more intense in the late 1990s, raising questions about the accountability of the EU's supranational executives.

The term 'executive power' is derived from the classical constitutional framework, wherein the legislature decides, the executive enacts, and the judiciary adjudicates. Whereas these powers, in some political systems, are each concentrated in the hands of a specific political actor, the EU boasts a more complex division of power, not least in regard to the organisation of the executive. In the EU, namely, executive power is vested both in the member states (each of which is responsible for implementing EU legislation through its own bureaucracy) and in several supranational organs (each of which has been delegated important competencies in the formulation and enactment of

EU policy). This unusual organisational structure has sometimes been described as a dual executive.

My attentions in this chapter are focused exclusively on the three main instances of supranational executive power in the EU: the Commission, the ECB, and the European regulatory agencies. More specifically, I concentrate on the delegation of executive power and the checks placed on its exercise, with a particular focus on the implications thereof for accountability. What powers have been delegated, and why? What kinds of mechanisms are in place for overseeing executive power, and why? To what extent does the resulting pattern of delegation and oversight present a problem for accountability? In addressing these questions, I draw on the increasingly voluminous empirical and theoretical literature on this topic. I conclude that executive power in the EU is subject to a variegated pattern of oversight and accountability. The Commission and the European agencies operate within relatively tight constraints. The ECB, however, enjoys extensive discretion in the exercise of its powers. The question of whether or not this pattern is cause for concern – in terms of its impact on democratic accountability – is the subject of normative debate.

This chapter proceeds along the following steps. In the section that follows, I describe how issues of delegation, oversight, and accountability are addressed by scholars who take positive and normative approaches to executive politics. In the subsequent three sections, I account for the principal patterns and points of contention with regard to the Commission, the ECB, and the European agencies as executive actors. Finally, I summarise the argument and lay out its verdict on the issue of accountability in EU politics.

Executive accountability: positive and normative approaches

The extent to which executive actors can be held accountable is of central concern both to rational-choice theorists, with their interest in positive questions of delegation and oversight, and to democratic theorists, with their interest in normative questions of accountability and legitimacy. Whereas principal-agent theory (hereafter P-A theory) is the dominant approach taken to the analysis of executive politics in the EU, the question posed by normative democratic theory is whether delegation to non-majoritarian executive institutions is democratically desirable or legitimate.

The strong position of *rational-choice institutionalism* in the study of EU executive politics owes much to the import of theories and methods from the literature on legislative-executive relations in American politics. Since the early 1980s, P-A analysis has been the favoured theoretical approach of American scholars for understanding the delegation of powers by the US Congress to the regulatory agencies of the executive branch, as well as the autonomy of the latter from their legislative principals. The study of EU politics in general, and of executive politics in particular, represents the most recent frontier of the contractual paradigm in political science (for overviews, see Tallberg 2002; Kassim and Menon 2003).

The analytical core of P-A theory is the principal-agent relationship, which arises whenever one party (the principal) delegates certain functions to another party (the agent), in the expectation that the latter will act in accordance with his wishes. P-A theory posits that this relationship is inherently problematic, since what is optimal for principals is not necessarily optimal for agents, who may have their own private interests at heart. Furthermore, principals rarely enjoy full insight into the actions of their agents; the latter thus have an opportunity to pursue their own interests at the expense of the former's – to 'shirk' their work, in the vocabulary of P-A theory. However, principals are not helpless in the face of such shirking by agents. By establishing oversight mechanisms, principals can monitor their agents' doings and sanction their transgressions, thus inducing them to comply with their wishes.

In the standard application of the P-A model to EU politics, scholars have conceptualised the member states as principals who have delegated certain powers to the supranational institutions, and so been faced with a problem of oversight. This way of framing the relationship between states and supranational institutions has served to focus the attention of EU scholars on the two issues of prime analytical importance in P-A analysis: namely: (a) why do principals delegate powers to agents? and (b) to what extent are agents able to take advantage of the situation to pursue their own private preferences?

The general answer offered by rational-choice institutionalists to the first question is functionalist in nature. Delegation is explained in terms of the anticipated effects for the delegating party: the latter is likely to resort to it when expected benefits outweigh expected costs. More specifically, the P-A literature calls attention to a number of ways in which delegation can serve to reduce transaction costs, notably by: (a) facilitating credible policy commitments (delegating powers to agents insulated from the day-to-day pressures of electoral politics allows politicians to bind themselves to a given policy) (b) reducing information asymmetries (setting up institutions and agencies in technical areas of governance grants politicians access to policy-relevant expertise) and (c) improving decision-making efficiency (detailed rule-making is handed over to agents, thus saving politicians' time and effort for policy decisions of a more general nature) (see, e.g. McCubbins and Page 1987; Epstein and O'Halloran 1999). In various studies of executive politics in the EU, scholars have sought to test whether these reasons for delegation properly capture the functions conferred on the supranational institutions. Rational-choice institutionalists have also carried on a debate over the relative explanatory power of alternative logics of delegation – credibility-based or efficiency-based.

In an offshoot of this research on the sources of delegation, scholars in recent years have paid increasing attention to the degree of discretion allowed to agents within the powers delegated to them (Epstein and O'Halloran 1999; Huber and Shipan 2002). Discretion is commonly understood as the net of the powers delegated to agents and the various oversight mechanisms established by principals (i.e. delegated powers – oversight mechanisms = discretion). All principal-agent relationships are likely to involve some degree of agent discretion, inasmuch as oversight mechanisms are costly to institute and to operate. The main question that has motivated P-A theorists is how to explain variations in the degree of discretion, which is thus conceptualised as a question of institutional design. In terms of the reasons for delegation, this research hypothesises that the degree of discretion is positively related to the demand for credible commitments and for policy-relevant expertise. Inspired by the work of American politics scholars, students of executive politics have started exploring the patterns and sources of discretion that characterise the delegation of power within the EU.

Where the agency stage is concerned, P-A analysis suggests that agent autonomy is a function of the extent and efficacy of oversight mechanisms. The general literature offers some well-established ways of categorising forms of oversight (McCubbins and Schwartz 1984; McCubbins *et al.* 1987). First, it is common to distinguish between two different but complementary forms thereof: *ex ante* administrative oversight and *ex post* oversight. *Ex ante* methods delimit the scope of the agent's activity, the legal instruments at his disposal, and the kinds of procedures he must follow. *Ex post* oversight, by contrast, involves the establishment of institutional mechanisms for monitoring agent behaviour and sanctioning potential shirking. A second influential distinction is that between 'police-patrol' oversight and 'fire-alarm' oversight: the first consists of centralised, active, and direct monitoring on the part of the principal; the second involves decentralised, reactive, and indirect monitoring by parties affected by the agent's actions. With regard to sanctions, P-A theorists have identified an array of potential instruments, including cutting an agent's budget, reversing appointments, overriding decisions through new legislation, and revising an agent's institutional mandate. Drawing on these general categorisations and inventories, students of EU politics have sought to identify the kinds of mechanisms set up by member-state principals for controlling their supranational agents. On this basis, they have generated specific hypotheses about the scope for agency and autonomy.

In a challenge to the positive approach, *normative democratic theory* takes on executive politics from a quite different direction. It puts the spotlight on the normative implications of delegation by democratically elected governments to non-majoritarian institutions – institutions which are directly accountable neither to the voters nor to their elected representatives. These are issues that rational-choice institutionalists have either neglected or regarded as unproblematic. The scholarly debate on legislative-executive relations in the US, for example, has paid little attention to normative concerns. Similarly, P-A theorists in EU studies have remained focused on positive questions. (There typically is, however, an unstated assumption in the broader literature on European integration: namely, that the delegation of power to supranational institutions has furthered the process of European unification, and thus been good for Europe.)

More specifically, it is the ideal of competitive or majoritarian democracy that presents the most interesting challenge to the positive perspective of P-A theory. Highly simplified, this model of democracy stresses the need for citizens to be able to choose between competing political elites with alternative agendas (Schumpeter 1943; Dahl 1967). It is this model of democracy that, in a variety of versions, informs the design of representative government in national political systems. In a strict interpretation of this theory, delegation to non-majoritarian institutions risks undermining the principles of democratic governance. First, the act of delegation in itself means that part of the authority to govern is shifted from the realm of democratic contestation to that of technocratic governance (which is especially problematic if this power is difficult to retrieve effectively). Second, the mechanisms for holding non-majoritarian institutions democratically accountable are, by definition, absent or underdeveloped. And third, the political room for manoeuvre enjoyed by non-majoritarian institutions may give rise to autonomous actions contrary to the interests of the democratic representatives who empowered them.

While not unique to the EU, these problems of democratic legitimacy have received particular attention in Europe, where the delegation of power to supranational institutions and agencies is often considered an important component of the EU's 'democratic deficit' (e.g. Lord 1998; Schmitter 2000; Karlsson 2001; Arnull and Wincott 2002). Problems typically mentioned include technocratic decision-making, lack of transparency, insufficient public participation, exploitation of supranational discretion, and inadequate mechanisms for oversight and accountability. This critique has been aimed at all three main forms of supranational executive power in the EU. This critique usually comes, moreover, with specific prescriptions attached as to how this aspect of the democratic deficit ought to be addressed, with proponents of competitive or majoritarian democracy generally endorsing a parliamentarisation of the EU – through an enhanced role for the European Parliament (EP) in the formulation of legislation, in the appointment of the Commission, and in the supervision of all supranational executives.

Whereas the large majority of rational-choice institutionalists have remained silent in this normative debate, some have taken a position in defence of non-majoritarian institutions (Majone 1998; Moravcsik 2002). These theorists have emphasised the positive role played by delegation in government *for* the people, rather than its role in limiting government *by* the people. First, they argue that delegation to non-majoritarian institutions is normatively justified, since it tends to produce better outcomes for citizens – by enhancing the efficiency of decision-making, securing political rights against majority rule, and offsetting the imperfections of majoritarian institutions. Second, these theorists point out that delegation to supranational institutions largely takes place in areas which are excluded from democratic control in most national political systems as well; thus it replaces, mainly, the increasingly ineffective efforts of national bureaucrats. Third and finally, they stress that non-majoritarian institutions in the EU are in fact subject to various forms of oversight, even if these do not involve direct democratic accountability. Foremost among these are the procedural requirements to which such institutions are subject – procedures which supply, in the view of these observers, an important source of legitimacy.

The next three sections of this chapter lay out the dominant forms of supranational executive power in the EU. I describe the powers delegated to the Commission, to the ECB, and to the European agencies; the mechanisms available for controlling these institutions; and the scholarly debate between rational-choice institutionalists and normative democratic theorists on the extent to which gaps in oversight generate problems of accountability.

The European Commission as EU executive

The Commission enjoys more far-reaching executive powers than any other administration or secretariat serving an international organisation. However, EU governments have been careful to match the delegation of powers to the Commission with measures for checking their exercise. While not accountable to the European electorate directly, the Commission is broadly accountable to the European Parliament and the member-state governments; and its ability to pursue a political agenda of its own is relatively limited. Whether accountability would best be enhanced by politicising the Commission or imposing tighter procedural requirements on it is a subject of debate among EU scholars.

Delegation of powers to the Commission

Through the Union treaties they have ratified, the member states of the EU have delegated powers to the Commission in three principal areas: agenda-setting, enforcement, and implementation. As agenda-setter, the Commission enjoys exclusive authority to present proposals for new legislation in policy areas within the first pillar of EU cooperation: internal market policy, environmental policy, social policy, regional policy, and agricultural policy. In addition, the Commission has the power, along with the member states, to present proposals within the second and third pillars of EU cooperation, which consist of foreign and security policy and justice and home-affairs policy, respectively. As guardian of the treaties, moreover, the Commission has been granted the power to monitor the compliance of member states with EU rules, and to initiate infringement proceedings against those that violate these rules, with the possibility of imposing sanctions in cooperation with the European Court of Justice. When it comes to implementation of EU policies, finally, the Commission is vested with the authority to adopt regulations within the framework of legislation adopted by the Council and the Parliament; to manage EU spending programs in areas such as agriculture, regional aid, and research; and to execute EU law directly in such areas as competition policy and external trade policy.

The delegation of executive power by member states to the Commission has generated extensive interest among EU scholars, who have sought to identify the reasons for this delegation, the specific functions delegated, and the degree of discretion enjoyed by the Commission within these powers. This research, within which P-A analysis has constituted the main approach, may be divided into two strands: the focus of the first is on the delegation of treaty-based powers; that of the second is on the delegation of implementation powers to the Commission, by means of secondary legislation.

The literature in the first category testifies to a close fit between the functionalist predictions of rational-choice institutionalism and the actual powers delegated to the Commission by the treaties. It was Mark Pollack who first observed the close match (1997); subsequently, his conclusion has been strengthened by research into the negotiations behind the founding treaties (Rittberger 2001), and by in-depth studies of the Commission's treaty-based powers of agenda-setting, enforcement, and implementation.

Three different findings have emerged from the research in this regard. First, scholars have argued convincingly in favour of a rationalist interpretation of the Commission's unusual agenda-setting role, stressing either (a) the logic of credible commitments or (b) the need to reduce information asymmetries (Moravcsik 1998; Majone 2001; Pollack 2003). According to the first explanation (which is most consistent with the data), the member states pre-committed themselves – when they delegated a monopoly on formal agenda-setting to the Commission – to a particular agenda of supranational integration. According to the second, the conferral of an agenda-setting role on the Commission helps to reduce technical information deficits, by allowing the member states to profit from the policy expertise of the Commission in the formulation of EU legislation.

Second, research on the Commission's function as guardian of the treaties strongly suggests that delegation in this area can be adequately explained by the logic of credible commitments (Tallberg 2003). The discretion accorded the Commission is exceedingly far-reaching, for EU governments have effectively abstained from supervising this institution in its enforcement of state compliance. Furthermore, historical data confirm that, when delegating enforcement powers to the Commission, EU governments have indeed been motivated by a desire to safeguard their commitments.

Third, research into the delegation of issue-specific powers of implementation through the treaties suggests that the logic of credible commitments is at play there too (Pollack 2003). In the particular areas where member states have chosen to delegate far-reaching implementation powers to the Commission and to allow it extensive discretion – such as competition policy and external trade policy – the role of the Commission has typically been so designed as to safeguard state commitments.

In the second strand of research on delegation, scholars have examined the conferral of powers of implementation on the Commission through secondary legislation. Questions animating this research include why the Council and the Parliament delegate authority over implementation to the Commission in some issue areas but not others, and why they tend to permit the Commission greater discretion in the exercise of this authority in some areas than in others. Drawing on the work of P-A theorists in the US context, EU scholars have developed and tested hypotheses about executive delegation in Europe (Franchino 2002, 2007). Their findings indicate that variations in the amount of delegation and discretion reflect several factors: the level of conflict within the Council, the decision rule operating in the Council, the degree of conflict between the Council and the Commission, and the complexity of the policy area. Formulated in terms of rationales of delegation, this research suggests that the delegation of authority over implementation to the Commission through secondary legislation is motivated both by a need for efficient policy-making and by a demand for credible-commitment devices.

Overseeing the Commission

What, then, are the mechanisms by which EU governments can oversee the Commission, and to what extent does the Commission's exercise of its powers display gaps in oversight and accountability? Pollack (1997, 2003) has presented the most comprehensive inventory of oversight mechanisms; other researchers have offered in-depth treatments of the design, evolution, or use of specific oversight mechanisms (e.g. Gabel and Hix 2002; Tallberg 2003). Expressed in P-A terms, EU governments have established a system of police-patrol oversight through the comitology committees that supervise the implementation work of the Commission; as well as a system of fire-alarm oversight in the shape of institutional checks, administrative law, and judicial review. The sanctions available to the member states, too, are familiar from legislative-executive relations in American politics, and include powers of appointment and censure, the possibility of cutting the Commission's budget, the right to overrule Commission decisions through new legislation, the option of non-compliance, and the ultimate prerogative of revising the Commission's institutional mandate at the next review of the EU treaties.

The design of the system of comitology committees is a topic that has generated an impressive amount of research. Part of the explanation for the interest in this relatively arcane aspect of EU politics lies in the fact that a model contrary to that advanced by rational-choice institutionalists has been put forward. In two frequently cited articles, Christian Joerges and Jürgen Neyer (1997a, 1997b) argue that the comitology committees, rather than constituting oversight mechanisms for member governments, provide fora for national and supranational experts to meet, deliberate, and engage in joint problem-solving. Joerges and Neyer submit that the comitology committees can be most accurately described as engaged in deliberative problem-solving – even if these committees may have been set up originally to secure governments a voice in the adoption of EU regulations. Rational-choice institutionalists have responded to this challenge by investigating the Council's choice of comitology procedure, generally concluding that member-state governments calculate the likely consequences of alternative comitology procedures carefully, and thus tend to perceive this system as an oversight mechanism (Dogan 1997; Franchino 2000; Pollack 2003).

The research on supranational agency has been driven by the question of when, where, and how the EU's supranational institutions are capable of implementing their desired political agendas. This literature stretches across all three main functions of the Commission, and across a range of issue areas. An overall conclusion in this research is that independent influences are more likely to appear where the Commission enjoys a higher degree of discretion within its delegated powers. Furthermore, this literature strongly suggests that the Commission is relatively more constrained than the European Court of Justice (ECJ), and that the close cooperation of the latter institution often figures as a key component in cases where the Commission succeeds in pursuing a supranational agenda unsupported by member-state governments (Schmidt 2000; Tallberg 2000; Pollack 2003). These findings contrast with those in the literature on the Commission as policy entrepreneur (Sandholtz and Zysman 1989; Cram 1997), which has portrayed the Commission as wielding substantially greater influence in EU politics.

Empirical studies of the Commission's capacity to exploit its formal agenda-setting power for its own purposes indicate that the need for member-state approval in the Council (as well as for the approval of the Parliament, in many cases) seriously limits the scope for independent supranational influence (Pollack 2003: Chapters 5–6). Rationally anticipating the risk that its legislative proposals will be dismissed by the Council, the Commission tends to present proposals with a high likelihood of adoption. Research on the enforcement function of the Commission shows how the guardian of the treaties, in tandem with the ECJ, has been able to exploit its discretion in order to strengthen the EU's enforcement regime (Tallberg 2000, 2003). Finally, research on the Commission's powers of implementation points to a relatively greater scope for supranational influence, but also to variation across issue areas. In the field of external trade, the Commission's mandate is subject to member-state oversight through the Council's 133 Committee; the scope for autonomous action is thus reduced (Meunier and Nicolaïdis 1999; Pollack 2003: Chapter 5). In the area of competition policy, by contrast, there is a relatively greater scope for supranational agency and influence, often secured through the benign help of the ECJ (Schmidt 1998, 2000; Pollack 2003: Chapter 5).

A problem of accountability?

This empirical record on delegation and oversight has generated a vigorous debate on the normative dimension of the Commission as executive actor. Proponents of majoritarian democracy at the European level emphasise the negative implications of delegation to the Commission, the low legitimacy of this supranational executive, and the virtues of a parliamentarisation of the Commission and the EU (e.g. Dehousse 1995; Mancini 1998; McKay 1999). This argument tends to be developed through a comparison with national political systems, which yields the conclusion that delegation to the Commission has created an executive that possesses exceptional control over the political agenda, yet is relieved of standard requirements of democratic accountability. The placing of a monopoly on formal agenda-setting in the hands of this bureaucracy means that citizens are deprived of the possibility of influencing the political agenda of the EU executive through the normal route of electoral contestation, with its competing elites and alternative political agendas. By the same token, the procedures for appointing and dismissing the Commission mean effectively that this executive cannot be voted out of office, should citizens be disappointed with its performance.

This analysis translates into a distinct normative position on the democratisation of the EU, which is seen as best achieved through a parliamentarisation of the Union. This standpoint is generally associated in the political debate with a federalist vision of the EU. The most important components of this reform alternative are the development of the Parliament into a full-blown co-legislator alongside the Council in a bicameral legislative structure, and the transformation of the Commission into a true European government appointed by the Parliament and accountable to it.

A second distinct position in the normative debate on the Commission's executive power takes the status quo in defence, and cautions against an increasing politicisation and parliamentarisation of the Commission. The most consistent advocate of this perspective is Giandomenico Majone (1998, 2002), who warns that the progressive parliamentarisation of the Commission risks compromising its credibility as an independent regulator, without necessarily enhancing its democratic legitimacy (see also Moravcsik 2002). If EU governments delegate powers to the Commission mainly in order to secure credible policy commitments, then the subjection of the Commission to stronger parliamentary control would risk undoing the virtues of this arrangement. No longer insulated from political pressure and majoritarian swings, the Commission would be unable to function as an impartial long-term guarantor of collective decisions, with negative effects for the credibility and consistency of EU policy.

Rather than seeking to strengthen the Commission's democratic accountability by developing a European parliamentary system, defenders of this position argue, we should accord greater recognition to the legitimacy that flows from appropriate procedural requirements (Majone 1998). The requirements of procedural legitimacy in this context are that powers be delegated to the Commission through democratic procedures, that the Commission leadership be chosen by elected politicians, that the Commission's decision-making follow well-defined procedures, and that its decisions be argued for and open to review.

The European Central Bank as EU executive

The establishment of the ECB as the joint central bank of the member states in the euro-zone constitutes an exceptional example of monetary delegation. Through the Maastricht Treaty, the member states delegated the execution of monetary policy in the euro-zone to the Governing Council of the ECB. In comparison with other executive actors in the EU, as well as with central banks at the national level, the ECB enjoys remarkable independence. While motivated by a desire to achieve a stable, non-inflationary monetary policy, the absence of direct or indirect control over the ECB represents a potential accountability problem.

To date, empirical research on this topic has mainly been preoccupied with the 'why' question. How, that is, can we explain that states normally protective of their national sovereignty agreed to delegate exclusive authority over monetary policy to a supranational central bank, even while abstaining from conventional methods for overseeing its exercise? By contrast, the other prominent question in the research on delegation – the degree of oversight – has not so far figured as a topic, even if the ECB's conduct of monetary policy has been the subject of studies by economists. This absence of research on agency is best explained by the perception of ECB shirking as a non-issue, given the bank's own preference for price stability – the target chosen by its principals for the conduct of monetary policy.

Two different answers have been proffered in the existing research as to why the governments of the member states have seen fit to delegate executive power over monetary affairs to the ECB. Rational-choice institutionalists typically present the establishment and design of the ECB as motivated by the functional logic of credible commitments. They support this argument with data on the negotiation of the Maastricht Treaty (Moravcsik 1998; Majone 2000). By placing power over monetary policy in the hands of an independent central bank, and charging this bank with the securing of price stability, EU governments committed themselves to a non-inflationary monetary policy.

The alternative interpretation, informed by sociological institutionalism, has been put most pointedly by Kathleen McNamara (2002). McNamara questions the functional rationale for delegation to the ECB, which she views instead as the latest example of the diffusion across industrialised countries of the organisational model of the independent central bank (see, also, Verdun 1999; Marcussen 2000). In McNamara's (2002: 48) account, 'governments choose to delegate not because of narrow functional benefits but rather because delegation has important legitimising or symbolic properties which render it attractive in times of uncertainty or economic distress. The spread of central bank independence should be seen as a fundamentally social and political phenomenon, rooted in the logic of organisational mimicry and global norms of neoliberal governance.'

However, the area of research on the ECB as executive actor that boasts the liveliest scholarly debate bears on the question of democratic accountability and oversight. The ECB is effectively relieved of most of the oversight mechanisms normally put in place for holding executive actors accountable to their principals. The members of the Executive Board serve the longest terms of any EU civil servants, and these terms are non-renewable. It furthermore deliberates in secret, and the voting records and transcripts of its meetings are not made public. The ECB is not accountable to any other EU institution, although it has agreed to testify regularly before the European Parliament. The Maastricht Treaty identifies price stability as the sole objective of the ECB, but the Bank enjoys complete discretion in formulating monetary policy to meet this goal. Finally, the statutes of the Bank can only be revised with the unanimous agreement of all member states on a new treaty, with subsequent ratification in all countries.

The point of contention in the scholarly debate is the appropriateness of such remarkable independence in light of democratic theory (for analyses of this debate, see de Haan and Eijffinger 2000; Elgie 2002; Jabko 2003). Critics of the existing arrangement typically highlight the lack of transparency in ECB decision-making, as well as the lack of accountability vis-à-vis both the member-state governments and the European Parliament (e.g. Verdun 1998; Berman and McNamara 1999; Buiter 1999). The EU governments, according to this view, went further than necessary in ensuring the Bank's independence when they were negotiating over its founding statutes. Even as compared with other independent central banks, the ECB is lacking in democratic accountability. Neither the Federal Reserve nor the Bank of England, for instance, keep the records of their proceedings permanently secret. Nor are such formidable obstacles placed in the way of any revision of their statutes.

Defenders of the ECB's independence typically justify this arrangement in terms of the need for maintaining the bank's credibility, as well as its capacity to function as the impartial guarantor of the long-term public interest; moreover, they lay considerable stress on the mechanisms of transparency and accountability that do exist (e.g. Majone 1998; Issing 1999). The ECB's legitimacy does not, in this view, derive primarily from any democratic properties on the part of its decision-making procedures, but from the capacity of the Bank to fulfil the objectives of monetary policy set out by the member-state governments when they founded it. Defenders also stress that, in practice, the ECB has increased its accountability and transparency beyond what the treaty requires, for example by appearing before the Parliament and by publishing information on monetary policy.

European agencies, analysts arrive at radically different conclusions on the nature of executive accountability in the EU, depending on which normative democratic perspective they espouse.

Champions of strong mechanisms for accountability typically find the executive arrangements that exist within the EU at present to be highly unsatisfactory. Not only are they removed (albeit in varying degrees) from effective accountability and oversight; in addition, the mechanisms that do exist tend to be overrated. In this view, the parliamentary oversight of the Commission, the transparency policy of the ECB, the statutes governing the European agencies, the general threat of treaty revision – all serve to create an illusion of accountability. In practice, namely, these institutions only can be held accountable for their actions and decisions with great difficulty – if at all. Defenders of the existing order, by contrast, find the arrangements in place to be broadly acceptable in terms of accountability. The executive institutions of the EU have been established through democratic decisions; they are subject to various forms of oversight, and their powers can be retrieved by the member states at any point. It would also be wrong, as these scholars see it, to apply more stringent standards to executive arrangements at the EU level than we do to corresponding arrangements at the national level. Finally, they suggest, we must recognise the potential trade-off between accountability and other central values – efficiency, for example – that we wish to see characterise EU institutions.

Notes

1 This chapter draws on Tallberg (2007).

10 The European Central Bank – independent and accountable?

Daniel Naurin

The European Central Bank (ECB) has the power to decide over monetary policy in the Euro-zone.[1] Its decisions have a tremendous impact on the lives of European citizens, affecting inflation, unemployment, and interest rates. The ECB makes policy independently from the democratically elected institutions of the European Union and its member states. Comparative studies of central banks show that the ECB has an unusually high degree of independence (Amtenbrink 1999). The rationale for this independence – founded in the economic theory of time-inconsistency – is that elected politicians are poor decision-makers when it comes to monetary policy (Kydland and Prescott 1977). Politicians care about being re-elected, not about the long-term health of the economy. If they can, they will use their powers to manipulate interest rates and money supply during election years, regardless of the long-term damage that may result. If the ECB is to perform well in its monetary policy, then, it must be able to take decisions without pressure from public opinion or from short-sighted elected politicians.

The value of central-bank independence has been widely accepted among both academics and practitioners, leading to a global trend to cut ties between governments and central banks (McNamara 1998). Independent central banks, in this view, give credibility to the monetary policy being pursued. Market actors trust independent banks to focus on price stability irrespective of public opinion; and election years no longer represent uncertainty, or tempt policy-makers to resort to inflationary policies. Paradoxically enough, however, there is also broad agreement that the ECB and other central banks must be 'democratically accountable'. According to a common position on the matter, the ECB should be surrounded – precisely because it is unusually independent – by particularly stringent mechanisms for accountability (Trichet 2001). But how can an 'agent' be both independent and accountable? If it anticipates being held accountable for its actions by the 'principal', is it not less independent by definition?

Not surprisingly, perhaps, the position of the ECB itself and of the members of its Executive Board is that we can have the best of both worlds (see, for example, Issing 1999; Padoa-Schioppa 2000; Trichet 2001). The ECB, according to this argument, is an example of an institution which has been given both a high degree of independence (which serves to safeguard efficient policy-making), and a high degree of accountability. This optimistic conclusion has received backing from several comparative academic studies measuring the accountability of different central banks (Briault *et al.* 1996; Eijffinger and de Haan 2000; Bini-Smaghi and Gros 2001). According to the indices used in these studies, the ECB is not at any rate less accountable than are those central banks with a lower degree of independence from political institutions. If these studies are any indication, then, a negative relationship between independence and accountability may not be inevitable.

In this chapter, I analyse two of the arguments made in this debate. First, I discuss the claim advanced by the ECB: that a negative relationship between independence and accountability is not inevitable, and indeed that independence and accountability are 'two sides of the same coin'. Second, I scrutinise the argument that the ECB is subject to a sufficient level of democratic accountability. I find that the idea that the ECB encompasses the best of both worlds – independence and accountability – relies on a missing link between accountability and transparency. The illusion of accountability, to cite the theme of the book, is upheld by an unsustainable assumption that transparency – and in particular the ECB's version of it – is a sufficient condition for accountability. In practice, press conferences have become a substitute for popular sanctions. Irrespective, therefore, of why we prize accountability in the first place – for the sake of democracy, legitimacy, or efficiency – the ECB is unlikely to have enough of it.

How independent is the ECB?

The legal status of the ECB is laid down in the Treaty of the European Union, which was negotiated among the heads of state and government in Maastricht in 1991. The main decision-making body within the ECB is the Governing Council, which consists of the six members of the Executive Board and the fifteen (as of 2008) national central-bank governors from the Eurozone states. The majority enjoyed by the national-bank governors reflects the general character of the EU as a balance between national and supranational actors. It bears noting, however, that the national-bank governors are expressly prohibited – like the members of the European Commission and the judges on the European Court of Justice – from taking national interests into account when making decisions at the European level.

The ECB is an extraordinarily independent central bank, in three ways. First, it gets generally high marks by the criteria usually used to measure central-bank independence (see, for example, Amtenbrink 1999). The members of the Executive Board are appointed by the heads of the member states. Once in office they cannot be replaced, even if they are considered to be performing poorly. Members of the Executive Board can only be removed from office if they become physically or mentally incapable of doing their job, or if serious misconduct on their part (such as corruption) has been discovered. The term of office is long (eight years) and re-election is forbidden, reinforcing the members' independence still further. The national-bank governors, for their part, are appointed and replaced at the national level, and they may seek re-election. They too, however, cannot be replaced during their term for political reasons, or in response to their performance (unless, once again, grave misconduct has come to light). Nor can the ECB's decisions be overridden. In this the ECB differs from the Bank of England, for example, the decisions of which can – under specific and extraordinary circumstances – be blocked by elected politicians, who may also assume control of monetary policy for a time.

The independence of the ECB is furthermore protected by a provision in the treaty that prohibits governments and other bodies from giving instructions to the bank. Article 108 in the Treaty on European Union states that:

> When exercising the powers and carrying out the tasks and duties conferred upon them by this Treaty and the Statute of the ESCB, neither the ECB, nor a national central bank, nor any member of their decision-making bodies shall seek or take instructions from Community institutions or bodies, from any government of a Member State or from any other body. The Community institutions and bodies and the governments of the Member States undertake to respect this principle and not to seek to influence the members of the decision-making bodies of the ECB or of the national central banks in the performance of their tasks.

In sum, the ECB is not to take instructions from anyone when framing its policies, and elected politicians are forbidden to try to influence its decisions.

A second factor contributing to the unique position of the ECB – and one not figuring among the standard criteria for central-bank independence – is the absence of any powerful political counterweight in the framing of economic policy at the European level. The normal arrangement at the national level is different. Central banks at that level do indeed decide over monetary policy, but they do not make their decisions in isolation from the fiscal policy pursued by the national government, or (particularly in corporatist countries) from the wage co-ordination carried out by employers and trade unions. However, the fiscal side of the Economic and Monetary Union is relatively weakly developed as yet, and the member states often take diverging positions. As a result, there is no political actor at the European level capable of balancing the ECB in the way normal at the national level. Governments and labour-market organisations must adapt to the monetary policy of the ECB, rather than the other way round.

The third way in which the ECB has an unusually strong position is that its legal status is grounded in the EU treaties, and is therefore difficult to change. If elected politicians want to pull the most fundamental emergency brake on the ECB, and take back some of the powers that have been delegated to it, they must make changes in the treaties themselves. We know from the history of the EU, that treaty revisions aimed at withdrawing powers from the supranational institutions are unlikely to succeed, since unanimity among the member states is required, and the member states usually have different preferences (Pollack 2003). Theoretically speaking, a revision of this kind is possible; in practice, however, the risk faced by the ECB that its power will be curtailed by treaty reform is low.

Why do we need accountability?

The ECB, then, is independent from democratically elected political institutions; furthermore, the rationale for this is clearly explicated in contemporary economic theory. So why is democratic accountability on the part of the ECB nonetheless 'crucial', to quote former Executive Board member Tommaso Padoa-Schioppa (Padoa-Schioppa 2000)? To say that accountability is important is a cliché. Why is it, more precisely, that we care about the accountability of the ECB? The answer to this question is important because it affects which types of accountability mechanism we seek out and consider to be sufficient.

In the debate on the independent status of the ECB, at least three different arguments are made for why accountability is important. One common argument is that we need accountability in order to safeguard democracy. We are all democrats, and in democracies the exercise of important political powers – and monetary policy is in that category – should be held to popular account. Delegating such powers without providing reasonable mechanisms for accountability simply breaches an intrinsic democratic principle. It is our duty as democrats not to let this happen. But while this is a reasonable argument, the dilemma we apparently face is a serious one. Let us assume that economic theory is right that an independent central bank leads to lower inflation, a stronger economy, and greater economic wealth. Will we still be loath in that case to challenge the democratic principle? (Of course, if Padoa-Schioppa and other defenders of the present arrangement are right, we do not have to choose: we can have the best of both worlds.)

A second type of argument made for democratic accountability is that it is necessary for securing the legitimacy of the ECB and the monetary-policy system. If citizens perceive the ECB as out of control, the argument goes, they will not accept it; and some sort of systemic crisis may occur. The assumption here seems to be that European citizens prefer democratic control to price stability. Alternatively, citizens fail to understand that price stability requires an independent central bank; such a view would be inconsistent, however, with the rationalistic assumptions of the theory of time-inconsistency. It should be noted that the argument from legitimacy does not require that the ECB actually be accountable. It is enough that the public be given the impression that the bank stands under democratic control. Such a (hypocritical) solution would in fact suffice, assuming it is sustainable, to secure both legitimacy and price stability.

A third reason why accountability might be thought important is that there is a risk that not even an independent central bank will always act in the interests of the general public. The member states may have decided, through their elected politicians, that price stability is to be the top goal for monetary policy in the Euro-zone. However, Article 105.1 of the Treaty also states that, 'without prejudice to the objective of price stability', the ECB 'shall support the general economic policies in the Community'. Monetary policy necessarily involves trade-offs (at least over the short term) between price stability and other economic goals – such as low unemployment and high economic growth, the pursuit of which may require the lowering of interest rates. One way in which the interests of the bank and of the public might diverge is that the two may put a different value on price stability as against low unemployment. As Fisher points out, central bankers may develop a deflationary bias: 'Shielded as they are from public opinion, cocooned within an anti-inflationary temple, central bankers can all too easily deny that cyclical unemployment can be reduced by easing monetary policy' (Fischer 1994, cited by de Haan 1997).

In addition, Euroland is an unusually heterogeneous currency area, with strong regional identities and interests. Strong mechanisms for ensuring accountability at the European level are therefore necessary, if the general European interest is to be safeguarded, or at least different national interests balanced. The bank may also fail to act in the interests of citizens due to sheer incompetence. Thus, even if the view that independent banks tend to outperform their politically controlled counterparts is correct, that is still no guarantee against unskilful policy-making. Accountability is therefore important.

In general, principal-agent theory teaches us that delegating powers is risky, as the agent may have incentives to shirk (Pollack 2003). Accountability can keep the agent on track. As we saw in the introduction, however, we confront a dilemma here: introducing mechanisms for accountability which are anticipated by the agent can have the effect, in practice, of thwarting the purpose of the delegation (which in this case is to keep the hands of elected politicians off monetary policy). So even if there are good reasons – rooted in basic democratic principles and in considerations of legitimacy and efficiency – for holding an agent accountable, how can we do this without reducing said agent's independence? What precisely is the argument of those who claim we can have the best of both worlds – or, in Padoa-Schioppa's words, that 'independence and accountability are two sides of the same coin' (2000: 28)?

Two sides of the same coin?

The proposition that there is no necessary negative correlation between independence and accountability has been supported by several academic economists. The idea that such a negative relationship is a 'myth' is also familiar to political scientists, from the works of Majone (1996b). In the context of the ECB, champions of this view adduce three different arguments.

The first such argument, and the least convincing one, is the bare common assertion that accountability is a 'necessary condition' for independence (Trichet 2001). The statement is a cliché; rarely does it contain any more

substance than to signal that the person making it values both independence and accountability. Sometimes, however, the position is more thought-out, as when Eijffinger and de Haan cite the legitimacy argument in favour of accountability, arguing that an unaccountable ECB would not be sustainable in the long run. It is 'not possible', they argue, to uphold independence without accountability. 'A central bank, continuously conducting a policy which lacks broad political support, will sooner or later be overridden' (de Haan 1997: 417; see also Eijffinger and de Haan 2000). This argument does not show, however, that independence and accountability are not negatively related. It merely states that failing to institutionalise sufficient mechanisms for accountability may result in a collapse of the system (which is hardly a comfort for those seeking to evaluate the present status of the ECB!). As for whether such a radical override is actually likely, given the treaty-based status of the ECB – that is a different question.

The claim that accountability does not undermine the Bank's independence figures in two further (mutually related) arguments as well. It is the 'clearly defined targets' for monetary policy on the one hand, and the provisions for 'transparency' on the other, that account for this happy result, according to adherents of these two views. Indeed, according to several comparative studies of central-bank accountability, clear objectives and transparency strengthen accountability by definition – and without undermining independence. In the index of central-bank accountability created by Eijffinger and de Haan (2000), eight of the thirteen criteria defining accountability relate to clear objectives and transparency (e.g. reporting requirements, parliamentary hearings, clear prioritisation of objectives, and publication of the minutes of meetings) (Eijffinger and de Haan 2000). In the index used by Briault, Haldene, and King, three out of four criteria bear on transparency (parliamentary hearings, publication of minutes, and publication of inflation reports; the fourth criterion relates to the existence of an override mechanism) (Briault *et al.* 1996). Even more striking is the index formulated by Bini-Smaghi and Gros, in which all fifteen criteria relate to transparency and clear objectives (Bini-Smaghi and Gros 2001).

In practice, clear objectives and transparency largely *define* accountability in these studies. It is true that Eijffinger and de Haan include other criteria as well: the existence of an override mechanism, the possibility of changing the status of the bank by means of a simple majority in Parliament, and the existence of a procedure for dismissing a central-bank governor on grounds of poor performance. But since their index is a simple additive one, transparency and clear objectives weigh heavily within it (as they do in the other indices mentioned).

Why give such weight to transparency in an accountability index? The underlying assumption is as follows: the greater the opportunities for citizens, political actors, and market players to evaluate the performance of the bank, the more fully said bank can be held to account. The idea is further that transparency offers a mechanism for accountability which does not

undermine the independence of the agent. Before discussing the link between transparency and accountability in greater detail, let us consider how transparent (and *thus* accountable, according to the above logic) the ECB actually is.

Transparency as 'the public's need to understand'

When it comes to 'clear objectives' the treaties are clear: price stability is the top priority for monetary policy in the Euro-zone. On the other hand, the ECB is free to define more precisely what is to count as price stability (which it has defined as 'inflation rates of below, but close to, 2 per cent over the medium term'). In the indices devised by Eijffinger and de Haan and by Bini-Smaghi and Gros, the fact that the ECB has quantified its target in this way serves to raise its accountability ranking. On the other hand, the fact that it is free to change its definition if it fails to reach the target does not affect its ranking negatively. It has set out a clear target, which constitutes a sufficiently strong commitment – so the assumption goes – to make such a scenario unlikely.

Where transparency is concerned, the ECB considers itself very ambitious and successful. The ECB President, Jean-Claude Trichet, has claimed that the ECB 'is one of the most transparent central banks in the world' (Trichet 2001: 3). Others have criticised the ECB for lacking transparency. In particular, members of the European Parliament have demanded that the ECB make its minutes and voting records public, as certain other central banks do.

The legal requirements for the ECB with respect to transparency are not particularly demanding. According to Article 113.3 (TEU), the ECB shall produce an annual report on its activities. Furthermore, 'the President of the ECB and the other members of the Executive Board may, at the request of the European Parliament or on their own initiative, be heard by the competent committees of the European Parliament'. Article 15.1 in the *Statute of the European System of Central Banks and the European Central Bank* further states that activity reports are to be produced at least quarterly.

Amtenbrink concludes that the ECB can basically decide for itself how transparent its activities will be. Even the provision in the treaty stating that the ECB 'may' be heard by the European Parliament does not, according to Amtenbrink, imply that the Parliament can force members of the Executive Committee to attend hearings (Amtenbrink 1999; see also Begg 2007: 41f). Nor is it specified what information shall be contained in the annual and quarterly reports.

Certain central banks, like the American Federal Reserve and the Bank of England, publish the minutes of their meetings at some delay, including the outcome of any votes taken. Article 10.4 of the Statute of the ECB states that 'the proceedings of the meetings [of the Governing Council] shall be confidential. The Governing Council may decide to make the outcome of its

deliberations public.' So far, the ECB has decided to keep all documentation of its meetings, such as minutes and voting records, secret.

Even so, the ECB claims to be among the most transparent (and *thus* accountable) of central banks. An argument is even made, in fact, that the bank's decision not to publish its minutes and voting records enhances the transparency of its proceedings. Executive Board member Otmar Issing has furnished us, through speeches and articles on the topic, with the most thorough explication of this argument. Transparency, according to Issing, is not just a question of having access to information; it is also a question of understanding that information:

> The 'public's right to know' has to be balanced by the 'public's need to understand'. What matters for transparency is therefore clarity as well as openness. For a new and supranational institution like the ECB, it is particularly important that it sends clear and coherent messages to the markets and the wider public. More 'words' do not necessarily mean 'more information', and 'more information' does not necessarily and by itself contribute to greater clarity.
>
> (Issing 1999: 508)

Issing objects to a 'legal-political' interpretation of transparency, in which the dissemination of information is 'exclusively "demand-driven"', i.e. the public is granted access to 'raw data' from the policy process on its own demand. When such 'legal-political' transparency obtains, Issing observes, 'the public decides the extent to which information is provided and the central bank has no right to limit the "supply side"' (Issing 2006). But this type of transparency – which could eventually result 'in regular television broadcasts of the meetings' – gives rise to several problems, according to Issing. First, it leads to a situation of 'information overflow'. 'Data are often not self-explanatory'; too much information will confuse people rather than inform them. Understanding requires interpretation, which the ECB itself provides in its communications at monthly press conferences, as well as in bulletins, speeches, and interviews.

Another argument against publishing minutes and voting records fastens on the great importance of the ECB's speaking with one voice. The public disclosure of internal debates and diverging opinions, revealing 'who said what and who voted this or that way', would be a 'distraction' for the public and the financial markets watching the ECB. Issing furthermore fears that, if the votes cast by national-bank governors were made public before their home 'constituencies', the deliberations of the Governing Council would risk becoming politicised along national lines (notwithstanding the fact that, formally speaking, its members are forbidden to regard their home member states as constituents). To communicate a coherent picture of its policy, the ECB must present a united front.

Thus, 'demand-driven' transparency – where the public rather than the ECB controls what information it has access to – does indeed restrict the independence of the ECB. By contrast, the type of transparency promoted by the ECB itself allows it to control the supply of information, thus offering the best of both worlds: transparency (which in this view is equal to accountability) and independence.

The single transparency measure most emphasised by Trichet, Issing, and the other Executive Board members is the monthly press conference. The Governing Council has two meetings per month. One of these is followed by a press conference, at which the president makes an introductory statement explaining the decisions taken and outlining the reasoning behind them. Questions from the press thereupon follow. The press conference is published on the internet.

In addition, the President of the ECB appears four times a year before the European Parliament's Committee on Economic and Monetary Affairs. These sessions last about two hours. They include an introductory statement by the President and questions from the MEPs, with a maximum of two questions per person. Both the introduction and the questions and answers are published on the internet. The ECB webpage, finally, features a fair number of speeches by Executive Board members laying out the ECB's view on various topics. In Trichet's words, 'explaining tirelessly the reasons and the reasoning that underpin the decisions of the Governing Council is a key part of our collective duty' (Trichet 2001: 4).

The academic measures of accountability mentioned earlier do not distinguish between demand-driven and supply-controlled transparency (to use Issing's terms). The indices give equal weight to holding a press conference and publishing minutes. Thanks to its communication measures, therefore, the ECB scores relatively well on transparency and *therefore* accountability, in spite of its extraordinary independence. In both of the above-mentioned indices of accountability – those devised by Eijffinger and de Haan and by Bini-Smaghi and Gros – the ECB takes the silver medal. The Bank of England comes in first, while the central banks of Canada, the United States, and Japan (and the former German Bundesbank as well) trail behind the ECB.

An alternative 'economic' definition of transparency is that offered by Geraats, for whom transparency is 'the absence of asymmetric information between monetary policy makers and other economic agents' (Geraats 2002: 533). It is clear that 'supply-controlled' transparency – with the unlimited opportunities it gives the agent to manipulate the information revealed – does not fall in that category. Rather, if one is to accept the conclusion that the ECB does indeed encompass the best of both worlds – both independence and accountability – one must accept the following two things as well: first, the particular definition of transparency used by the ECB (i.e. supply-control: the ECB itself decides how transparent it will be); and second, the assumption that a high degree of such transparency brings with it an abundance of accountability. In the section that follows, I discuss the latter assumption.

Sufficiently accountable? – examining the missing links

There are no formal rules providing for any sanctions against the ECB. There is no way to replace the members of the Executive Board or of the Governing Council. Nor is there any way of lowering their wages, or otherwise affecting them personally. There is no way to give them instructions. There is no emergency brake to pull; no override mechanism. And there is a merely theoretical chance – which is very slim in practice – of rewriting their mandate by revising the treaties. Transparency, therefore, is the only remaining mechanism for ensuring accountability. Is it a reasonable conclusion that the ECB is sufficiently accountable?

To be able to say anything on that matter, we must go back to the previous question: namely, what is the point of accountability in the first place? If the point is to live up to valuable democratic principles, then the ECB's status as a 'supply-controlled' transparent institution should be evaluated against said principles. If one believes the main point of accountability is to prevent the directors of the ECB from 'shirking', or from placing their own preferences before the public interest, then the question is whether the transparency measures in place are likely to prevent such behaviour. If it is legitimacy that is primarily sought, then the important question is whether the present level of transparency increases trust in the ECB among European citizens, political actors, and/or financial-market actors (depending on which of these audiences one considers most important). Of course, one may value accountability for more than one of these reasons. Unless one has a clear view of why accountability is important, however, one cannot evaluate whether the ECB's present level of accountability is sufficient. I shall consider each of these arguments in turn.

Let us assume the point of accountability is to secure democracy. Are clear objectives and transparency enough in that case? Democracy is a contested concept with many meanings. A fairly non-controversial way of categorising different democratic ideals is in terms of three types: participatory democracy, representative democracy, and deliberative democracy. Needless to say, the scope for direct citizen participation in the monetary policy of the ECB is basically non-existent. But what about the other two democratic ideals?

Accountability is crucial in a system of representative democracy, but it is also a problematic concept. 'What do we really mean by this ubiquitous admonition to "hold people accountable"?', asks Behn in his study of the subject. 'The phrase rolls off one individual's tongue and into another's ears without registering in either's mind. To "hold people accountable" has become a cliché and, like all clichés, is a substitute for thinking' (Behn 2001). There may be no watertight uncontested meaning of accountability in a representative democracy, but on one point Behn's argument is irrefutable. Accountability in a representative democracy is more than just a question of giving an account of one's actions, i.e. explaining and justifying them (which would appear to be the dictionary definition of the term). 'Somehow the dictionaries have not caught up with the vernacular. When people seek to hold someone accountable, they are usually planning some kind of punishment' (Behn 2001: 4). According to Behn, 'accountability means punishment' (Behn 2001: 3).

The editors of another key book on the topic say the same:

> Governments are "accountable" if citizens can discern representative from unrepresentative governments and can sanction them appropriately, retaining in office those incumbents who perform well and ousting from office those who do not. An "accountability mechanism" is thus a map from the outcomes of actions (including messages that explain these actions) of public officials to sanctions by citizens.
>
> (Manin *et al.* 1999: 10)

Accountability without a stick is not compatible with the idea of representative democracy. Clear objectives and transparency do not furnish any formal mechanisms whereby citizens can punish the ECB for its actions. In a legal sense, therefore, the ECB is not accountable, as that notion is understood in theories of representative democracy.

On the other hand, clear objectives and transparency may facilitate public criticism of the ECB, which can be seen as a type of stick. Is it reasonable to assume that the ECB will do everything it can to fulfil its objectives, thus avoiding such criticism? Is this stick heavy and hard enough to ensure both that principles of representative democracy are respected and that the risk of agency-shirking is minimised?

First of all, 'public criticism' is not necessarily democratic. It depends on where the criticism comes from. Criticism of the ECB is normally voiced by elite actors, such as political parties, media actors, lobby groups, and (especially) financial-market players. The extent to which these voices are representative of the broader public (in terms of values, beliefs, and opinions) is an empirical question, the answer to which may vary from case to case. Issing too recognises, in fact, the risk that public criticism in practice would be the voice of the financial markets, rather than of European citizens:

> Not surprisingly, the strongest and loudest criticisms therefore come from financial market players. Consequently, central banks are exposed to the temptation of tailoring their communication entirely to the interests of those players, thus running the risk of being towed along by the financial markets. This risk is all the greater since market participants under certain circumstances may develop their own expectations which the central bank would then be obliged to more or less fulfil.
>
> (Issing 2006)

On paper, at least, the most promising channel for subjecting the ECB to public criticism would appear to be the 'monetary dialogue', which is the term used for the appearances of the ECB President before the European

Parliament. EP elections are problematic in many respects: they are 'second-order national elections', with campaigns that deal mainly with national issues; and voter turnout is low by the standards of national elections. Even so, the European Parliament is directly elected by the citizens. As long as MEPs do not take Article 108 too seriously (which forbids them to try to influence ECB policy), the 'monetary dialogue' could make for a democratic criticism with some bite – thus ensuring a type of accountability. According to Jabko, however, the monetary dialogue in the European Parliament is a rather feeble affair, at any rate compared with the hearings which the chairman of the Federal Reserve must attend at the U.S. Congress:

> In the US the power of Congress can be felt in the staging of Congressional hearings. The chairman of the Federal Reserve stands in the witness box and must answer questions asked by a small number of Congressmen who sit above him like judges. These hearings last as long as the people's representatives deem necessary. In the EU, the president of the European Central Bank addresses members of the European Parliament from above. He sits on a platform, next to the chair of the Economic and Monetary Affairs Committee, and takes questions from the floor. The hearings only last two hours and MEPs are only allowed to ask two questions, which are therefore not very difficult to fudge. The contrast with the US situation could hardly be more striking.
>
> (Jabko 2005:10f)

In my view, it is doubtful that these quarterly sessions – each lasting only two hours, including the President's own introduction – are sufficient to secure accountability as understood in a representative democracy. If the ECB fails to secure price stability, or in some other way misuses its powers, what chance do European citizens have to hold the ECB accountable after such a session? It takes very low expectations to answer that question in the affirmative.

In the deliberative-democratic ideal, on the other hand, accountability is a less central concept overall. Democracy in this concept is less about power and sanctions, and more about arguing and engaging one's fellow citizens in dialogue. The heart of democracy is deliberation – rational exchanges of argument for and against different policies, values, and beliefs. Versions of this ideal are many and varied, of course, and participatory notions are less relevant in this context. But deliberative democracy can also be applied to the elite level. Does a proponent of deliberative democracy have reason to be satisfied with the present specification of the ECB's objectives, or with the efforts at communication made by its leadership?

In fact there is much, in the explanations given by ECB Executive Board members of their views on transparency and accountability, that resembles the deliberative-democratic ideal. The 'monetary dialogue' with the European Parliament and the 'tireless' explaining of reasons in speeches and press conferences is emphasised. There is no doubt that the ECB has been active in communicating its message (an activity at the core of its definitions of transparency and accountability). But there is also no doubt that a key factor for deliberative democrats is missing here, or at least its presence cannot be verified. Presenting one's case publicly is just the first part of the concept of deliberation. The second part is being receptive to the arguments of others (Gutman and Thompson 1996). Deliberating actors do more than just try to get their own message across. They also listen sincerely to the arguments of others, and they are prepared to revise their positions in light of what they hear. Dialogue is a two-way street. Where reciprocity is lacking, there is no deliberation – only rhetorical action (Schimmelfennig 2001).

The methodological challenge of distinguishing deliberation from rhetorical action may be insurmountable (Naurin forthcoming). We are unable to verify that the ECB takes the comments of MEPs or other public figures into serious account when formulating its policies; nor can we establish that it does not. Of course, no one likes to be criticised; it might therefore be reasonable to assume that, if not for deliberative then for rational reasons, the ECB does take such views into account. But there is one circumstance which makes it very hard to describe the 'monetary dialogue' as a deliberative setting: Article 108. The purpose of deliberation is to try to change people's minds through rational argument. Article 108, however, constitutionally prohibits the ECB from listening too seriously, and it forbids MEPs and any other representative-democratic actors to try to influence the ECB. This is not a situation characterised by reciprocity; hence it does not qualify as a deliberative setting.

My conclusion is therefore that, notwithstanding its clear objectives and (supply-controlled) transparency, the ECB is not sufficiently accountable – not if the point of accountability is to fulfil basic democratic principles. If neither sanctions nor reciprocity obtain, the ideals of neither representative nor deliberative democracy are satisfied. A completely different type of argument would be to claim that the ECB's status is democratically justified because it was determined by democratically elected politicians. According to such an argument, however, there would be no need to worry about the accountability of the ECB in the first place. It would in that case be the governments of the member states which are to be held to account – for creating the system. But the ECB itself does not argue in this fashion; its academic champions do not do so either. The common view – which is the focus of attention here – is that the ECB should be accountable in its own right.

Let us turn now to the second argument for the importance of accountability. The idea here is that, while clear objectives and (supply-controlled) transparency do not satisfy democratic principles, they may be sufficient for preventing agency-shirking, i.e. they may keep the ECB focused on the preferences of European citizens, rather than on those of special (national, financial-market, or central bankers') interests. There is evidence that institutionalising a 'giving-reasons requirement' into public law affects the behaviour of bureaucrats (Shapiro 2001). Again, however, the weak spot for the ECB is the fact that there is no hard stick at the end. Article 108, moreover, gives a totally contrary signal here. It seems reasonable to assume the ECB will care about criticism which may affect its status (which probably means, in particular, criticism from the financial markets). If it does not wish to listen, however, it simply need not do so. As Begg notes, in reference to the appearances of the ECB President before the European Parliament, 'it is not obvious that [these hearings] create incentives for central bankers to modify policy. … If the principles (whether governments or citizens) do not like what they see, there is not much they can do about it' (Begg 2007: 41). It is hard to imagine that sufficient accountability mechanisms are in place here to prevent shirking.

The third argument for the importance of accountability fastens on legitimacy. Are clear objectives and (the ECB's definition of) transparency sufficient to secure acceptance and trust? Ferejohn has explained why public authorities and other 'agents' may have an incentive to render their doings even more transparent than the contract with their 'principal' originally enjoined. The motive for so doing is to secure the principal's trust, as a result of which still greater powers may end up being delegated to the agent. Ferejohn interprets the transparency reforms implemented by the US Congress historically as a rational strategy aiming at increasing the chance that the people would accept the transfer of still greater powers to the federal government (Ferejohn 1999). In the case of monetary policy and the ECB, there is hardly any power left to be delegated. But the logic may also apply to the possibility of power being withdrawn. The risk of such a treaty revision is already low, but a high degree of public legitimacy may reduce it still further.

The idea that transparency affects the degree of legitimacy does seem reasonable, although there are few empirical studies of the link.[2] It is more questionable, in my view, that making statements and answering questions – the ECB's own version of transparency – will help the ECB to secure legitimacy if it fails to reach its policy goals, or in other ways performs poorly. What might instead happen in that case is that the people will feel growing frustration, due to the absence of any real mechanisms for holding the bank to account.

Conclusion

If contemporary economic theory is to be believed, independent central banks make better monetary policy than do politically controlled banks. If the degree of central-bank independence is too low, therefore, the principle of representative democracy is thwarted: the people's representatives, after all, are supposed to act in the interests of the people (Pitkin 1967). Time-inconsistent politicians who only care about the next election do not live up to this ideal. Yet solving the problem by handing over powers to independent experts also challenges democratic principles. Furthermore, even independent banks may be prone to shirking and vulnerable to pressures from special interests. There are accordingly good reasons to institute decent accountability mechanisms for central banks. The problem is that such mechanisms tend to restrict the independence sought in the first place.

Since both independence and accountability are valuable objectives in this case, there is a great demand for solutions that seem to secure both. It is no surprise that members of the ECB's Executive Board consider their score on both counts to be high. More problematic, in my view, is the support furnished by academic scholars to the view that well-developed PR activities are enough to gain high marks on indices of accountability. With these indices, defenders of the ECB's present construction have helped the Bank to handle the difficult debate on democratic legitimacy. Rather than being forced to discuss what is a reasonable balance between the two values of independence and accountability (a different balance than the present one is of course possible, for instance through an override mechanism), representatives of the ECB can simply point to the indices mentioned and argue that the two are not negatively related. A greater sensitivity to the distinction between transparency and accountability might have enabled scholars to avoid the dubious political role they have played here, in which they have helped uphold the 'illusion of accountability'.[3]

There is no doubt that clear objectives and transparency (at least of the demand-driven type, which implies access to documents and not just PR) are positively related to accountability, as that notion is understood in theories of representative democracy. It could probably even be seen as a necessary condition for accountability (Naurin 2006). The principal must be able to monitor the actions of its agent. But transparency is not a sufficient condition; it is therefore unsuitable as a criterion in unweighted additive indices of accountability. Transparency may facilitate public criticism; but for the latter to work as a form of democratic accountability, it must be representative of citizens' views and must affect the behaviour of the agent. In view of the ECB's present institutional design, we can only hope that its supply-controlled transparency will contribute to such an outcome.

Notes

1 A previous version of the main arguments presented in this chapter has been published (in Swedish) as Naurin, D. (2003) 'Den Europeiska Centralbanken: oberoende med ansvarsutkrävande?', in U. Bernitz, Gustavsson, S. and Oxelheim, L. (eds) *Valutaunionen, Författningsfrågan och Östutvidgningen*, Stockholm: Santerus.

2 For overviews of the research on the effects of transparency on market actors and economic behaviour, see Geraats 2002; Crowe and Meade 2007; and the special issue of *European Journal of Political Economy* edited by de Haan, Eijffinger, and Rybinski 2007.

3 One of these scholars – Lorenzo Bini-Smaghi – has subsequently become a member of the ECB Executive Board.

11 Civil society participation and accountability

Thomas Persson

The alleged democratic deficit and the waning legitimacy of the European Union have inspired scholars and practitioners to look for new ways of improving accountability in the EU. While acknowledging the weakness of representative channels in the Union, and the difficult road ahead before parliamentarisation is accomplished, they have shifted their attention to the direct involvement of civil society in the European political system. Letting stakeholders and civil society take active part in policy-making is considered to offer a promising complement to representative democracy (cf. Smismans 2006; Finke 2007; Kohler-Koch and Rittberger 2007). Greater societal involvement in EU policy-making will expose decisions to public scrutiny and, in the long run, contribute to the emergence of a European public sphere. Thus, it is believed, participatory and deliberative arrangements hold the potential to generate a better democratic legitimation of European governance (Steffek and Nanz 2008).

At the heart of this new strand of political thought and practice is a broader view on the meaning of accountability. Mark Bovens, for instance, argues that a lack of trust in European governance has created an urge 'for more direct and explicit accountability relations between public agencies, on the one hand, and clients, citizens and civil society, on the other hand' (Bovens 2007a: 457). Hence, accountability is no longer considered to be furnished solely through the representative channels of the Union, i.e. when voters hold office-holders to account. It also finds expression in participatory and deliberative arrangements, in which stakeholders and civil society are involved more directly in policy-making and implementation. In this vein, the European Commission has committed itself to 'opening up the policy-making process to get more people and organisations involved in shaping and delivering EU policy', with an eye to promoting 'greater openness, accountability and responsibility for all those involved' (Commission 2001a: 3). Thus, both scholars and EU officials regard *social accountability* as a possible remedy for accountability deficits in the EU (Bovens 2007b).

In this chapter, I seek to assess the prospects for this new view on accountability, on the basis of empirical findings from one important policy-making process in which new measures for societal involvement have been tested: the overhaul of European chemicals policy.[1] This law-making process is generally considered an early test of the new governance strategy by the Commission, since it entailed inviting the public, stakeholders, and civil society to give their input throughout most of the legislative process. The question we must answer, then, is this: to what extent have the new participatory and deliberative measures tested in this policy-making process provided stakeholders and civil society with new opportunities to hold policy-makers to account? The test is a limited one, but it ought to make possible at least a tentative conclusion on the potential role of social accountability in European governance.

This test indicated, if I may anticipate a little, that the chemicals-policy overhaul was, at least to some extent, more transparent, more inclusive, and more responsive than is EU-level decision-making generally. Transparency, inclusiveness, and responsiveness are all prerequisites for accountability. Accountability itself, however, must be furnished primarily through the traditional representative bodies of the Union. Accordingly, those who decided on the new EU chemicals law were directly (in the case of the European Parliament) and indirectly (in the case of the Council) accountable to European citizens, and thus subject to the general democratic deficit of the Union. Moreover, European citizens have no way of holding the stakeholders and civil society organisations that were involved to account. Thus, while weak mechanisms of accountability (transparency, inclusiveness, and responsiveness) were improved, stronger ones were not changed in any way.

The chapter will unfold as follows. First, I discuss the scholarly debate on the promise and the pitfalls of participatory and deliberative governance. I then review some reforms that have been introduced in this vein at the EU level. Following this, I try to shed some light on the strengths and weaknesses of the new approaches to participatory and deliberative governance, using insights drawn from my review of how chemicals are approved in Europe. I conclude with a discussion of whether participatory and deliberative governance can live up to its promise.

The promise of participatory and deliberative governance

While still contested (see, for example, Moravcsik 2008), the democratic deficit and the waning popular legitimacy of the Union are nowadays widely acknowledged (Føllesdal and Hix 2006). European integration comes with a decline in traditional representative channels of democracy, since EU policy-making by-passes national parliaments, and the European Parliament has failed to furnish any adequate substitute for them. Declining public confidence in the representative channels of the Union weakens its capacity for action and reform (Hix 2008); while, at the same time, the 'parliamentary path' towards a democratisation of the EU falls short of offering a solution. Inspiration for reform has therefore come – even more in the case of the EU than elsewhere – from alternative models of democracy.

In particular, participatory and deliberative models of democracy have gained ground since the late 1990s (Grenwood 2007; Kohler-Koch and Rittberger 2007).

Notwithstanding this, however, the idea of societal involvement in policy-making is hardly new, whether at the national or the European level. The European Commission, for instance, has always been open to stakeholders and organised civil society, since they supply expertise and serve as a check and balance on political institutions as well as each other.[2] Yet, the traditional notion of societal involvement has mainly been based on the functional needs that these groups fill in improving the effective problem-solving capacity of the Union (i.e. the output-oriented legitimation they provide). The Commission has regarded external expert advice as a way to improve the quality of policies; in exchange, interest groups get an opportunity to influence policy and to defend and promote the interests of their members. Thus, in accordance with neo-pluralist theory, consultations have helped the Commission to arbitrate between competing priorities, and to gain acceptance for its policies from those affected by them.

Since the 1990s, however, there has been a shift in how the Commission and academic scholars seek to promote civil society involvement. The focus now is on the way in which participation by stakeholders and civil society can contribute to the input-oriented legitimation of European governance (cf. Finke 2007; Greenwood 2007). Proponents of this new mode of governance claim that civil society associations can partially compensate for the structural deficiencies of traditional representative channels in the Union. The involvement of civil society in EU policy-making contributes to political bargaining between those who are affected by EU polices and those who make the decisions (Héritier 1999). Hence, the main thrust of participatory-democratic ideals lies in the enhanced democratic legitimation for political decisions to which the *participation* of civil society can contribute. Furthermore, proponents of the involvement of civil society in EU policy-making are often influenced by the ideals of *deliberative* democracy. According to this view, it is not participation *per se* that offers a remedy for the Union's legitimacy problem, but public deliberation and an open exchange of ideas. An element of popular scrutiny and oversight will thus be added to European governance, and the development of a European public sphere furthered (Eriksen and Fossum 2000).

Yet, while these lines of thought emphasise the positive effects that enhanced input from stakeholders and civil society can have on the Union's democratic legitimacy, my concern here lies with *accountability*. The purest form of democratic accountability works through representative channels, whereby voters hold those whom they have elected to account for their actions. Such a system presupposes not only that voters have access to information and can monitor the actions of their representatives, but also that they can impose sanctions on them, e.g. by voting them out of office (cf. the introductory chapter of this volume). It is important to note, however, that this ideal of delegated authority and representative accountability takes its model from political institutions on the national level.

Since governance at the European level (and the global level too) functions through a much wider variety of institutional forms, then accountability too must also take multidimensional forms (cf. Keohane's chapter in this volume; Fischer 2004; Bovens 2007a, 2007b). Accountability may thus have many faces, although not all of them can be considered democratic. Thus, Mark Bovens claims that scholars debating business responsibility and corporate governance have paid 'more attention to the role of non-governmental organisations, interest groups and customers or clients as relevant "stakeholders", not only in determining policy, but also in rendering account' (Bovens 2007a: 457). It may well be possible to transfer this form of accountability – known generally as *social accountability*, in which stakeholders and civil society are given a special role in rendering account – to the level of European governance.

However, once we start speaking of accountability through participatory and deliberative arrangements with stakeholders and civil society (rather than through representative channels), the concept seems to become more slippery. It has become equated – not least when invoked by the Commission – with openness and responsibility, rather than with the ability of citizens actually to hold EU officials to account. The Commission has argued, for example, that accountability means that the institutions of the Union 'must explain and take responsibility for what [they do] in Europe' (Commission 2001a: 3). But responsibility is a much wider concept than accountability. Giving persons responsibility means allowing them to act on their own premises; the concept thus relates more to personal liability. Accountability is in question when certain persons act on behalf of others, implying a duty on the part of the former to justify their actions, and an opportunity on the part of the latter to impose sanctions (Mulgan 2000).

In what follows, I seek to assess the extent to which the involvement of civil society in EU policy-making can really contribute to enhanced accountability, and if so how. I shall consider a couple of aspects that, for theoretical reasons, I regard as important to this matter. First, *transparency* and accountability are intimately connected. For citizens to be able to hold those wielding power to account, they must at the least have access to information on policy deliberations, decisions, and the policy-making process. Hence, transparency can be considered a necessary but insufficient condition for accountability. Second, *responsiveness* and accountability are closely associated, since both reflect the idea of a binding relationship between citizens and their representatives. Responsiveness, however, can be viewed as a softer form of the phenomenon, since it concerns the concordance between the actions of representatives and the preferences of citizens. Accountability goes further, in the sense that it relates not only to compliance with popular demands, but also to the justification given for one's actions and the possibility of facing consequences for them (Mulgan 2000; Bovens 2007a, 2007b; Hüller and Kohler-Koch 2008).

Now, let me underline that I regard stakeholders and civil society as intermediary agents between the Union and the wider public. They serve as a 'transmission belt'. On the one hand, they aggregate and articulate the preferences of the people; on the other, they help scrutinise the activities of the Union and its officials on citizens' behalf (Steffek and Nanz 2008: 3). For this to function properly, it is not only necessary that policy-making be transparent and responsive, but also that participatory and deliberative arrangements be put in place that adhere to basic notions of political equality. If only a limited part of civil society is represented, not all relevant citizen viewpoints will be transmitted to public officials, and public scrutiny and debate will be narrowed down. Hence, I will take *inclusiveness* in policy-making as an indicator of whether it is open, and whether it invites a broad variety of viewpoints. This may not be an element of the same instrumental value for accountability as transparency and responsiveness; nevertheless, it is a core value for any notion of democracy (Hüller and Kohler-Koch 2008).[3]

These weaker forms of accountability can play an important role in ensuring that the activities of Union bodies are scrutinised and that wrongdoing on the part of public officials is highlighted, i.e. 'whistle-blowing' and 'blaming and shaming'. However, they are not to be equated with stronger mechanisms of accountability, since they do not enable stakeholders and civil society organisations to impose formal sanctions on those wielding power. Moreover, we must recognise that stakeholders and civil society organisations are not synonymous with EU citizens; nor do they generally live up to democratic ideals in their internal life. In general, citizens are not able – unless they are members of the organisation in question – to hold these mediating associations to account. We ought not, accordingly, to expect the new participatory arrangements to provide strong mechanisms of accountability. But have they provided any weaker forms, such as openness and transparency? Before assessing this, let us take a closer look at the participatory arrangements furnished by the Commission.

Reforms for improved participation and deliberation

Inspired by an explicit desire to improve the democratic legitimacy of the EU, the Commission launched a new governance strategy at the beginning of this century, with the White Paper on European Governance (Commission 2001a). The Commission has a long tradition of consulting experts and organised interests in order to ensure the support of stakeholders for its legislative initiatives. When European integration began, for example, the Commission established close ties with various European federations of associations, such as those for farmers, employers, and trade unions. Input and support from such organisations was perceived as necessary for improving the quality of regulations, and for the efficient implementation of Community policies. Consultation with general interest groups, such as environmental and consumer organisations, was less developed, and it mainly took the form of bilateral contacts. Except in the case of the advisory group with socio-economic participation laid down in the Treaties – i.e. the European Economic and Social Committee – consultations were long, informal and *ad hoc* (Kohler-Koch and Finke 2007).

From the mid-1980s onwards, the Commission started pursuing a 'social dialogue' on the social dimension of the internal market with the European social partners, i.e. employers' and trade-union organisations. Contacts were established with new actors and new instruments for consultation were introduced, such as the European Social Policy Forum. The Commission started consulting not just with directly affected stakeholders, but with groups representing a more general interest as well, like organisations for human rights and for women's rights. At the same time, 'partnership' arrangements in connection with European regional policy involved new public and private actors in the formulation and implementation of programmes. These new patterns of consultation are 'characterized by the broadening and deepening of societal involvement' (Kohler-Koch and Finke 2007: 210).

However, with the White Paper on European Governance, the Commission introduced a qualitatively different consultation policy. It proposed to open up the policy-making process to more people and more organisations, and to promote 'greater openness, accountability and responsibility for all those involved' (Commission 2001a: 3). The White Paper acknowledged the insufficiency of the output approach to legitimacy, i.e. the idea that the Union ultimately derives its legitimacy from the efficiency of its outcomes. It argued that the legitimacy of the Union could no longer rest solely on its 'ability to remove barriers of trade or to complete an internal market'; instead, 'its legitimacy today depends on involvement and participation' – in other words, an input approach is needed too (Commission 2001a: 11). Hence, the new goal for the Union was 'to open up policy-making to make it more inclusive and accountable' (Commission 2001a: 8).

Following the White Paper on European Governance, the Commission also introduced new instruments – e.g. public online consultations – in an effort to give better opportunities for a wide range of societal groups and individual citizens to make their voices heard. The role of civil society has been further emphasised by introducing the principle of participatory democracy into the draft of the EU Constitutional Treaty (Article I-47), and later into the draft of the Lisbon Treaty as well (Article 11 in the consolidated version of the Treaties). Notwithstanding these developments, however, the Union's democratic aspirations are largely founded in the principle of representative democracy; participatory and deliberative arrangements, while important, are a complement to this ideal. However, the impact of these new practical steps is quite unknown. Empirical research on the effects of the Commission's participatory regime is sparse. I will therefore attempt, in what follows, to assess the effects on accountability of the new participatory and deliberative arrangements established by the Commission.

Lessons from the chemicals-policy overhaul

In order to get a better idea of how participatory and deliberative governance works in practice, let us consider the political process leading to the adoption of a new European system for the regulation of chemicals. This policy overhaul is particularly interesting, for at least two reasons. First, the aim of the new regulatory framework is to address market failures arising from the integration of the single market. At the same time, strong environmental requirements may put trade and the international competitiveness of European industry at risk. Consequently, the adoption of a new scheme for chemicals regulation in the EU requires that a balance be struck among important interests. The salience and cross-cutting nature of this policy area, moreover, make it susceptible to broad engagement on the part of stakeholders and civil society. Second, the process leading up to the adoption of the REACH system (as the new policy is known) can be viewed as an early test of the EU's new governance strategy. It illustrates the type of participatory and deliberative political process that is thought to provide a remedy for the Union's legitimacy problems (see, e.g. Greenwood 2007: 352). In fact, it has recently been argued that 'we could very plausibly hold up the REACH reform process as blue print for participatory law-making' (Heyvaert 2008: 198).

And, indeed, the draft legislation for a new chemicals policy was the result of lengthy deliberations. Following the Commission's adoption in 2001 of the White Paper, extensive consultations were initiated with stakeholders and civil society organisations on a strategy for a future chemicals policy (Commission 2001b). Having gathered new information from this round of consultations, conferences, and public hearings with regulators, scientists, businesses, civil society associations, and representatives of member states and applicant countries, the Commission proceeded to revise its legislative draft proposal. It also invited stakeholders, civil society, and the general public to take part in a public Internet consultation, held between May and July 2003, in which the workability of the proposed REACH system would be assessed (Persson 2007a). Once the online consultation had been concluded, the Commission analysed the contributions and was set to make appropriate changes in its proposal. At this stage, however, massive lobbying campaigns were launched, directed at the responsible directorates-general. Then, after its adoption by the College of Commissioners in October 2003, the final version of the REACH proposal was sent to the Council and the European Parliament under the co-decision procedure (Commission 2003). This final version provoked, once again, a flood of reactions – from the chemicals industry and environmental organisations alike. In fact, throughout the entire phase of policy-shaping and decision-making in the legislative institutions of the

Union, massive lobbying campaigns were launched by both industry and environmental organisations. And although the Council and the Parliament were in near agreement on central components of the REACH proposal, they failed to close a deal in the first reading. Negotiations continued throughout 2006. Finally, the EU's two law-making bodies came to a compromise, and in December 2006 the resulting version of the proposal was adopted by both institutions (Pesendorfer 2006; Selin 2007). Now then, did this lengthy law-making process make for any improvement in transparency, inclusiveness, responsiveness, and ultimately accountability?

A more transparent, inclusive, and responsive policy-making process?

Given the above characterisation of the policy-making process – from initiation through policy-shaping and up to the time of the final decision – it is quite clear that the new measures for involving stakeholders and civil society have helped make the process more open and transparent. The Commission worked hard on making information on the new policy public at all stages of the process. And, since groups and organisations got engaged at an early stage, they helped to raise awareness about this technical policy, and to make the new scheme for chemicals regulation a subject of public debate, at least to some extent. To be sure, chemicals policy bears on the environment and on the health, safety, and welfare of Europeans; all the same, ordinary citizens may find it hard to participate in the debate concerning it, due to the technical character of the issue. Nevertheless, the consultation on the new chemicals law sparked a Europe-wide public debate, albeit one largely restricted to elite actors with a common interest in the field.

In particular, environmental organisations used the Internet to conduct Europe-wide public campaigns in favour of stricter regulations; while animal-welfare groups, for instance, called for greater limitations on the use of animals for testing. Businesses and their associations, on the other hand, took a somewhat different strategy. They relied more on traditional lobbying and informal contacts with policy-makers, although they also warned publicly about the detrimental effects that stricter regulations might have on European industry (Friedrich 2008: 159). Taken together, it is fair to say that the policy-making process on REACH was fairly transparent, and that it was widely debated as well (if not so much among European citizens in general, then at least among mediating organisations and their representatives).

One thing that helped make chemicals policy the subject of public debate is the fact that it is commonly thought to activate two competing 'advocacy coalitions', each positioned at their respective end of the policy spectrum: namely, environmentalists and industrialists (Pesendorfer 2006; Selin 2007). In line with this, our own findings suggest that the views of different actors on REACH are captured well by a single underlying dimension that mirrors respondents' attitudes toward EU-level regulation of chemicals. That is, opinions on REACH are ordered along a dimension running from pro-to anti-regulation. However, the pattern of contestation over EU regulation of chemicals is not so simple (Lindgren and Persson 2008a). On the contrary, there are important groups and associations – e.g. those of workers and consumers – which are positioned between the two extremes. The views of consumer representatives, in fact, are closer to those of business representatives than to those of environmental representatives. Moreover, the fact that there is only a limited disparity between the views of business and worker representatives in this area indicates that the issue is not simply one of left or right; indeed, there is some room, on environmental issues of this type, for an anti-regulation cross-class coalition between European labour and capital. Workers and trade unionists share the concerns of business for the competitiveness of the European chemical industry, since jobs will be lost if production moves out of Europe. This contributed, we would argue, to the mobilisation of a broad range of stakeholders and civil society organisations on the question. Consequently, the pattern of participation became more inclusive than it would likely have been had the issue not been polarised and politicised in this way.

This heterogeneity of interests was also reflected in a broad participation by different interests in the public online consultation that preceded the final Commission proposal. An impressive number of proposals – almost 6,400 – were submitted to the Commission in the course of eight weeks during 2003. Nevertheless, data from this consultation reveal a pattern of unequal participation. Business and industrial interests were considerably better represented in the consultation than were trade unions, consumers, or groups representing the interests of the environment. The participation of NGOs (Non-Governmental Organisations) was in general rather low, as was – predictably enough – that of ordinary citizens. Industry answered for nearly two thirds of the participants (65 per cent); NGOs accounted for a mere 6 per cent. Other categories, such as public authorities, political parties, academic institutions, and individual citizens, provided the remaining 29 per cent. These results are not very surprising. They accord closely with those found in previous research on interest representation in the EU, and they confirm the strongly pro-business character of policy-making processes in Brussels (Persson 2007a).

It still remains to be determined whether this unbalanced participation, in quantitative terms, is also reflected in other stages of the policy-making process than the policy-shaping phase. We should not be too optimistic about this. Other studies have pointed to the fact that, 'despite the Commission's efforts to create an accessible, transparent and inclusive policy process', it has in practice 'created asymmetric access to policy processes' (Friedrich 2008: 157). Notwithstanding these findings, however, the consultation on REACH may not have been 'business as usual', since it triggered several Europe-wide campaigns with thousands of participants representing workers, consumers, animals, and the interests of the environment. It is quite clear, then, that the online consultation on REACH had a mobilising effect on many so-called diffuse interests, and that it created a broad public debate on the question.

Online consultations may thus be an improvement on traditional instruments for consultation. In comparison with, for instance, advisory committees, expert groups, and *ad hoc* consultations between the Commission and certain groups of stakeholders, public online consultations are more easily accessible for a broader part of the European community. They have lowered the threshold for many citizens and organisations to take an active part in EU policy-making. They accordingly promote openness and transparency in EU policy-making, and they may serve to encourage Europe-wide public debates on EU affairs. The task for future reforms should be to enhance the general level of participation – and not just of active citizens and well-organised interests, but also of average citizens and diffuse interests – so that participation becomes more inclusive and equal.

Thus far we have ascertained that the chemicals law-making process did indeed contribute to better transparency, and in some respects to more inclusive involvement from civil society as well. But what about responsiveness to the preferences of stakeholders and civil society? As our review of the debate has shown, many scholars and practitioners have been arguing for enhancing input legitimacy – so that the preferences of those involved are sufficiently considered – through promoting the participation of stakeholders and civil society on important European issues. Others warn, by contrast, that this strategy may not serve to increase the overall legitimacy of the EU, since greater input legitimacy may have the effect of undermining the Union's output legitimacy – i.e. that policy outcomes are efficient and effective (Höreth 2001). Judged from this angle, reforms aimed at increasing the Union's input legitimacy through greater participation and deliberation may serve only to reshuffle the legitimacy problem.

However, within the context of the political process leading to the adoption of a new regulatory scheme for chemicals, there seems to be a rather strong positive relationship between input and output legitimacy, inasmuch as actors that were more likely to hold the quality of the policy-making process in high regard were also more likely to view the resulting outcome as efficient. Our findings rely on data from an expert survey with more than 600 respondents from over 40 countries.[4] Respondents who viewed the policy-making process on REACH as open, transparent, and inclusive were substantially more likely to view the proposed regulatory scheme as a Pareto-optimal solution that improves the environment and health protection without damaging industrial competitiveness. Our results thus provide empirical support for the claim that increased input legitimacy, through participation by stakeholders and civil society, is a viable method for overcoming the Union's legitimacy crises (Lindgren and Persson 2008b).

That said, we must be careful not to exaggerate the significance of the findings from a single case study. More research is therefore needed, if we are to have a better basis for judging whether the new participatory and deliberative measures can provide a remedy for legitimacy problems in the EU. In order to judge the generality of our results it would be fruitful to compare the findings presented here with those found in other policy areas in which provisions have been made for participation and deliberation by stakeholders and civil society.

Respondents to the survey may consider the policy-making process to have been responsive to the preferences of participants, but it still remains to be ascertained whether the process actually did display such responsiveness. Dawid Friedrich (2008) has sought to evaluate the responsiveness of the process in question to key concerns of industry, consumers, workers, and environmental associations. His analysis shows that, in the initial phase of the process – i.e. shortly after the release of the White Paper – business concerns were satisfied in a lesser degree, and other concerns in a higher. In the later stages of the process, however, the balance between the environmental and economic aspects shifted in favour of the latter. Another author even describes the final proposal as a clear-cut victory for businesses and industry: 'a neo-liberal interpretation of the Lisbon strategy which includes a dangerous shift in environmental policy making' (Pesendorfer 2006: 95).

In fact, throughout the policy-making process, the discussion became increasingly polarised and politicised, which quite naturally made it impossible to respond to all the claims put forward by stakeholders and civil society organisations. Business associations, together with conservative and liberal Members of the European Parliament, were also able to prolong the legislative process into the next legislative term. This made it possible to water down certain measures, since the newly elected parliament was more conservative and pro-business than its predecessor. A general conclusion, therefore, is that the policy-making process was more responsive to environmental concerns in the early stages, while business and industry were more in touch with policy-makers during the final stages (Pesendorfer 2006; Selin 2007; Friedrich 2008).

A more accountable policy-making process?

As we have just seen, the chemicals-policy overhaul has expanded the role played by weak mechanisms of accountability. The result, at least to some extent, has been to enhance transparency, inclusiveness, and responsiveness. Where stronger mechanisms of accountability are concerned, however, the results are more discouraging. European citizens have not gained any new instruments for holding policy-makers accountable. The power to sanction the law-making bodies of the Union can still only be exercised through representative channels – either directly (through the Parliament) or indirectly (through the Council). Efforts of either kind, however, run up against the democratic deficit of the Union. The Parliament, on the one hand, suffers from its well-documented weaknesses: both its inability to mobilise citizens to take part in its elections, and its lack of parties and electoral campaigns focused on European rather than national issues. Thus, while EP elections provide European citizens with a potential opportunity to hold one of its legislative institutions to account every fifth year, this method for holding leaders accountable does not, in fact, work very well. As for the Council, there is no coordinated mechanism through which European citizens can hold their representatives on that body to account. Instead, it is up to each country to supply its own citizens with this opportunity through national elections – during which European issues tend to play an insignificant role.

Furthermore, the present study (as well as, for instance, Louisa Parks' chapter in this volume) has pointed to the limited contribution made by civil society to remedying this situation. The involvement of stakeholders and civil society organisations in public policy-making furnishes them with opportunities to influence policy. They may thus help to scrutinise Union activities and to trigger Europe-wide debates, and the long-run effect thereof will be likely to promote the emergence of a European public sphere. However, they cannot impose any formal political sanctions on Union bodies; the only punishment they can impose is through 'whistle-blowing' and 'blaming and shaming'. Nor are stakeholders and civil society organisations themselves accountable in any direct way to citizens (unless one happens to be a member of such an organisation). In the same way as in national political systems, then, the involvement of stakeholders and civil society in EU policy-making may contribute significantly to ensuring that policy-makers are more in touch with the preferences of those affected by their actions. Yet this may in turn create other democracy problems. After all, who is scrutinising the scrutinisers?

Another reason for caution is that participatory and deliberative arrangements may serve in the long run to impede already existing representative channels. Fewer people may be expected to engage in political parties and representative institutions when they have other organisations at their disposal through which they can channel their engagement. If citizens conduct their activities more and more in single-issue movements and special-interest organisations, we risk a situation in which it will be hard to find people who are willing to take responsibility for weighing different interests against each other. In the end, someone has to take responsibility for the totality of policies pursued, and not just the constituent parts thereof. This is a major challenge for democracy, both in the EU and elsewhere. My concern, then, is that the new approach may serve to undermine the efficient functioning of existing representative channels. The Commission itself does not seem to see any trade-off between different models of democracy, and it tries to combine them in an unrelated manner. But we should recognise that representative democracy may be put at a disadvantage when participatory and deliberative arrangements are on the rise.

On the other hand, if one believes participatory and deliberative arrangements to be a remedy for the Union's democratic deficit, it is quite clear by now that expectations have been set too high. Participatory and deliberative arrangements can never replace representative channels. They can at most be an important supplement, not a democratically acceptable replacement. My impression is that both scholars and practitioners – those to whom I referred earlier – tend to overlook the problem that can arise when stakeholders and civil society organisations are increasingly involved in policy-making. In the normal case, namely, these mediating organisations do not themselves live up to the standards of democracy they exist to protect.

In conclusion, then, the evidence from the chemicals-policy overhaul is quite discouraging, notwithstanding all the great expectations that were raised about how participatory and deliberative measures would improve EU accountability. All the same, we should not be unduly pessimistic about the improvements accomplished by these new measures. Arrangements for increased involvement on the part of civil society tend to promote transparency, inclusion, and responsiveness. And while these are not to be equated with accountability, they are all pre-conditions for it. As such, they may make an important contribution to European governance.

Conclusion

Great hopes are now being placed, both by academic scholars and by practitioners, in civil society as a means for improving European governance. Proponents of participatory and deliberative democracy hold that greater societal involvement can provide a cure for the declining democratic legitimacy of European governance. With the involvement of stakeholders and civil society in policy-making, better opportunities arise for holding policy-makers accountable, as do better opportunities for ensuring that the policies promulgated accord with the wishes of European citizens. In this chapter, I have sought to assess whether these ideas appear justified in light of the empirical findings from a study of one particular policy-making process: the EU chemicals-policy overhaul, which is generally considered an early test of the new governance strategy.

Since accountability is fundamental to democracy, any evaluation of participatory and deliberative arrangements in EU policy-making is well-advised to pay it close heed. However, the empirical results are discouraging. New participatory and deliberative arrangements permeated the EU law-making process in respect of the chemicals-policy overhaul, and these arrangements did indeed contribute, at least to some extent, to enhanced transparency, inclusiveness, and responsiveness. And transparency, inclusiveness, and responsiveness are necessary conditions for accountability, albeit insufficient ones. The policy-making process was thus more transparent, and the policy in question became the subject of public debate in a higher degree than most EU policies (although largely among elite actors, not among a larger public). A broad range of societal groups was included, and some individual citizens too; the pattern of participation, however, was an unequal one. The policy that was ultimately adopted, finally, is generally regarded as having responded to the concerns of most of the stakeholders and civil society organisations involved, although more favourably in the case of some than of others.

However, the new arrangements include no new mechanisms for holding policy-makers accountable. It remains the case, then, that those wielding power can only be held accountable through the traditional representative channels of the Union (i.e. the Parliament and the Council). Indeed, the new arrangements for policy-making help to diffuse responsibility for policy, since stakeholders and civil society organisations become deeply engaged in policy-making, even as European citizens have no chance to hold them to account. My conclusion, therefore, is that social accountability is merely *illusory*. The involvement of stakeholders and civil society in EU policy-making gives an erroneous impression that such methods can improve accountability, whereas in fact they help to hide important problems of European governance. Or, in the words of Hüller and Kohler-Koch (2008: 172): 'When it comes to civil society input in the process of policy formulation and decision-making, the principles of openness and participation apply and instruments have been introduced that have broadened access and voice. But institutionalised accountability is lacking.'

In sum, it is important that institutionalised forms of civil society participation, such as consultations, be seen in the light of the formal decision-making framework of the EU, in which democratic legitimacy is primarily derived from the involvement of the Council and the Parliament. At most, institutionalised consultations and better communication between EU institutions and civil society can serve as an important complement to traditional channels of political representation. Yet the new participatory and deliberative arrangements discussed here probably offer the best way forward, even if they cannot solve the EU's democratic deficit or, for that matter, its legitimacy problem. The alternative would be to institute more closed and secretive decision-making processes unresponsive to the demands of European citizens – surely not an approach likely to enhance the legitimacy of the Union.

Notes

1 The new EU chemicals policy is usually called REACH, for Registration, Evaluation and Authorization of Chemicals (Commission 2003). It grew out of concerns about the shortcomings of the previous regulatory framework – which was widely considered to be insufficient and exceedingly complex – and replaced it with a single system. The overall objective of the new system was to make the chemical industry accept more responsibility, while also safeguarding the Single Market and the competitiveness of European industry.

2 Civil society is a contested concept, and I will not attempt any further contribution to the discussion on it here. In general, it refers to a separate sphere of society – separate from the state, the economy, and private life. Given my present purpose, it would be unwise to provide a more exact definition that might exclude certain kinds of associations. My understanding of civil society here is very practically oriented, and I try to assess all kinds of groups, associations, and organisations which act as intermediaries between the spheres. Since some of these groups may not fall within civil society as traditionally understood, I sometimes use the concept of stakeholders as well (for further discussion on the concept of civil society, see for instance Smismans: 2006; Finke 2007).

3 My analytical categories are close to those used by Hüller and Kohler-Koch (2008: 151). In their assessment of the democratic value of involving civil society in EU policy-making, these authors cite the principles of 'reciprocity, publicity, and accountability.'

4 For more information on the survey, see Lindgren and Persson 2008a.

12 Improving accountability in the European Union – the potential role of NGOs

Louisa Parks

In his contribution to this volume, Robert Keohane notes that the conditions for democracy in the classical sense are simply not present at the global level (and thus not at the regional level either). When looking at accountability at the international level, he suggests, we should pay careful attention to the role of *information*. And it is precisely information that lies at the centre of what non-governmental organisations (NGOs) regard as the key to accountability in the European Union (EU). Information helps enhance three important things – transparency, access to institutions, and participation in policy-making – all of which may be described as prerequisites for accountability (Bovens 2007b: 107). The aim of this chapter is not to portray NGOs working at the European level as some kind of panacea for problems of accountability within the EU (although a discussion of their potential role necessarily forms a central part of this chapter). It is rather to propose that, since NGOs are well-established and active actors at the EU level, it is important that we not overlook any potential role they may play in securing an effective accountability regime in the EU.

Bearing this in mind, the chapter will unfold as follows. After briefly outlining the reasons why NGOs are valid actors to consider when thinking about problems of accountability, I review their possible roles (and limitations) in improving EU accountability. In the course of this discussion, it becomes obvious that the potential role of NGOs in alleviating the Union's accountability problems relates less to accountability in its classical definition than to a 'new form' of horizontal accountability, which has been labelled 'social accountability' (Bovens 2007b: 112). Drawing on Bovens' suggested framework for assessing forms of accountability (Bovens 2006: 24) connected with information-provision (which may be understood as a pre-condition for the establishment of accountability relationships), I present material from interviews with NGO actors. I then seek to evaluate the situation with respect to the provision of information to NGOs by European institutions, and I make some tentative but concrete suggestions – on the basis of the views presented – as to how the situation can be improved and the chances increased that NGOs will become effective actors in social accountability. I further argue that, if we wish to see NGOs make their (necessarily small) contribution to solving the EU's accountability problem, we will need to introduce greater transparency and openness, particularly in the Council and the Commission. The European Parliament, furthermore, will need to be assigned a larger role in the institutional balance of power. NGOs, for their part, will need to organise themselves in broader and more permanent coalitions in order to play the role of broker between EU institutions and smaller groups.

The possible contributions of NGOs to EU accountability

At a general level, NGOs play an important role in the EU. As one subdivision within the more general category of interest groups, they provide a valuable source of information for European institutions. When the Commission goes about drafting legislation, it tries to consult as widely as possible, for the reason (amongst several others, as we shall see below) that the number of its staff is very small as compared with the size of its remit. The Commission is therefore obliged to seek information from a wide range of third parties. NGOs are one such source of information, and they are considered to be important contributors to the legislative process (Commission 2001a). Within the larger category of interest groups, moreover, they furnish an important counterbalance to industrial interest groups, inasmuch as they present the views of concerned citizens, or at least – if we regard their representative functions as debatable – the views of citizens who are economically disinterested. NGOs also provide information and opinions to the European Parliament, another EU institution whose resources are stretched (in the sense that its members must follow numerous issues – most of them highly technical – at once). In addition, because NGOs in fact consist in their vast majority of networks of national-level organisations, they are important in diffusing information about what the EU does back to the national level (as well as – via their collective members – to EU citizens).

The question of real relevance here, however, is this: can NGOs play a role as accountability actors in the EU? It is generally accepted that indeed they may: by serving as a check and balance, by scrutinising the work of EU institutions, and by blowing the whistle on any wrongdoing. Their views on accountability in the EU are therefore interesting to consider. Any role they might play in providing accountability aside, their opinions are qualified and informed, due to their proximity to the EU machine and their understanding of it. The concept of accountability, as recent work has made clear, remains extremely contested (Bovens 2007b: 105). In a strict sense its meaning is straightforward. It denotes the ability to hold an actor to account for actions he/she has taken. In a political sense, it refers to the ability of one forum to hold another to account, and to sanction it where necessary. In the EU, for example, a strict accountability relationship exists between the European Parliament and the Commission: the former may remove the latter from office, if in its judgement it acted wrongly. The EU itself, however, uses a much looser definition of accountability, which 'serves not only as a synonym for "clarity", "transparency", and "responsibility", but is also equated with much broader concepts such as "involvement", "deliberation", and "participation"' (Bovens 2007b: 105). When the potential role of NGOs in EU accountability is considered, it is this stricter definition of accountability that must stand.

In terms of this definition of accountability, NGOs play but a limited role, in the sense that they cannot plausibly threaten to sanction any power-holders directly. They can only hope to bring wrongdoing to the attention of those with the power to sanction (in the case of the EU, either the European Parliament or European citizens themselves). Their role, then, is only important in terms of *weak* accountability, as that expression is understood in this volume. They may scrutinise Union institutions, and blow the whistle on any wrongdoing or shady dealings they discover therein, drawing the attention of those with formal powers of accountability to problems that may otherwise have gone unnoticed. Another important reason why NGOs cannot be involved in stronger accountability relationships (or in vertical ones) with EU institutions is that they themselves do not meet the democratic criteria they tend to expect from those very institutions. The level of internal democracy in NGOs varies widely: their governance ranges from the extremely hierarchical to the highly deliberative. But they are never democratic in the sense that their rank-and-file are able to 'throw the rascals out'.

With these limitations duly noted, it may nevertheless be argued (and it has been) that 'standardized procedures of accountability' may not be sufficient for the EU as a complex and unprecedented governmental organisation (Puntscher Riekmann 2007: 134). The weak accountability mechanisms in which NGOs may be involved in relation to the EU can be grouped under the heading of social accountability, as defined by Bovens (2006: 17), who notes that, 'In reaction to a perceived lack of trust in government, there is an urge in many western democracies for more direct and explicit accountability relations between public agencies on the one hand and … civil society on the other' (Bovens 2006: 17). The author also, however, notes that the extent to which these mechanisms can be classed as 'full accountability mechanisms' is limited, for the reasons already mentioned (Bovens 2006: 18). It is my aim in this chapter to contribute to answering one aspect of this question. Bovens provides a convincing framework for approaching such an empirical investigation, in the form of a series of questions that must be asked of any given accountability relationship.[1] I shall borrow elements from his framework here.

Bovens' framework for assessing accountability includes questions designed to investigate the provision of information, the quality of debate, and the procedures for judgement. The empirical evidence outlined below goes some way towards answering the questions contained in the first of these categories. Although answering all of the questions set out by Bovens (2006: 24) would of course be preferable, it is of paramount importance first to understand the relationship between NGOs and EU institutions in terms of information-provision, since this forms the pre-condition for any accountability relationship. Without transparency in information-provision, in other words, the quality of debate and the ability to pass judgement are compromised. And, as the evidence will show, this relationship is far from the ideal situation as yet, in terms of allowing a fruitful role in social accountability for NGOs. The questions put by Bovens about the provision of information are as follows: 'Does the actor provide information about his conduct in a timely fashion? Is the information reliable? Is the information sufficient?' (Bovens 2006: 24). Affirmative answers, of course, would point to positive prospects for NGOs in ensuring EU accountability. I concentrate on these aspects of information-provision in the following section, which is based on interviews with a range of NGOs working on EU issues.[2] I then proceed to discuss the quality of this information-provision, bearing in mind its role as a pre-condition for (a weak form of) social accountability in the EU. Where appropriate, finally, I extend the discussion to other areas.

Perceptions of the EU and its institutions amongst NGOs

The views presented below are from interviews carried out with representatives of NGOs involved in four campaigns, each on a specific European issue.[3] It bears recalling that the opinions expressed are shaped by the nature of these campaigns. Simply put, the campaigns differ in their primary targets; i.e. some may focus more closely on one institution, others on another. More specifically, the campaigns focused on legislation that followed the co-decision procedure pay closer attention to the European Parliament, especially in cases where the Commission did not consult widely.[4] Similarly, other campaigns are more oriented to the Commission or to the Council. However, the four campaigns cover just two broad subject areas, with one legislative and one non-legislative campaign considered for each. The NGOs involved in each campaign thus overlap in each subject area, ensuring a wider coverage of opinions relating to the full range of EU institutions. That said, it should also be noted that the campaigns were selected as a result of their contested nature. The Commission, as the initiator of legislation – and thus naturally the prime target of NGOs' efforts (Greenwood 2003: 33) – takes a great deal of the blame for unfavourable proposals. This is in line, however, with the EU's institutional balance; it may thus be considered a true reflection of the situation. I have arranged the views expressed by NGO staff members according to institution. Let us begin with their comments on the Commission.

The Commission – open to some but not others?

Perceptions of information-provision by the Commission amongst the groups interviewed follow two general themes: transparency and access. Transparency is a major theme mentioned in relation to the Commission. A majority state that the Commission is not the most transparent of institutions;

moreover, they offer parallel comments to the effect that, were it to become so, many of the problems thought to plague the institution would be solved. In the judgement of those interviewed, the flow of information essential to accountability has been blocked:

> If you want, the big difference between our lobbying activity and the industry activity is that they need to lobby behind closed doors. And they are successful. When we open, when the institution, when the decision-making process is like a glass, a building of glass, transparent, and peoples, citizens are one of the key players, then they have lost![5]

More specifically, the problem of transparency is often connected to comitology and agencies. This is especially important to recall in view of the fact that the aim behind the creation of independent agencies – which has been extensive in recent years, due to the newly acquired power of the Parliament over comitology procedures – was to overcome this very problem. Yet these agencies are particularly frowned upon by NGOs, on account of their secretive and labyrinthine nature. The European Food Safety Authority, for example, comes under severe attack from environmental groups. They question its independence, and they accuse it of consistently favouring the biotech industry in its decisions. They furthermore aver that its procedures remain secret. One group goes so far as to claim the Authority is 'trying to actively undermine the European legislation'.[6] In a similar vein, secretive processes within the Commission during the development of legislative proposals are seen as encroaching on the most institutionalised of EU mechanisms for consultation: i.e. the social dialogue. Even where dialogue does take place, the ETUC is beginning to be sceptical about how far its views are really taken into account in the subsequent drafting of legislation: ' … but we have the impression that this is more for the gallery, to ease, to keep trade unions calm, but that it's not a real dialogue in the sense that they are taking our points up and trying to do something with it. It's more, let's come together, let's talk, give the impression of dialogue, and then hope that we will take less action and pose less pressure than otherwise.'[7]

Nevertheless, many of those interviewed believe the Commission is steadily improving in terms of transparency. A greater number of documents are now widely available, and they are often passed on in advance. The gap between different views on the transparency of the Commission depends on whether the group in question is a relatively 'conservative' one, or whether it has a background of more direct forms of action: the difference between the WWF and Greenpeace, for example, or that between the ETUC and a more radical left-wing trade-union group. The size of the group can also be a factor: smaller groups do not find it easy to get information, especially when they lack an office in Brussels. This is linked to another of the subjects discussed below in connection with the Commission: the importance of personal contacts.

Let us move now to the next of the above-mentioned themes: access. This is the subject mentioned most often by the groups interviewed in connection with the Commission, and the opinions expressed are varied and sometimes contradictory. According to many of those interviewed, access to the Commission is easy. Those most positive in this regard are, once again, the more 'conservative' groups. However, respondents from the less well-organised and/or conservative groups also say that, when they create 'noise' around an issue, the Commission does react (although some take the view that it ought to react earlier). One of the most important techniques here is to demonstrate to the Commission the extent of popular support that a given group enjoys: ' … I think in Brussels it's very often forgotten, and kind of the Commission feels like oh, it's Solidar, it's this office in Brussels, and they come to talk to me and it's the same, I guess it's the usual suspects. So it's very important every now and then to say, no it's not us, it's La Ligue in France and it's Lega Cooperative in Italy and like, whoever. And to actually make that clear'.[8] While none of the groups reports receiving no response at all from the Commission, the *quality* of their contacts with it varies. The variation, they believe, depends on several different factors.

First, the quality of dialogue with the Commission may depend on whether or not industry is also involved. Although anecdotal, the evidence from the interviews shows that, where industry is involved and has an interest in the question, the voices of NGOs tend to be drowned out. Indeed, respondents accuse the Commission of actively preferring industrial groups to NGOs, and of making private contacts with them outside the open arenas for dialogue: 'Because I have been in the meetings with DG Trade, and I always have the impression that there we are very strong, but that the biotech companies are never there. So in the end they are going by other circles or in another way to lobby the commission'.[9] Industry also has greater resources on its side, as well as sheer numbers. NGOs further complain that, once industry has a foothold, they are often excluded from events such as roundtable discussions, stakeholders' meetings, and other gatherings. Or else they get invited, but the events in question become interminable – with meeting after meeting taking place, and the possibility of concrete action receding ever further into the background.

Second, when the Commission deals with NGOs, it tends to give preferential treatment to groups that it funds: 'networks who are actually funded by the Commission through programmes, usually they have – it's true – some kind of privileged access to key people at the Commission. Because they have been given the task of implementing some objective'.[10] This is of course understandable. If a group is paid to represent a certain group of people by the Commission, or to carry out a certain project, it is natural for the Commission to view it as a valid partner for discussion. Paradoxically enough, however, being funded by the Commission – or, to be more precise, being forced to seek funding from it – can contribute, in the opinion of the EAPN, to widening the gap between the European-level group and its national membership, by making the former less representative of a particular constituency and therefore less useful in terms of accountability. This is because seeking funding from the Commission usually entails taking part in a project in which very specific types of action are prescribed: 'if you have to start chasing funding then you can find a very big gap between what you would like to do and what you're doing'.[11] On the one hand, therefore, the Commission tends to prefer the bigger, well-established groups which receive its funding; on the other, it is the smaller, less well-funded groups that may well be more representative of their collective national members.

Third, and perhaps most importantly, groups highlight the need for personal contacts within the Commission in order to ensure access. The main problem here is that contacts between the Commission and NGOs are often limited to the directorate-general (DG) within the former which is regarded as the 'natural' counterpart of the NGO in question; NGOs often meet with frustration, therefore, when they try to arrange meetings to discuss issues for which the responsibility lies with another DG.[12] The Commission is thus viewed as open when it sees the group in question as an *asset* to itself. In other words, NGOs are used in internal power struggles between different DGs (not that this is necessarily bad, seen from an NGO standpoint). In the succinct words of one interviewee, 'in Brussels, there's a lot of lobbying on lobbyists on lobbying'.[13] Thus, respondents do not regard the Commission as a *unitary* institution, but rather a system consisting of several units, each with its own particular character. NGOs state that their relations with their 'natural' DG are close and of good quality, and that the latter's vision of what a policy should be is largely the same as their own. But contention arises where a subject falls under the purview of another DG, at the same time that both the NGO in question and the other DGs take the view that it should not. When good-quality contacts remain compartmentalised in this manner, any real consideration of the views of all 'stakeholders' (to use the Commission's parlance) will remain elusive. The consultation processes themselves, moreover, are questioned by a fair few of the groups interviewed. Several cite the guidelines for consultation following from the Commission's White Paper on Governance, and bring up cases where the Commission failed to follow its own rules. One interviewee pointed out that '[although] it is true that now nearly all networks have these kinds of structures of dialogue, they all depend on goodwill. So. A new Director General of DG Employment could in theory say no, I'm not interested in bi-annual meetings with the Social Platform. And I don't care if it was always done or not.'[14]

Council and Parliament – poles apart

The title of this section points to the fact that, while NGOs regard the Council as nearing the impenetrable (from the European level), they view the Parliament almost as a natural ally. Before discussing this, however, let us consider some of the views expressed on the EU as a single unit. The general view on information-provision in the EU as a whole is that a single group acting alone has little chance of being noticed. In other words, a single organisation representing twenty-seven or more organisations at various national levels is not enough to be noticed at the EU level, or at least not in practical terms. EU institutions, as interviewees see it, react to coalitions of different groups with similar positions, or to permanent coalition platforms, like the Social Platform or the European Trade Union Confederation (ETUC). Cross-issue coalitions in particular – wherein public concerns are pitted against private ones – are seen as crucial amongst environmental NGOs. If various kinds of NGOs can be assembled in a campaign coalition, access to several different institutions (or to groups within these[15]) can be facilitated. Social NGOs rely, precisely for this reason, on a more permanent coalition structure; after all, many of the groups in question are extremely small at the European level, and they dispose of few resources. Thus, one of the principal roles of the Social Platform – aside from providing its members with the advantages arising from information-sharing and resource-pooling – is to facilitate their access to EU institutions.

The accountability of the EU, in terms of its response to the requests put by NGOs for meetings and for information, is thus conditioned by the need for groups to band together. Indeed, a 'representativity' requirement is specified by the Commission – with reference to all EU institutions – in its 2001 White Paper on Governance (Commission 2001a). For the smallest groups working at the EU level, therefore, working solo becomes ineffective – they must join coalitions in order to be heard. Yet coalitions are not easily formed around all subjects. The main preoccupation of one small NGO may not top the list of priorities for other groups. Smaller NGOs may therefore only manage (or wish) to join in coalitions on the broader issues that interest them, and to leave other matters by the wayside. In addition, the EU institutions (and the Commission in particular) may take advantage of such coalitions in order to avoid more detailed and widespread consultations: 'they love having a nice easy organisation to come to, and then they feel that they've consulted everyone'.[16] Member organisations of the Social Platform, for instance, have had such an experience. On many occasions, namely, members of the Social Platform with specific and in-depth knowledge on certain issues have been overlooked in favour of the Platform as a whole. Among some organisations, in fact, the EU (and the Commission in particular) is seen as having created such requirements in order to provide itself with easy, one-stop shops for consultation, thus making its accountability credentials seem stronger than they really are. And since many of those interviewed complain of a significant gap between what the EU says and what it does, it would appear that much of the dialogue taking place between NGOs and EU institutions involves little more than lip service to inclusion on the part of the latter.

Unsurprisingly, the European Council and the Council of Ministers are generally perceived to close their doors to the groups dealt with here. Very little of what happens in these intergovernmental bodies at the European level is visible, and documentation is often hard to come by. It seems that small progress has been made on this front, notwithstanding the decision to hold Council meetings in public and to make documents available. However, NGOs working at the level of the EU still regard these bodies as key elements in an effective accountability relationship, especially where the legislative process is concerned. Simply put, they do not target these bodies themselves; rather, they encourage their national collective members to do so, since they know the systems and individuals involved much better. Efforts are made to meet with the permanent representations of member states in Brussels; however, these contacts are always supplemented by actions carried out at national level, and indeed they are sometimes replaced by them. As a result, problems with information-provision at European level are not really a great hindrance to the work of these groups, which think of the national-level organisations more as their component parts, and as accountable to national voters.

The rotating presidency of the Council of Ministers and the European Council is also considered important for the fortunes of NGOs. A well-disposed presidency can steer the discussion or initiate a debate where there had been none, and more generally set the tone and agenda for its six-month stint. As one respondent put it, the Council presidency 'is important. I think I first realised this when the Italian presidency was there. And all of the, for example, the round table on social inclusion, the one topic was family. Because that was their answer to all problems on social inclusion, why don't we discuss family? You know, and at that moment you realise that there is an agenda-setting'.[17] An ill-disposed presidency, of course, can block a process for the duration of its tenure, should it so wish. Some NGOs also report good contacts and working relationships with those preparing (well-disposed) presidencies, hinting at a possibly hidden arena of cooperation between NGOs and the Council that may previously have been overlooked. For example, a representative of the EEB makes the following observation: 'Now we are working for the new [presidency programme], Austria. And we are pushing a lot, since you know that Austria is part of the so-called blocking minority. So Austria is calling for a proposal, the adoption of a proposal on EU rules on coexistence including GM-free zones. This is how we are working'.[18] Where accountability and the availability of information are concerned, however, such contacts are completely dependent on the goodwill of the presidency, and are by no means guaranteed. The pot-luck nature of the (at time of writing) rotating presidency cannot be judged, on the whole, to have been helpful for increasing transparency and the flow of information around the activities of the Council.

In general, the European Parliament is seen by NGOs as the most open and democratic of EU institutions, and indeed as their most natural ally. The connection between the institution's openness and its position as a classically democratic body is neatly summed up by a representative of the Social Platform:

> Well, the European Parliament has always been very open. Because by nature they are there to represent citizens, and they have a keen interest in accessing the expertise that we have on specific topics. Because they have to be experts in everything, so it's of course very difficult for them.[19]

A link is also made between the Parliament's open nature and its need for information *from* NGOs. Members of the European Parliament (MEPs) must cope with a wide range of issues without access to the expertise enjoyed by other institutions – the Commission has the expertise of its officials and agencies, the Council that of its secretary-general – so they turn to NGOs for information and expert opinions on matters under discussion.[20] For some groups, however, the fact that MEPs are obliged to follow many dossiers at once is a reason for not going into any real detail when visiting them, and for sticking to short, simple political messages. Either way, the flow of information between NGOs and the European Parliament representing citizens' interests in various issues is judged to be vigourous (in both directions), with NGOs being actively consulted by MEPs on a variety of issues. A certain impact of ideological preferences can be discerned, in that MEPs are sometimes more accessible to certain groups than to others. On the whole, however, no significant barriers are mentioned.

If, however, we extend the discussion on information and the European Parliament to the issue of the latter's importance for European accountability, we find that the power of this institution is seen to vary – according to legislative procedure and policy competence. For example, the European Parliament is a much more important target in a campaign focused on legislation passed under the co-decision procedure than in one focused on the initiation of legislation. And yet, the perception of the Parliament as democratic and therefore able to exert pressure on other institutions (other actors being aware that MEPs are the 'elected people on the European level'[21]) has the consequence that, where the institution is not a target as such, it is still used as a conduit for channelling NGO opinions, and as a space for 'making noise'. The hope is then that the Parliament will hold other institutions to account. In both of the campaigns carried out by the NGOs examined, for example, there was no co-decision legislation involved, and indeed no institutionalised role for the Parliament as such; yet in both cases, information meetings, conferences, and lobbying were directed at the Parliament. In sum, because the European Parliament is a fairly democratic institution, it is exploited in order to underline widespread support for NGO positions, and to draw the attention of other European institutions. The democratic credentials of the European Parliament are used to underline the *lack* of democratic credentials possessed by other EU institutions, in an attempt to shame them into action.

Assessing information flows and social accountability in the EU

It is impossible to draw any detailed conclusions about the quality of information-provision (in terms of promptness, reliability, and sufficiency) between the EU and NGOs. As the views laid out above indicate, this relationship relies on many different circumstances on both sides: e.g. the size and nature of the particular NGO, whether it works in coalition with others or not, the institution from which it wishes to obtain information, and the issue in question. Information that is available to all may certainly be reliable; it may not, however, always be sufficient – not while informal contacts play a large role in dealings with EU institutions, and bodies like the Council remain cloaked in secrecy. The timing of information is also extremely important when it comes to the EU, especially in connection with legislation: information received too late can be meaningless, inasmuch as positions have already been adopted. As we saw above, however, no general comments were ventured on these themes, precisely because situations differed from one issue to another, from one institution to another, and even from one committee or directorate-general to another. Indeed, it seems the only general conclusion we can draw is that the quality of information-provision depends on too many contingent factors for a positive assessment to be possible. Unless this pre-condition is fulfilled, a social accountability relationship cannot be established, and an effective role for NGOs in holding the EU to account would seem difficult to imagine. Such a relationship may indeed be occasionally observed; upon closer inspection, however, the circumstances under which it arises prove to be difficult to reproduce.[22]

It would appear, therefore, that standardising or stabilising some of the factors affecting the quality of information-provision would be a good first step towards enhancing the possible role of NGOs in EU accountability – not to mention their role as stakeholders in legislative processes and policy-making. In this vein, and with an eye to the evidence presented here, I would venture to make some suggestions. It bears stressing that these suggestions are based on the subjective views of NGO staff presented earlier; and they should only be followed, of course, if increasing the role of NGOs in social accountability is considered desirable. If that is the goal, however, the following steps may be of some use. First, consultation procedures between the Commission and all other parties should be made more transparent. Participants in organised dialogue are disclosed; however, it is claimed that informal contacts often take place – contacts which can be influential for subsequent legislative texts. Along similar lines, the way in which the Commission follows up on consultation – in terms of how it gets translated into draft legislation and other decisions – should be made clearer.[23] A fixed code for consultation could perhaps be an answer here. Light also needs to be shed on comitology procedures and the work of agencies: transparency should apply there too, together with clear standards for information-provision. With regard to the Commission, finally, efforts must be made to solve the problem of the 'natural partner' DG. The input of NGOs (or indeed of interest groups of any type) matters most when the dossier is held not by a DG acquainted with their work and accustomed to considering their views, but by another DG unfamiliar with their standpoint. Some mechanism guaranteeing a balance in dialogues with various civil-society groups, or simply better coordination between different sections of the Commission, would contribute to solving this problem. Of course, such a measure could also be applied to all of the institutions at the receiving end of lobbying efforts. It might furthermore alleviate the problems noted above in connection with the need to form coalitions.

The only institution in relation to which significant problems with information-provision are charged is the Council of Ministers: documents from this source, according to those interviewed, continue to be unavailable. It is true that European-level NGOs rely on their national members to carry out actions in this area; nevertheless, the former have sought their own access to Council documentation. Increased access to such documents would go some way towards remedying the situation here, although it remains the case that national-level conditions probably play a greater part in determining the role of NGOs in regard to the accountability of this particular institution, as well as that of the European Council. At the other end of the scale, NGO representatives describe the European Parliament as the most open and democratic of the European institutions, and as the natural ally of NGOs seeking to represent citizens' concerns. They see it as an accessible arena, with MEPs being more or less willing to meet with all kinds of groups and to provide information to them. The only problem identified in connection with the Parliament is its varying level of power over EU decisions. Where the co-decision procedure applies, the Parliament gives NGOs a good chance to influence the text of the resulting legislation. But this procedure is not followed, of course, for all EU legislation and decision-making. Yet, even in cases where the Parliament does not have much power over a decision, NGOs still ascribe it worth as an open arena in which to make noise: if it is made there, such noise will more likely be noticed by other EU institutions. In this way, NGOs exploit the Parliament's role in providing accountability in the strict sense. According to this logic, then, we can increase the accountability of the EU by strengthening the role of the Parliament at the European level, with co-decision becoming the default procedure for as many decisions as possible (as prescribed by the draft Constitutional Treaty), and the Parliament being involved more formally in other decisions as well.

Where the NGO side is concerned, I would recommend that more permanent coalitions be formed among small groups working on related subjects. This will provide the Commission and other actors with a more visible partner for dialogue (and particular questions can then be referred to the relevant experts within the coalition). It will furthermore contribute both to overcoming the problem of smaller NGOs' being overlooked[24] (and to minimising the difficulties arising from the Commission's favouritism towards groups receiving its funding. If, however, a more neutral 'middleman' (the neutrality and effectiveness of which will need to be ensured) is placed between those requesting information and those being asked, it may be possible to ensure that more radical and critical groups, as well as simply less resource-rich ones, gain a level of access to the institution which they had not previously enjoyed.

Conclusion

In this chapter, I have presented evidence about how NGOs active at the European level perceive problems of accountability in the European Union, especially in connection with information-provision. I have proceeded on the assumption that NGOs cannot help make the EU accountable in the classical or strong sense, because they lack (quite rightly) the power to impose sanctions. Instead, they may contribute to accountability in a weaker form – what Bovens (2007b) terms 'social accountability' – in which their role is to monitor the behaviour of EU institutions and to draw attention to any wrongdoing. However, if the potential for such forms of accountability is to be realised, there must be a good level of information-provision between the parties (Bovens 2006: 23). Accordingly, I gathered interview evidence from the staff members of NGOs – based for the most part in Brussels and active on EU issues – with an eye to discovering how they perceive the situation in this respect, as well as how they see other questions pertinent to accountability.

The results of this admittedly limited study have shown that, while the outlook is not entirely dim for the potential role of NGOs in EU accountability, there are several problems that must be rectified before the pre-condition of high-quality information-provision can be said to be met. The main problems indicated in the interviews have to do with smaller groups being overlooked in favour of larger groups (or EU-funded ones), and more generally with transparency and access in the case of the European Commission, with secretiveness in the case of the Council, and with lack of power in the case of an otherwise exemplary European Parliament. I have therefore suggested that, if NGOs are to contribute their weak form of social accountability to the overall effort to solve the conundrum of EU accountability, the problems identified need to be addressed. I have made some tentative suggestions to this end, in line with the evidence. These relate in the main to improving transparency in the Commission and the Council, and to increasing the relative power of the European Parliament. Where the NGO side is concerned, I have argued that larger and more permanent coalition structures will help smaller groups achieve better access to information, and increase their chances of being consulted. The truth remains, however, that NGOs play but a small role, albeit a useful one. Their contribution lies in their monitoring of EU institutions. The changes suggested above will help NGOs make their small contribution to resolving the EU's problem of accountability, and thus to rendering it more legitimate.

Notes

1 A relationship which need not only apply, in my opinion, after a decision has been taken (which is the view taken by certain other scholars: e.g. Harlow and Rawlings 2006). Indeed, given the 'social' nature of the accountability in question (NGOs lack the power to apply sanctions), a more constant exchange of accountability throughout the decision-making process – in which calling attention to shortcomings may yet shame institutions into changing their positions – is infinitely more useful.

2 See note 3.

3 The interviews were carried out to gather evidence for the author's PhD at the European University Institute, Florence (Parks 2009). The issues studied were: (1) GMOs and the question of 'coexistence'; (2) REACH – the European chemicals legislation; (3) the proposed changes to the Lisbon agenda (in 2005); and (4) the directive on Services in the Internal Market (often known as the Bolkestein directive). For each of these campaigns, I identified core groups active on the subject at the European level. Staff members responsible for campaigning and/or the subject area were contacted and, where possible, interviewed. The interviews generally lasted about one hour, and followed a semi-structured format.

4 As was the case with the campaign on the Services Directive. See Parks (2006: 3) and Fazi and Smith (2006: 62).

5 Interview with the Vice-President of the European Environmental Bureau. Brussels, 6 April 2005. This quote also highlights a perception of industrial groups as enjoying privileged access or influence – a perception that will be explored further below.

6 Interview with the EU Policy Director for Genetic Engineering, Greenpeace European Unit. Brussels, 23 March 2005.

7 Interview with a Political Advisor, European Trade Union Confederation. Brussels, 13 September 2005.

8 Interview with the Social Affairs Co-ordinator, Solidar. Brussels, 16 September 2005.

9 Interview with the Assistant to the GMO Campaign, Friends of the Earth Europe. Brussels, 25 March 2005.

10 Interview with the President of the Platform of European Social NGOs and Director of AGE Europe. Brussels, 15 September 2005.

11 Interview with the Vice-President of the Platform of European Social NGOs and Director of the European Anti-Poverty Network. Brussels, 15 September 2005.

12 For example, the 'natural' DG for a farmers' group would be DG Agriculture, for an environmental group DG Environment, and so forth.

13 Interview with a Policy Officer, Uni-Europa. Brussels, 21 March 2006.

14 Interview with the Social Affairs Co-ordinator, Solidar. Brussels, 16 September 2005.

15 For example, according to Women in Europe for a Common Future, more conservative groups such as the WWF may be given a friendlier reception by right-wing members of the European Parliament. Moreover, including NGOs representing a range of affected sectors can help environmental groups gain access to otherwise 'hostile' DGs within the Commission, according to the AER.

16 Interview with a Policy Officer, secretariat of the Platform of European Social NGOs. Brussels, 20 September 2005.

17 Interview with the Social Affairs Co-ordinator, Solidar. Brussels, 16 September 2005.

18 Interview with the Vice-President of the European Environmental Bureau. Brussels, 6 April 2005.

19 Interview with the President of the Platform of European Social NGOs and Director of AGE Europe. Brussels, 15 September 2005.

20 Of course, the Parliament does have some expert internal services: e.g. legal services, services for its various committees, and services for the established political groups. I would nevertheless argue, however, that MEPs have less access to such expertise than do members of the other EU institutions.

21 Interview with the Social Affairs Co-ordinator, Solidar. Brussels, 16 September 2005.

22 A recent and unique example of such an occurrence took place in connection with the Directive on Services in the Internal Market. Widespread mobilisation by trade unions in Brussels, throughout the EU, and especially in France – where the issue was effectively linked with the debate then raging over the draft Constitutional Treaty – helped ensure that this legislation was significantly watered down (see Parks 2009). Circumstances of this kind, in which ordinary citizens were peculiarly aware of EU issues, are clearly difficult to reproduce.

23 This suggestion is also taken up by NGOs themselves, in their response to the Commission's White Paper on the European Communication Policy (Commission 2006). See the conclusions of Fazi and Smith (2006) for more details on this suggestion, as well as others.

24 Although such coalitions bring with them a host of problems for other work; for problems within the Social Platform, see for example Cullen 2005.

13 Taking accountability seriously

Sverker Gustavsson, Christer Karlsson and Thomas Persson

Accountability analysis is no isolated or self-contained academic island. An historic turning of the tide has occurred in this area. It took place twenty years ago, when the Berlin Wall was torn down. Prior to that time, there was not much discussion of the kind found in the preceding twelve chapters, or in three closely related volumes from recent years (Kohler-Koch and Rittberger 2007; Niznik and Ryabinska 2007; Curtin and Wille 2008).

During the Cold War, the existence of an iron curtain cutting through Europe determined how the EU's accountability problem was perceived. The key concept was 'permissive consensus' (Lindberg and Scheingold 1970: 249–78). According to this notion, citizens accepted European integration even though they were unable to hold its supranational decision-makers to account. The underlying rationale was that citizens, while not very interested in European integration, were nonetheless well-disposed to it – leaving decision-makers free to take the necessary steps towards an ever closer Union. Against the background, moreover, of the more flagrant democratic deficiencies east of the iron curtain, the shortcomings in the West could be easily overlooked.

However, after the breakdown of the Soviet Union and the dissolution of the Warsaw Pact, it was not possible to view the matter from such a broad geopolitical and historical perspective. Scholars, politicians, and opinion-makers were then faced with a problem which they had never before encountered. Now that the Cold War had suddenly disappeared from the historical scene, what could induce citizens to accept an executive, a legislature, a central bank, and a court of justice beyond electoral reach at the supranational level? Why should they accept such a political order?

From permissive consensus to illusion of accountability

To remedy this situation, solutions have been sought along three different lines. Advocates of the first two acknowledge the democratic deficiencies of the Union, and try to solve the problem of accountability either by introducing 'limited democratic politics' (Føllesdal and Hix 2006; Hix 2008), or through an 'informal pact of confidence' that restricts the competences of the suprastate while also avoiding democratic reforms that might destabilise the entire integration project (Bartolini 2006, 2008; Scharpf 2008, 2009). Champions of these two positions share a concern with the Union's accountability problem, but make different suggestions for its solution.

Proponents of the third position, however, deny that the EU has such a problem. A great many politicians and opinion-makers at both Union and national levels take this view, making the standpoint in question yet more crucial to assess. According to this view, the democratic deficit does not exist. In fact, the claim goes, the EU's democratic status is on par with that of national political systems, while being far higher than that of other international organisations (Moravcsik 2002, 2008; Majone 2005). But how is it possible, after the end of the Cold War, to maintain that the EU's democratic credentials are sufficient?

Our answer to this question is that those making this claim have shifted from defending a permissive consensus to upholding an illusion of accountability. It is no longer possible to justify the institutional set-up of the Union by citing historical and geopolitical circumstances. Accordingly, defenders of current arrangements have now taken to defending them on the grounds that they do in fact meet the criteria for accountability. However, the arguments made in support of the current 'constitutional settlement' are founded on too formalistic an analysis of existing mechanisms of accountability in the EU. Take, for example, the contention that there is no accountability deficit in the Union. This argument is based on the mere existence of a full range of *formal* opportunities for holding decision-makers accountable: directly, via the European Parliament (EP); and indirectly, via elected national officials.

Our own analysis, by contrast, is focused on the *real* opportunities citizens have to hold decision-makers to account in the European political system. As explained in this volume's introductory chapter, we distinguish five claims made on behalf of the proposition that the Union's accountability problem has been solved. The upshot of all of them is that the current situation is satisfactory. The contributors to this volume examine each claim under its respective heading: 'rethink the meaning of accountability'; 'delegated power and accountability'; 'hold the legislature accountable'; 'hold the executive accountable'; and 'accountability through civil society'.

Due to the insights furnished by the contributions to this volume, we believe we have substantiated our hypothesis: that the accountability mechanisms offered by the EU are illusory. As we have seen, European citizens are indeed able, in a formal sense, to hold the executive and legislative branches of the Union to account. In practice, however, these provisions are not sufficient – either because they are weak, or because they fail to reach their full potential. Quite obviously, then, the above-mentioned five claims serve to deceive us, by creating the false impression that the problem has been solved. We would argue, accordingly, that the EU is far indeed from having succeeded with the 'third transformation' discussed in the introductory chapter.

Having so concluded, our next step should be to ask whether our scholarly understanding has benefited from this analytical turn: i.e. from thinking about the Union along the lines of the permissive consensus to analysing it in terms of an illusion of accountability. We should thereupon ask whether this turn has resulted in policy mistakes.

Our answer to the first question is a definite 'yes'. Analysing the current structures of European integration in terms of an illusion of accountability is a clear improvement over the former practice of describing them as an ongoing process that must be accepted because there is 'no alternative'. Now then, establishing that we confront an illusion is not the same as saying that all of the conceptual and empirical analyses that have been offered in the great debate on the future of the EU have been in vain, from the standpoint of furthering our scholarly understanding. On the contrary, our discipline has learnt a great deal during these last twenty years – not only about politics in general, but also more specifically about the actual structure and workings of the particular quasi-federal machinery that marks the EU.

It is not equally apparent, however, whether this turn from permissive consensus to illusion of accountability has been for the better or the worse in terms of its tendency to promote policy mistakes. Our answer here is: 'that depends'. In our view, responsible politicians and opinion-makers during the last twenty years have been far too reluctant to tell the truth, and far too inclined to manipulate public opinion through the misuse of political language. Even more than in national politics, we would say, political elites in all member states have been governed by pragmatism in the approach they have taken to EU affairs. There seem to be very few among their number who advocate a more principled approach.

Notwithstanding this, our refutation of the five illusory claims makes it possible to give better policy advice. The point we wish to make – and we want to stress its practical importance – is the following: According to the theory of permissive consensus, the judgement of those in power simply had to be accepted, because there was no alternative. The opposite perspective – that an illusion of accountability prevails – makes for a broader range of alternatives. According to this approach, decisions are accepted because they reflect the real power structure.

From a superficial point of view, the two assertions in question – that 'there is no alternative', and that 'outcomes reflect the real power structure' – would appear to issue in the same policy advice. If we look at the matter more carefully, however, this proves not to be the case. The real power structure, after all, consists of more than just economic hardware and populism. Sophisticated ideas and strong long-term institutions are also part of it. Thinking in terms of institutions – which occupy the grey zone between realism and idealism – means thinking in materialist and idealist terms at the same time. On the one hand, it means understanding that economic hardware and electoral populism exist, and that they must be taken into consideration. On the other hand, it also means realising that ideas can be institutionalised in such a way that hardware and populism do not always, or entirely, have the upper hand.

Taking accountability seriously

There is a certain experience that participants in intellectual and academic milieus all over Europe during the last twenty years have shared. Our Italian colleague Stefano Bartolini has described it very elegantly and exactly. He speaks of 'a certain amount of fearful complicity' in which many contemporary academics and intellectuals have engaged, due to their 'strong awareness of the difficulties of the project'. The fear of being taken hostage by populist anti-EU movements is threatening to make us prisoners of the wartime dictum: 'silence, the enemy is listening to you' (Bartolini 2008: 7). It is not acceptable, however, to downplay the problems currently faced by the EU, or the challenges that lie ahead. If we mean to take accountability seriously – and constitutionalism and legitimacy as well (Bartolini 2008) – we must tell it like it is.

'Telling it like it is', as we see it, means two things:

First, when analysing and debating accountability in the EU, we must resist the temptation to change the established meaning of the term and to tailor it to fit present circumstances. If we stretch and misuse the term, we will leave the underlying problem unresolved, and we will make it hard to identify the options and find solutions to the current impasse.

Second, we must discuss the current accountability deficit openly. We must not refrain from telling the truth, even when no simple solution is at hand. It may very well be that calling attention to the problematic aspects of European integration – like the absence of effective mechanisms for accountability – will provide further fuel for the debate on the democratic deficit and decrease public support for the EU. However, it is not for us to decide who the enemies are, or to be bothered with who may be listening. Our task is rather to describe how the Union has developed, how its present structure works, and what options for the future can be distinguished – even if no simple solution is at hand.

The illusion of accountability and the absence of opposition

In the introductory chapter to this volume, we asked whether EU citizens have real opportunities to hold decision-makers accountable, or whether the current institutional set-up in the Union instead merely creates an illusion of accountability. Having examined different aspects of the EU political system, we do find a number of *weak* accountability mechanisms which allow citizens to monitor and evaluate the actions of EU decision-makers. However, when we look for *strong* accountability mechanisms – tools which make it possible for citizens to impose sanctions on their representatives – we come up rather empty-handed.

Strong mechanisms for holding the most important decision-makers to account do exist: MEPs can be held directly accountable via EP elections, and members of the Council of Ministers can be held indirectly accountable via national elections. In theory, therefore, citizens are able to sanction their representatives. Nevertheless, the real opportunities furnished by these channels in this respect are severely limited, for neither type of election is fought on European issues (Hix 2008). This means that EU citizens are never presented with any real alternatives. Nor is there any clear opposition to which they can turn should they feel discontent with the actions of their national governments or the EP party groups.

The key point we want to make here is this: as long as we persist in upholding the illusion of accountability, and in refusing to acknowledge that no effective tools are available for sanctioning the most important decision-makers in the Union, we will never find a solution to the quandary. It is only by breaking this illusion that we can identify the underlying problem – the critical factor that prevents the strong formal mechanisms now in place from performing effectively. This underlying problem, as we see it, is the *absence of opposition* in the EU.

In his contribution to this volume, Sverker Gustavsson argues that the right of opposition is a historically given constraint that puts a limits on the use of accountability avoidance. Otherwise put, opposition is necessary for accountability to be possible in practice. 'Political opposition gives voice. By losing opposition we lose voice', as Peter Mair puts it (Mair 2007: 17). We would like to add that, in losing voice, we lose alternatives – and without alternatives, elections cannot work as effective mechanisms for accountability. We run the risk of ending up with a situation where voters are hard-pressed to see any meaningful differences between the options set before them. What we have then is 'opposition within the cartel' (Mair 2007: 14): a state of affairs where voters still have the formal right to remove office-holders, but where the differences in respect of real policies are so marginal that there is no 'classical opposition', as Otto Kirchheimer (1957) would have described it.

It all comes down to this: in the absence of opposition, not even strong accountability mechanisms can offer EU citizens real opportunities to hold their representatives to account in practice. As we have argued, breaking the illusion of accountability is a necessary step on the road to restoring opposition in the EU – both at the level of the Union, and at the level of its member states. Unfortunately, the next steps on this journey are not easily identified. Certain reforms could be proposed, however, that would serve to strengthen opposition and thereby also accountability (Hix 2008).

The problem with all such reforms is that they require of political elites that they give up the freedom they have hitherto enjoyed to act on EU affairs without having their hands tied by mandates derived from genuine electoral contests. We do not believe they will be easily persuaded to do so. For one thing, politicians always prefer to work as freely as possible from external constraint. For another, their space for manoeuvring and striking deals at the

European level would be restricted. We must presume, therefore, that political elites will continue to try to prevent European issues from being politicised and publicly debated.

Still, we believe our task is to tell it as it is, and to give the public the whole story. We hope thereby to stimulate an enlightened and forward-looking public debate on these crucial issues. Some of our more 'realistic' colleagues may think this is a bad idea. Too radical a debate, they fear, will disturb the sensitive equilibrium we have achieved – an equilibrium they believe to be essential for 'integration by stealth'. In our view, however, there is no greater realism than speaking truth to power.

Bibliography

Abromeit, H. (1986) *British Steel. An Industry between the State and the Private Sector*, Leamington Spa: Berg Publishers.

—— (1998) *Democracy in Europe*, Oxford: Berghahn Books.

—— (2002) *Wozu braucht man Demokratie?*, Opladen: Leske & Budrich.

—— (2007) 'Probleme einer Demokratisierung der Europäischen Union – oder: Warum es so schwer ist, einen gemeinsamen Nenner zu finden', in N. Bandelow and W. Bleek (eds) *Einzelinteressen und kollektives Handeln in modernen Demokratien*, Wiesbaden: Verlag für Sozialwissenschaften.

Abromeit, H. and Stoiber, M. (2007) 'Criteria of democratic legitimacy', in A. Hurrelmann, S. Schneider and J. Steffek (eds) *Legitimacy in an Age of Global Politics*, Basingstoke: Palgrave.

Aghion, P. and Tirole, J. (1997) 'Formal and real authority in organizations', *Journal of Political Economy*, 105: 1–29.

Agné, H. (2007) 'The myth of international delegation: limits to and suggestions for democratic theory in the context of the European Union', *Government and Opposition*, 42: 18–45.

Amtenbrink, F. (1999) *The Democratic Accountability of Central Banks: A Comparative Study of the European Central Bank*, Oxford: Hart.

Arnull, A. and Wincott, D. (eds) (2002) *Accountability and Legitimacy in the European Union*, Oxford: Oxford University Press.

Arrow, K.J. (1985) 'The economics of agency', in J.W. Pratt and R.J. Zeckhauser (eds) *Principals and Agents: The Structure of Business*, Boston, MA: Harvard Business School Press.

Balla, S.J. and Wright J.R. (2001) 'Interest groups, advisory committees, and congressional control of bureaucracy', *American Political Science Review*, 45: 799–812.

Bartolini, S. (2005) *Restructuring Europe*, Oxford: Oxford University Press.

—— (2006) 'Should the Union be "politicised"? Prospects and risks', *Notre Europe*, Policy Paper 19. Online. Available HTTP: <http:www.notre-europe.eu/uploads/tx_publication/Policypaper19-en_01.pdf> .

—— (2008) 'Taking "constitutionalism" and "legitimacy" seriously', *European Governance Papers*, discussion paper No 1. Online. Available HTTP: <http://www.connex-network.org/eurogov/pdf/discuss_paper_01_2008.pdf> .

Beach, D. (2003) 'Towards a new method of constitutional bargaining?', *The Federal Trust*, online paper 13/03. Online. Available HTTP: <http://www.fedtrust.co.uk>.

Begg, I. (2007) 'Contested meanings of transparency in central banking', *Comparative European Politics*, 5: 36–52.

Behn, R.D. (2001) *Rethinking Democratic Accountability*, Washington, DC: Brookings Institution Press.

Bergenstrand, K. (2004) 'The European intelligence and security community and the fight against terrorism', in O. Horvath and T. Brenners (eds) *European Cooperation against Terrorism (Conference Proceedings)*, Nijmegen: Wolf Legal Publishers.

Berman, S. and McNamara, K.R. (1999) 'Bank on democracy: why central banks need public oversight', *Foreign Affairs*, 78 (2): 2–8.

Bigo, D. (2008) 'Globalized (in)Security: the Field and the Ban-opticon' in D. Bigo and A. Tsoukala (eds) *Terror, Insecurity and Liberty: Illiberal Practices of Liberal Regimes after 9/11*, London: Routledge.

Bini-Smaghi, L., and Gros, D. (2001) 'Is the ECB sufficiently accountable and transparent?', *European Network of Economic Policy Research Institutes Working Paper* 007. Online. Available HTTP: <http://www.enepri.org/Publications/WP007.pdf>.

Blomgren, M. and Bergman T. (eds) (2005) *EU och Sverige: ett sammanlänkat statsskick*, Lund: Liber förlag.

Bobbio, N. (1987) *The Future of Democracy*, Cambridge: Polity Press.

Born, H. and Leigh, I. (2005) *Making Intelligence Accountable: Legal Standards and Best Practice for Oversight of Intelligence Agencies*, Oslo: Printing House of the Norwegian Parliament.

Bovens, M. (2006) 'Analysing and assessing public accountability: a conceptual framework', *European Governance Papers No. C-06-01*. Online. Available HTTP: <http://www.connex-network.org/eurogov/pdf/egp-connex-C-06-01.pdf>.

—— (2007a) 'Analysing and assessing accountability: a conceptual framework', *European Law Journal*, 13: 447–68.

—— (2007b) 'New forms of accountability and EU-governance', *Comparative European Politics* 5: 104–20.

Bovens, M., T'hart, P. and Schillemans, T. (2008) 'Does public accountability work?', *Public Administration*, 86: 225–42.

Briault, C., Haldene, A. and King, M. (1996) 'Independence and accountability', *Bank of England Working Paper*: No. 49.

Budge, I. (2006) 'Direct democracy', in R.A.W. Rhodes, S. Binder and B.A. Rockman (eds) *The Oxford Handbook of Political Institutions*, Oxford: Oxford University Press.

Buiter, W.H. (1999) 'Alice in Euroland', *Journal of Common Market Studies*, 37: 181–209.

Cheneval, F. (2006) 'Federalism and direct democracy: a Swiss tradition or a systemic necessity of composed politics?', paper presented to the CONNEX workshop 'One democracy or several', 20–22 January 2006, Darmstadt.

Commission of the European Communities (2001a) *European Governance. A White Paper*, COM (2001) 428 final.

—— (2001b) *White Paper: Strategy for a Future Chemicals Policy*, COM (2001) 88 final.

—— (2003) *Proposal for a Regulation of the European Parliament and of the Council concerning the Registration, Evaluation, Authorisation, and Restriction of Chemicals (REACH), establishing a European Chemicals Agency and Amending Directive 1999/45/EC and Regulation (EC) on Persistent Organic Pollutants*, COM (2003) 644 final.

—— (2005) *Communication to the Spring European Council – Working Together for Growth and Jobs: A New Start for the Lisbon Strategy*, COM (2005) 24.

—— (2006) *White Paper on a European Communication Policy*', COM (2006) 35.

Coosemans, T. (2004) 'L'Union européenne et le renseignement: perspectives de coopération entre les états membres, Brussels: GRIP. Online. Available HTTP: <http:www.grip-publications.eu/pub/rapports/rg04–3_renseignement.pdf>.

Council of the European Union (2005) 'Convention between the Kingdom of Belgium, the Federal Republic of Germany, the Kingdom of Spain, the French Republic, the Grand Duchy of Luxembourg, the Kingdom of the Netherlands and the Republic of Austria on the stepping up of cross-border cooperation particularly in combating terrorism, cross-border crime and illegal migration'. Online. Available HTTP: <http://register.consilium.europa.eu/pdf/en/05/st10/st10900.en05.pdf> .

Cram, L. (1997) *Policy-Making in the EU: Conceptual Lenses and the Integration Process*, London: Routledge.

Crowe, C. and Meade, E.E. (2007) 'The evolution of central bank governance around the world', *Journal of Economic Perspectives,* 21: 69–90.

Cullen, P.P. (2005) 'Conflict and cooperation within the platform of European social NGOs', in J. Bandy and J. Smith (eds) *Coalitions Across Borders: Transnational Protest and the Neoliberal Order,* Oxford: Rowman and Littlefield.

Curtin, D. and Wille, A. (eds) (2008) *Meaning and Practice of Accountability in the EU Multi-Level Context*, Mannheim: Mannheim Centre for European Social Research. CONNEX Report Series Nr. 07.

Dahl, R.A. (1965) 'Reflections on opposition in western democracies', *Government and Opposition*, 1: 7–24.

—— (1967) *A Preface to Democratic Theory*, Chicago IL: University of Chicago Press.

—— (1971) *Polyarchy*, New Haven, CT: Yale University Press.

—— (1979) 'Procedural democracy', in P. Laslett and J.S. Fishkin (eds) *Philosophy, Politics and Society*, 5th series, Blackwell Publishers; reprinted in R. Goodin and P. Pettit (eds) (1998) *Contemporary Political Philosophy*, Oxford: Blackwell.

—— (1982a) 'Federalism and the democratic process', *Nomos*, 25: 95–108.

—— (1982b) *Dilemmas of Pluralist Democracy*, New Haven, CT: Yale University Press.

—— (1989) *Democracy and Its Critics*, New Haven, CT: Yale University Press.

—— (1994) 'A democratic dilemma: system effectiveness versus citizen participation', *Political Science Quarterly*, 109: 23–34.

—— (1998) *On Democracy*, New Haven, CT: Yale University Press.

—— (1999) 'Can international organizations be democratic?', in I. Shapiro and C. Hacker-Cordón (eds) *Democracy's Edges*, Cambridge: Cambridge University Press.

Daun, A. (2005) 'Intelligence – Strukturen für die multilaterale Kooperation europäischer Staaten', *Integration*, 2: 134–49.

Daun, A. and Jäger, T. (2005) 'Intelligence cooperation in Europe', *Welttrends*, 48: 67–82.

De Haan, J. (1997) 'The European Central Bank: independence, accountability and strategy: a review', *Public Choice*, 93: 395–426.

De Haan, J. and Eijffinger, S.C.W. (2000) 'The democratic accountability of the European Central Bank: a comment on two fairy-tales', *Journal of Common Market Studies*, 38: 393–407.

De Haan, J., Amtenbrink, F. and Waller, S. (2004) 'The transparency and credibility of the European Central Bank', *Journal of Common Market Studies*, 42: 775–94.

Dehousse, R. (1995) 'Constitutional reform in the European Community: are there alternatives to the majoritarian avenue?', *West European Politics*, 18: 118–36.

—— (1997) 'Regulation by networks in the European Community: the role of European agencies', *Journal of European Public Policy*, 4: 246–61.

Depauw, S. (2003) 'Government party discipline in parliamentary democracies: the cases of Belgium, France, and the United Kingdom in the 1990s', *Journal of Legislative Studies,* 9: 130–46.

Dogan, R. (1997) 'Comitology: little procedures with big implications', *West European Politics*, 20: 31–60.

Dubnick, M. and Justice, J.B. (2004) 'Accounting for accountability', conference paper. Online. Available HTTP: <http:www.allacademic.com/meta/p60363_index.html>.

Eberlein, B. and Grande, E. (2005) 'Beyond delegation: transnational regimes and the EU regulatory state', *Journal of European Public Policy*, 12: 89–112.

Eijffinger, C.W. and de Haan, J. (1996) *The Political Economy of Central-bank Independence*, Princeton, NJ.: Princeton University Press.

—— (2000) *European Monetary and Fiscal Policy.* Oxford: Oxford University Press.

Elgie, R. (2002) 'The politics of the European Central Bank: principal-agent theory and the democratic deficit', *Journal of European Public Policy*, 9: 186–200.

Epstein, D. and O'Halloran, S. (1999) *Delegating Powers: A Transaction Cost Politics Approach to Policy Making under Separate Powers*, Cambridge: Cambridge University Press.

Eriksen, E.O. (2000) 'Deliberative supranationalism in the EU', in E.O. Eriksen and and J.E. Fossum, (eds) *Democracy in the European Union—Integration through Deliberation?* London: Routledge.

Eriksen, E.O. and Fossum, J.E. (eds) (2000) *Democracy in the European Union – Integration through Deliberation?* London: Routledge.

Euractiv (2005) 'Gijs de Vries on terrorism, islam and democracy'. Online. Available HTTP: <http:www.euractiv.com>.

European Convention (2002) 'Introductory speech by Giscard D'Éstaing to the convention on the future of Europe'.

—— (2003) 'Contribution franco-allemande à la convention européenne sur l'architecture institutionelle de l'Union', *CONV 489/03.*

European Council (2001) 'The future of the European Union—Laeken declaration'. Online. Available HTTP: <http://www.ena.lu>.

European Parliament (2001) 'Report on the existence of a global system for the interception of private and commercial communications', A5–0264/2001. Online. Available HTTP: <http://cryptone.org/echelon-ep-fin.htm>.

—— (2006) 'Decision to set up the temporary committee on the alleged use of European countries by the CIA for the transportation and illegal detention of prisoners'. Online. Available HTTP: <http:www.europarl.europa.eu/comparl/tempcom/tdip/default_en.htm>.

—— (2007) 'Resolution on the alleged use of European countries by the CIA for the transportation and illegal detention of prisoners'. Online. Available HTTP: <http:www.europarl.europa.eu/comparl/tempcom/tdip/final_ep_resolution_en.pdf>.

Everson, M. (1995) 'European agencies: hierarchy beaters?' *European Law Journal*, 1: 180–204.

Everson, M., Majone, G., Metcalfe, L. and Schout, A. (2001) 'The role of specialized agencies in decentralising EU Governance', report for the European Commission'. Online. Available HTTP: <http://europa.eu.int/comm/governance/areas/group6/contribution_en.pdf>.

Fazi, E. and Smith, J. (2006) 'Civil dialogue: making it work better', study commissioned by the Civil Society Contact Group. Online. Available HTTP: <http://act4europe.horus.be/module/FileLib/Civil%20dialogue,%20making%20it%20work%20better.pdf>.

Ferejohn, J. (1999) 'Accountability and authority: toward a theory of political accountability', in A. Przeworski, S.C. Stokes and B. Manin (eds), *Democracy, Accountability and Representation*, Cambridge: Cambridge University Press.

Finke, B. (2007) 'Civil society participation in EU governance', *Living Reviews in European Governance,* 2. Online. Available HTTP: <http://www.livingreviews.org/lreg-2007-2>.

Fink-Hafner, D. (2007) 'Europeanization in managing EU affairs: between divergence and convergence', *Public Administration,* 85: 805–28.

Fischer, E. (2004) 'The European Union in the age of accountability', *Oxford Journal of Legal Studies*, 24: 495–515.

Fischer, S. (1994) 'The costs and benefits of disinflation', in J.O. de Beaufort Wijnholds, S.C.W. Eijffinger and L.H. Hoogduin (eds), *A Framework for Monetary Stability*, Dordrecht: Kluwer.

Føllesdal, A. and Hix, S. (2006) 'Why there is a democratic deficit in the EU: a response to Majone and Moravcsik', *Journal of Common Market Studies*, 44: 553–62.

Fossum, J.E. and Menéndez, A. (2005) 'The constitution's gift? A deliberative democratic analysis of constitution making in the European Union', *European Law Journal*, 11: 380–410.

Franchino, F. (2000) 'The Commission's executive discretion, information and comitology', *Journal of Theoretical Politics*, 12: 155–81.

—— (2002) 'Efficiency or credibility? Testing the two logics of delegation to the European Commission', *Journal of European Public Policy*, 9: 677–94.

—— (2007) *The Powers of the Union: Delegation in the EU*, Cambridge: Cambridge University Press.

Friedrich, D. (2008) 'Democratic aspiration meets political reality: participation of organized civil society in selected European policy processes', in J. Steffek, C. Kissling, and P. Nanz (eds) *Civil Society Participation in European and Global Governance: A Cure for the Democratic Deficit?*, London: Macmillan.

Gabel, M. and Hix, S. (2002) 'The European Parliament and executive politics in the EU', in M. Hosli, A. Van Deemen and M. Widgrén (eds) *Institutional Challenges in the European Union*, London: Routledge.

Gat, A. (2007) 'The return of authoritarian great powers', *Foreign Affairs*, 86 (4): 59–69.

Geraats, P.M. (2002) 'Central bank transparency', *Economic Journal*, 112: 532–65.

Goldstein, J. and Keohane, R.O. (1993) 'Ideas and foreign policy: an analytical framework', in J. Goldstein and R.O. Keohane, *Ideas and Foreign Policy*. Ithaca, NY: Cornell University Press.

Grant, R.W. and Keohane, R.O. (2005) 'Accountability and abuses of power in world politics', *American Political Science Review*, 99: 29–43.

Greenwood, J. (2003) *Interest Representation in the European Union*, New York: Palgrave Macmillan.

—— (2007) 'Organized civil society and democratic legitimacy in the European Union', *British Journal of Political Science*, 37: 333–57.

Gustavsson, S. (1998a) 'Defending the democratic deficit', in A. Weale and M. Nentwich (eds) *Political Theory and the European Union*, London: Routledge.

——(1998b) 'Double asymmetry as normative challenge', in A. Føllesdal and P. Koslowski (eds) *Democracy and the European Union*, Berlin: Springer Verlag.

——(2003) 'Double asymmetry and its alternatives', in J. Hallenberg, B. Nygren and A. Robertson (eds) *Transitions. In Honour of Kjell Goldmann*, Stockholm: Department of Political Science.

——(2006) 'Designing European federalism', *Swedish Economic Policy Review*, 13: 163–83.

——(2008) 'The living constitution of the EU', in B. Kohler-Koch and F. Larat (eds) *Efficient and Democratic Governance in the European Union*, Mannheim: Mannheim Centre for European Social Research. CONNEX Report Series Nr. 09.

Gutman, A. and Thompson, D. (1996) *Democracy and Disagreement*, Cambridge, MA: The Belknap Press of Harvard University Press.

Harlow, C. (2002) *Accountability in the European Union*, Oxford: Oxford University Press.

Harlow, C. and Rawlings, R. (2006) 'Promoting accountability in multi-level governance: a network approach', *European Governance Papers No. C-06-02*. Online. Available HTTP: <http://www.connex-network.org/eurogov/pdf/egp-connex-C-06-02.pdf>.

Hegeland, H. (2006) *Nationell EU-parlamentarism: Riksdagens arbete med EU-frågorna*, Stockholm: Santérus Academic Press.

Held, D. (2004) *Global Covenant*, Cambridge: Polity Press.

Héritier; A. (1999) 'Elements of democratic legitimation in Europe: an alternative perspective', *Journal of European Public Policy*, 6: 269–82.

Heyvaert, V. (2008) 'The EU chemicals policy: towards inclusive governance?' in M. Everson and E. Vos (eds) *European Risk Governance: Its Science, its Inclusiveness and its Effectiveness*, Mannheim: Mannheim Centre for European Social Research. CONNEX Report Series Nr. 06.

Hix, S. (2008) *What's Wrong with the European Union and How to Fix It*, Cambridge: Polity Press.

Hix, S. and Marsh, M. (2007) 'Punishment or protest? Understanding European Parliament elections', *Journal of Politics*, 69: 495–510.

Holmstrom, B. (1979) 'Morale hazard and observability', *Bell Journal of Economics*, 10: 74–91.

Höreth, M. (2001) 'The European Commission's white paper on governance: a "tool-kit" for closing the legitimacy gap of EU policy-making', *ZEI Discussion Paper C94*, Bonn: University of Bonn.

Huber, J.D. and Shipan C.R. (2000) 'The costs of control: legislators, agencies, and transaction costs', *Legislative Studies Quarterly*, 25: 25–52.

——(2002) *Deliberate Discretion? The Institutional Foundations of Bureaucratic Autonomy*, Cambridge: Cambridge University Press.

Hüller, T. and Kohler-Koch, B. (2008) 'Assessing the democratic value of civil society engagement in the European Union' in B. Kohler-Koch, D. De Bièvre and W. Maloney (eds) *Opening EU-Governance to Civil Society: Gains and Challenges*, Mannheim: Mannheim Centre for European Social Research. CONNEX Report Series Nr. 05.

Issing, O. (1999) 'The eurosystem: transparent and accountable or "Willem in euroland"', *Journal of Common Market Studies*, 37: 503–19.

——(2006) 'Communication and transparency—how do central banks meet these demands?', speech by Otmar Issing, member of the executive board of the ECB, Frankfurt am Main, 18 January 2006. Online. Available HTTP: <http://www.ECB.int>.

Jabko, N. (2003) 'Democracy in the age of the Euro', *Journal of European Public Policy*, 10: 710–39.

—— (2005) 'The politics of central banking in the United States and in the European Union', *NEWGOV*, ref. no 19b/D04, June 2005.

Jacobsson, B. and Sundström G. (1999) *Invävd i Europa: en undersökning av den svenska statsförvaltningens EU-arbete*, Stockholm: SCORE.

Jepperson, R.L., Wendt, A. and Katzenstein, P.J. (1996) 'Norms, identity and culture in national security' in P.J. Katzenstein (ed.) *The Culture of National Security*, New York: Columbia University Press.

Joerges, C. and Neyer, J. (1997a) 'From intergovernmental bargaining to deliberative political process: the constitutionalization of comitology', *European Law Journal*, 3: 273–99.

—— (1997b) 'Transforming strategic interaction into deliberative problem-solving: European comitology in the foodstuffs sector', *Journal of European Public Policy*, 4: 609–25.

Johannesson, C. (2005) 'EU:s inflytande över lagstiftning i Sveriges riksdag', *Statsvetenskaplig Tidskrift*, 107: 71–84.

Kahler, M. (2004) 'Defining accountability up: the global economic multilaterals', *Government and Opposition*, 39: 132–58.

Karlsson, C. (2001) *Democracy, Legitimacy and the European Union*, Uppsala: Acta Universitatis Upsaliensis.

—— (2008) 'Deliberation at the European Convention: the final verdict', *European Law Journal*, 14: 604–19.

Kassim, H. and Menon, A. (2003) 'The principal-agent approach and the study of the European Union: promise unfulfilled?', *Journal of European Public Policy*, 10: 121–39.

Kassim, H., Menon, A., Peter, P.G. and Wright, V. (eds) (2001) *The National Co-ordination of EU Policy: The European Level*, Oxford: Oxford University Press.

Katz, R.S. (1987) 'Party government and its alternatives', in Katz, R.S. (ed.) *Party Governments*, Berlin: de Gruyter.

Katzenstein, P.J., Keohane, R.O. and Krasner, S.D. (1999) 'International organization and the study of world politics', in P.J. Katzenstein, R.O. Keohane and S.D. Krasner (eds) *Exploration and Contestation in the Study of World Politics*, Cambridge, MA: MIT Press.

Kelemen, R.D. (2002) 'The politics of "eurocratic" structure and the new European agencies', *West European Politics*, 25: 93–118.

Keohane, R.O. (1984) *After Hegemony*, Princeton, NJ: Princeton University Press.

—— (2003) 'Global governance and democratic accountability' in D. Held and M. Koenig-Archibugi (eds) *Taming Globalization*, Cambridge: Polity Press.

—— (2006) 'Accountability in world politics', *Scandinavian Political Studies*, 29: 75–87.

Keohane, R.O. and Nye, J.S. (2001) 'The club model of multilateral cooperation and problems of legitimacy', in R.B. Porter *et al.* (eds) *Efficiency, Equity and Legitimacy*, Washington, DC: Brookings Institution.

Kielmansegg, P.G. (1977) *Volksouveränität*, Stuttgart: Klett-Cotta.

Kiewiet, D.R. and McCubbins, M.D. (1991) *The Logic of Delegation: Congressional Parties and the Appropriate Process*, Chicago, IL: Chicago University Press.

Kirchheimer, O. (1957) 'The waning of opposition in parliamentary regimes', *Social Research*, 24: 127–56.

Klingeman, H., Volkens, A., Bara, J., Budge, I. and McDonald, M.D. (2006) *Mapping Policy Preferences II: Estimates for Parties, Electors and Governments in Eastern Europe, European Union, and OECD 1990–2003*, Oxford: Oxford University Press.

Kohler-Koch, B. and Finke, B. (2007) 'The institutional shaping of EU-society relations: a contribution to democracy via participation?', *Journal of Civil Society*, 3: 205–21.

Kohler-Koch, B. and Rittberger B. (eds) (2007) *Debating the Democratic Legitimacy of the European Union*, Lanham, MD: Rowman & Littlefield.

Kuflik, A. (1984) 'The inalienability of autonomy', *Philosophy and Public Affairs*, 13: 271–98.

Kydland, F. and Prescott, E. (1977) 'Rules rather than discretion: the inconsistency of optimal plans', *Journal of Political Economy*, 85: 473–90.

Larue, T. (2006) *Agents in Brussels. Delegation and Democracy in the European Union*, Umeå: Umeå University.

Lewin, L. (2007) *Democratic Accountability*, Cambridge, MA: Harvard University Press.

Lijphart, A. (1999) *Patterns of Democracy*, New Haven, CT: Yale University Press.

—— (2007) *Thinking About Democracy*, London: Taylor and Francis.

Lijphart, A, Rogowski, R. and Weaver, R.K. (1993) 'Separation of powers and cleavage management', in R.K Weaver and B.A. Rockman (eds) *Do Institutions Matter?*, Washington, DC: The Brookings Institution.

Lindberg, L. and Scheingold, S. (1970) *Europe's Would-Be Polity*, Englewood Cliffs, NJ: Prentice-Hall.

Lindgren, K.-O. and Persson, T. (2008a) 'The structure of conflict over EU chemicals policy', *European Union Politics*, 9: 31–58.

—— (2008b), 'Input and output legitimacy: synergy or trade-off? Empirical evidence from an EU survey', paper presented at the meeting of the Swedish Political Science Association, Uppsala University, September 26–27, 2008.

Lord, C. (1998) *Democracy in the European Union*, Sheffield: Sheffield University Press.

Lowenthal, M.W. (2002) *From Secrets to Policy*, Washington, DC: Congressional Quarterly Press.

Lupia, A. (2003) 'Delegation and its perils', in K. Strøm, W.C. Müller and T. Bergman (eds) *Delegation and Accountability in Parliamentary Democracies*, Oxford: Oxford University Press.

McCubbins, M.D and Page, T. (1987) 'A theory of congressional delegation', in D. Mathew, M.D. McCubbins and T. Sullivan (eds) *Congress: Structure and Policy*, New York: Cambridge University Press.

McCubbins, M.D. and Schwartz, T. (1984) 'Congressional oversight overlooked: police patrols versus fire alarms', *American Journal of Political Science*, 28: 165–79.

McCubbins, M.D., Noll, R.G. and Weingast, B.R. (1987) 'Administrative procedures as instruments of political control', *Journal of Law, Economics, and Organization*, 3: 243–77.

McKay, D. (1999) *Federalism and the European Union*, Oxford: Oxford University Press.

McNamara, K.R. (1998) *The Currency of Ideas: Monetary Politics in the European Union*, Ithaca, NY: Cornell University Press.

—— (2002) 'Rational fictions: central bank independence and the social logic of delegation', *West European Politics*, 25: 47–76.

Magnette, P. and Nicolaidis, K. (2004) 'The European Convention: bargaining in the shadow of rhetoric', *West European Politics*, 27: 381–404.

Magnette, P. and Papadopoulos, Y. (2008) 'On the politicization of the European consociation: a middle way between Hix and Bartolini', in D. Curtin and A. Wille, (eds) *Meaning and Practice of Accountability in the EU Multi-Level Context*, Mannheim: Mannheim Centre for European Social Reserach. CONNEX Report Series Nr. 07.

Mair, P. (2007) 'Opposition and the European Union', *Government and Opposition*, 42: 1–17.

—— (2008) 'Popular democracy and the European Union polity', in D. Curtin and A. Wille (eds) *Meaning and Practice of Accountability in the EU Multi-Level Context*, Mannheim: Mannheim Centre for European Social Research. CONNEX Report Series Nr. 07.

Mair, P. and Thomassen, J. (2008) 'Electoral democracy and political representation in the European Union', unpublished paper, European University Institute.

Majone, G. (1996a) 'Regulatory legitimacy', in G. Majone (ed.) *Regulating Europe*, London: Routledge.

—— (1996b) *Regulating Europe*, London: Routledge.

—— (1997) 'The new European agencies: regulation by information', *Journal of European Public Policy*, 4: 262–75.

—— (1998) 'Europe's "democratic deficit": the question of standards', *European Law Journal*, 4: 5–28.

—— (2000) 'The credibility crisis of community regulation', *Journal of Common Market Studies*, 38: 273–302.

—— (2001) 'Two logics of delegation: agency and fiduciary relations in EU governance', *European Union Politics*, 2: 103–22.

—— (2002) 'The European Commission: The limits of centralization and the perils of parliamentarization', *Governance*, 15: 375–92.

—— (2005) *Dilemmas of European Integration*, Oxford: Oxford University Press.

Mancini, G. Federico (1998) 'Europe: the case for statehood', *European Law Journal*, 4: 29–42.

Manin, B., Przeworski, A. and Stokes, S. (1999) 'Introduction', in A. Przeworski, S. Stokes and B. Manin (eds) *Democracy, Accountability and Representation*, Cambridge: Cambridge University Press.

March, J.G. and Olsen, J.P (1999) 'The institutional dynamics of international political orders', in P.J. Katzenstein, R.O. Keohane and S.D. Krasner (eds) *Exploration and Contestation in the Study of World Politics*, Cambridge, MA: MIT Press.

Marcussen, M. (2000) *Ideas and Elites: The Social Construction of Economic and Monetary Union*, Aalborg: Aalborg University Press.

Meunier, S. and Nicolaïdis, K. (1999) 'Who speaks for Europe? The delegation of trade authority in the EU', *Journal of Common Market Studies*, 37: 477–501.

Michels, A. (2007) *Theories and Core Principles of Dutch Democracy*, Eurogov, No C 07–01. Online. HTTP: <http://www.connex-network.org/eurogov/pdf/egp-connex-C-07-01.pdf>.

Miller, G. (2005) 'The political evolution of principal-agent models', *Annual Review of Political Science*, 8: 203–25.

Mitchell, R.B. (1994) *Intentional Oil Pollution at Sea*, Cambridge, MA: MIT Press.

Moravcsik, A. (1998) *The Choice for Europe: Social Purpose and State Power from Messina to Maastricht*, Ithaca, NY: Cornell University Press.

—— (2002) 'In defence of the "democratic deficit": reassessing the legitimacy of the European Union', *Journal of Common Market Studies*, 40: 603–34.

—— (2004) 'Is there a "democratic deficit" in world politics? A framework for analysis', *Government and Opposition*, 39: 336–63.

—— (2008) 'The European constitutional settlement', *The World Economy*, 31: 157–82.

Moravcsik, A. and Sangiovanni, A. (2003) 'On democracy and "public interest" in the European Union', in R. Mayntz and W. Streeck (eds) *Die Reformierbarkeit der Demokratie*, Frankfurt am Main: Campus Verlag.

Mulgan, R. (2000) 'Accountability: an ever-expanding concept?', *Public Administration*, 78: 555–73.

Müller-Wille, B. (2004) 'For our eyes only? Shaping an intelligence community within the EU', *EU Institute for Security Studies Occasional Paper 50*, Paris: EU-ISS.

Naurin, D. (2006) 'Transparency, publicity, accountability—the missing links', *Swiss Political Science Review*, 12: 90–98.

—— (2007) 'Network capital and cooperation patterns in the working groups of the council of the EU', *European University Institute Working Paper* RSCAS 2007/14.

—— (forthcoming 2009) 'Safe enough to argue? Giving reasons in the EU Council of Ministers', *British Journal of Political Science*.

Naurin, D. and Lindahl, R. (2007) 'Anmärkningsvärt starkt svenskt inflytande i EU', *Dagens Nyheter,* 31 March.

Neunreither, K. (2000) 'Political representation in the European Union: a common whole, various wholes, or just a hole?', in K. Neunreither and A. Wiener (eds) *European Integration after Amsterdam*, Oxford: Oxford University Press.

Niznik, J. and Ryabinska, N. (eds) (2007) *Political Accountability*, Warsaw: IFiS Publishers.

Norman, P. (2003) *The Accidental Constitution*, Brussels: EuroComment.

Nugent, N. (1999) *The Government and Politics of the European Union*, London: Macmillan.

Nye, J.S. (2004) *Soft Power*, New York: Public Affairs Press.

Official Journal of the European Union, 'Consolidated version of the Treaty on the European Union', 2008/C 115/01.

Padoa-Schioppa, T. (2000) 'An institutional glossary of the eurosystem', *ECB*. Online. HTTP: <http:www.ECB.int>.

Parks, L. (2006) 'No valentine for Bolkestein: a study of the campaign against the draft directive on services in the internal market', paper presented at the annual ESPAnet conference, 21–23 September 2006, Bremen.

—— (2009) *In the Corridors and in the Streets: A Comparative Study of the Impacts of Social Movement Campaigns in the EU*, Florence: European University Institute.

Parliamentary Assembly of the Council of Europe (PACE) (2007) 'Secret detentions and illegal transfers of detainees involving Council of Europe member states: second report – Explanatory memorandum', AS/Jur (2007).

Persson, T. (2007a) 'Democratising European chemicals policy: do online consultations favour civil society participation?', *Journal of Civil Society*, 3: 223–38.

—— (2007b) 'Explaining European Union adjustments in Sweden's central administration', *Scandinavian Political Studies,* 30: 204–28.

Pesendorfer, D. (2006) 'EU environmental policy under pressure: chemicals policy change between antagonistic goals', *Environmental Politics*, 15: 95–114.

Peters, G.B. and Pierre, J. (2006) 'Governance, accountability and democratic legitimacy', in A. Benz and Y. Papadopoulos (eds) *Governance and Democracy: Comparing National, European and International Experiences*, London: Routledge.

Pitkin, H. (1967) *The Concept of Representation*, Berkeley, CA: University of California Press.

Pollack, M.A. (1997) 'Delegation, agency, and agenda-setting in the European Community', *International Organization*, 51: 99–134.

—— (2003) *The Engines of European Integration: Delegation, Agency, and Agenda Setting in the EU*, Oxford: Oxford University Press.

Pollak, J. and Slominski, P. (2004) 'The representative quality of EU treaty reform: a comparison between the IGC and the convention', *Journal of European Integration*, 26: 201–26.

Priest, D. (2005) 'Help from France key in covert operations', *The Washington Post*, 3 July.

Puntscher-Riekmann, S. (2007) 'In search of lost norms: is accountability the solution to the legitimacy problems of the European Union?', *Comparative European Politics*, 5: 121–37.

Rabkin, J.A. (2005) *Law without Nations?* Princeton, NJ: Princeton University Press.

Ragin, C.C. (1987) *The Comparative Method: Moving Beyond Qualitative and Quantitative Strategies*, Berkeley, CA: University of California Press.

Reif, K. and Schmitt, H. (1980) 'Nine second-order national elections: a conceptual framework for the analysis of European election results', *European Journal of Political Research*, 8: 3–44.

Richardson, H. (2002) *Democratic Autonomy: Public Reasoning about the Ends of Policy*, Oxford: Oxford University Press.

Richelson, J. and Ball, D. (1985) *The Ties that Bind: Intelligence Cooperation between UK/USA Countries*, Boston and London: Allen & Unwin.

Risse, T. and Kleine, M. (2007) 'Assessing the legitimacy of the EU's treaty revision methods', *Journal of Common Market Studies*, 45: 69–80.

Rittberger, B. (2001) 'Which institutions for Europe? Explaining the institutional design of Europe's first community', *Journal of European Public Policy*, 8: 673–708.

Ross, A. (1952) *Why Democracy?*, Cambridge, MA: Harvard University Press.

Ruggie, J.G. (2004) 'Reconstituting the global public domain: issues, actors and practices', *European Journal of International Relations*, 10: 499–531.

Sandholtz, W. and Zysman, J. (1989) '1992: recasting the European bargain', *World Politics*, 42: 95–128.

Sartori, G. (1970) 'Concept misformation in comparative politics', *American Political Science Review*, 64: 1033–53.

—— (1987) *The Theory of Democracy Revisited*, Chatham, NJ: Chatham Publishers Inc.

Scharpf, F.W. (1994) 'Community and autonomy: multi-level policy-making in the European Union', *Journal of European Public Policy*, 1: 219–42.

—— (1999) *Governing in Europe*, Oxford: Oxford University Press.

—— (2008) 'Individualrechte gegen nationale Solidarität', in M. Höpner and A. Schäfer (eds) *Die Politische Ökonomie der europäischen Integration*, Frankfurt am Main: Campus Verlag.

—— (2009) *Legitimacy in the Multilevel European Polity*, Köln: Max-Planck-Institut für Gesellschaftsforschung, Working Papers 09/01.

Schimmelfennig, F. (2001) 'The community trap: liberal norms, rhetorical action, and the eastern enlargement of the European Union', *International Organization*, 55: 47–80.

Schmalz-Bruns, R. (2007) 'The Euro-polity in perspective: some normative lessons from deliberative democracy', in B. Kohler-Koch and B. Rittberger (eds) *Debating the Democratic Legitimacy of the European Union*, Lanham, MD: Rowman & Littlefield.

Schmidt, S.K. (1998) 'Commission activism: subsuming telecommunications and electricity under European competition law', *Journal of European Public Policy*, 5, 169–84.

—— (2000) 'Only an agenda setter? The European Commission's power over the Council of Ministers', *European Union Politics*, 1: 37–61.

Schmidt, V. (2006) *Democracy in Europe. The EU and National Politics*, Oxford: Oxford University Press.

Schmitter, P. (2000) *How to Democratize the European Union ... And Why Bother?*, Lanham, MD: Rowman and Littlefield.

Schumpeter, J.A. (1943) *Capitalism, Socialism, and Democracy*, London: Allen & Unwin.

Scott, C. (2000) 'Accountability in the regulatory state', in C. Harvey, J. Morison and J. Shaw (eds) *Voices, Spaces and Processes in Constitutionalism,* Oxford: Blackwell.

Selin, H. (2007) 'Coalition politics and chemicals management in a regulatory ambitious Europe', *Global Environmental Politics*, 7: 63–93.

Setälä, M. (2006) 'On the problems of responsibility and accountability in referendums', *European Journal of Political Research*, 45: 699–721.

Shapiro, I. (2001) 'The institutionalization of European administrative space', in A. Stone Sweet, W. Sandholz and N. Fliegstein (eds) *The Institutionalisation of Europe*, Oxford: Oxford University Press.

Shapiro, M. (2002) 'Two transformations in administrative law: American and European?', in K.H. Ladeur (ed.) *The Europeanisation of Administrative Law: Transforming National Decision-Making Procedures*, Aldershot: Ashgate.

Shavell, S. (1979) 'Risk-sharing and incentives in the principal and agent relationship', *Bell Journal of Economics,* 10: 55–73.

Shaw, J. (2003) 'What's in a convention? Process and substance in the project of European constitution-building', in J. Shaw, P. Magnette, L. Hoffmann and A.V. Bausili, *The Convention on the Future of Europe*, London: The Federal Trust for Education and Research.

Shklar, J. N. (1984) *Ordinary Vices*, Cambridge, MA: Harvard University Press.

Shorrock, T. (2008) *Spies for Hire: The Secret World of Intelligence Outsourcing*, Riverside, NJ: Simon and Schuster.

Slaughter, A-M (2004a) *A New World Order*, Princeton, NJ: Princeton University Press.

—— (2004b) 'Disaggregated sovereignty: towards the public accountability of global government networks', *Government and Opposition*, 39: 159–90.

Smismans, S. (2006) *Civil Society and Legitimate European Governance*, Cheltenham: Edward Elgar.

Spence, M.A. (1974) *Market Signalling: Informational Transfer in Hiring and Related Screening Processes*, Cambridge, MA: Harvard University Press.

Spitz, E. (1984) *Majority Rule*, Chatham, NJ: Chatham House Publishers.

Statewatch. (2005) 'SIS II: fait accompli? Construction of EU's big brother database underway'. Online. Available HTTP: <http:www.statewatch.org/news/2005/may/sisII-analysis-may05.pdf>.

Steffek, J. and Nanz, P. (2008) 'Emergent patterns of civil society participation in global and European governance', in J. Steffek, C. Kissling, and P. Nanz (eds) *Civil Society Participation in European and Global Governance: A Cure for the Democratic Deficit?*, London: Macmillan.

Steffek, J., Kissling, C. and Nanz, P. (eds) (2008) *Civil Society Participation in European and Global Governance: a Cure for the democratic deficit?*, London: Macmillan.

Strøm, K., Müller, W.C. and Bergman, T. (eds) (2004) *Delegation and Accountability in Parliamentary Democracies*, Oxford: Oxford University Press.

Svensson, A-C. (2000) *In the Service of the European Union. The Role of the Presidency in Negotiating the Amsterdam Treaty 1995–97*, Uppsala: Acta Universitatis Upsaliensis.

Tallberg, J. (2000) 'The anatomy of autonomy: an institutional account of variation in supranational influence', *Journal of Common Market Studies*, 38: 843–64.

—— (2001) *EU:s politiska system*, Stockholm: Studentlitteratur.

—— (2002) 'Delegation to supranational institutions: why, how, and with what consequences?', *West European Politics*, 25: 23–46.

—— (2003) *European Governance and Supranational Institutions: Making States Comply*, London: Routledge.

—— (2007) 'Executive politics', in K.E. Jørgensen, M. Pollack and B. Rosamond (eds) *Handbook of European Union Politics,* London: Sage.

TDIP, (2006) 'Letter to the President of the European Parliament'. Online. Available HTTP: <http:www.statewatch.org/cia/documents/coelho-letter-en.pdf>.

Touraine, A. (1997) *What is Democracy?* Boulder, CO: Westview Press.

Trichet, J.C. (2001) 'The euro after two years', *Journal of Common Market Studies*, 39: 1–13.

Tsebelis, G. (2002) *Veto Players*, Princeton, NJ: Princeton University Press.

Verdun, A. (1998) 'The institutional design of EMU: a democratic deficit?', *Journal of Public Policy*, 18: 107–32.

—— (1999) 'The role of the Delors committee in the creation of EMU: an epistemic community?', *Journal of European Public Policy*, 6: 308–28.

Waltz, K.N. (1979) *Theory of International Politics*, Reading, MA: Addison-Wesley.

Weaver, R.K. (1992) 'Political institutions and Canada's constitutional crisis', in R. K. Weaver (ed.) *The Collapse of Canada?*, Washington, DC: The Brookings Institution.

Weiler, J.H.H. (1999) *The Constitution of Europe,* Cambridge: Cambridge University Press.

Wendt, A. (1999) *Social Theory of International Politics*, Cambridge: Cambridge University Press.

Wetzling, T. (2008) 'European counterterrorism intelligence liaisons', in S. Farson, P. Gill, M. Phythian and S. Shapiro (eds), *PSI Handbook of Global Security and Intelligence – Volume 2*, Westport, CT: Praeger Security International.

Winkelmann, I. (1994) *Das Maastricht-Urteil des Bundesverfassungsgerichts vom 12. Oktober 1993. Dokumentation des Verfahrens mit Einführung*, Berlin: Duncker & Humblot.

Wolf, K-D. (2000) *Die neue Staatsräson*, Baden-Baden: Nomos.

Wolf, S. (2000) 'Ein Vorschlag zur Beseitigung von Repräsentations-und Legitimationsdefiziten in Rat und Europäischem Parlament', *Politische Vierteljahresschrift,* 41: 730–41.

Xifaras, M. (2006) 'Is democracy a meaningful concept to understand the evolution of French modern constitutional history?', paper presented at the CONNEX workshop 'One democracy or several?', 20–22 January 2006, Darmstadt.

Yin, R.K. (2003) *Case Study Research: Design and Methods*, London: Sage Publications.

Zweifel, T.D. (2006) *International Organizations and Democracy*, Boulder, CO: Lynne Reiner Publishers.

Index

Accountability: avoidance of 6, 35–36, 39–45, 47–48, 174; as checks and balances 29; through civil society 6, 9, 10, 141, 142–45, 148, 153; deficit of 5, 6–7, 141, 171, 173; defined 4; and delegated power 4, 6, 7–8, 60, 171; direct 8, 72, 74–76; electoral 31, 32, 37; *ex ante* 4–5; *ex post* 4; of the executive 6, 9, 112, 116–24; external 15, 16, 18; indirect 8, 72–74; illusion of 1, 4–6, 10, 73, 80, 125, 141, 154, 170–75; internal 4, 15; of the legislature 6, 8, 171; mechanisms of 1, 4–5, 18, 21, 68–69, 72, 74, 83–84, 86–93, 96, 112, 125, 130, 142, 145, 157, 173–75; pluralistic system of 11, 15, 18–21; as a power relationship 14; public 28–30, 102, 107; rethink the meaning of 6–7, 171; social 141, 144, 154, 155, 157, 165–67; strong 5, 7, 173; weak 5, 157, 173
Amsterdam Treaty *see* Treaty of Amsterdam
authority 54, 56, 118; alienated 7, 53, 59; delegated 4, 7, 52, 53, 59, 118, 144; retrieval of 56, 59
autonomy 14, 93, 114

Bartolini, Stefano 42, 48, 173
Bobbio, Noberto 3, 4
Bovens, Mark 36, 102, 141, 144, 155, 157, 167

central bank *see* European Central Bank
chemicals-policy 10, 142, 147, 151, 153
civil society 9, 44, 141, 145, 152, 166; global 13; participation of, to improve accountability 6, 9–10, 141, 143, 148, 153, 171
cleavage-management 39, 40, 41; as argument for avoiding accountability 39, 47
co-decision procedure 147, 164
competencies 2, 67, 75; delegated 7, 9, 111
concept-stretching 6, 23
confederalism 38, 49
consociational 32, 33, 40
constitutional balance of terror 38, 42, 44, 47, 49
Constitutional Treaty *see* Treaty establishing a Constitution for Europe
constitutionalism 43, 44, 50; transnational 43–45
control 9, 18, 54, 121; democratic 35, 96, 103, 115, 124, 129; mechanisms of, between principal and agent 84, 91, 92; ministerial 28
corporatism 32, 39
corruption 14, 16, 127
Council of the European Union 8, 104, 162, 163, 166, 174
Council of Ministers *see* Council of the European Union

Dahl, Robert 2, 3, 14, 46, 52, 59
delegation 4, 7–8, 51, 54, 60, 83, 93, 111, 113–15, 117–18, 121, 130; and accountability 4, 7, 9, 15, 60–65, 68–69, 74, 83–84, 94, 120; designs of 84–86; myth of international 59–60; to national bureaucrats at the European level 84, 86; and procedural democracy 52–54
democracy 1, 2, 13–14, 23, 26, 30, 41, 43, 52, 95, 115, 129, 145, 152, 155, 157; as an end in itself 31; competitive 115; concepts of 26–28, 30–31;

deliberative 135, 137, 143, 146, 153; direct 3, 27, 32; electoral 6, 11, 31, 33; global 6, 11, 15; liberal 13; majoritarian 115, 120; participatory 6, 11, 42, 135, 143, 153; representative 1, 24, 33, 135, 141, 146; transformations of 2–5, 44–45
democratic deficit 1, 24, 53, 72, 97, 115, 141, 151, 154; positions regarding 1–2, 170–71; procedural 37
democratic theory 53, 108, 112, 114, 122
democratic transformation *see* third transformation
democratisation 1, 24, 33, 96, 142
directorate-general (DG) 161, 165

EC Treaty *see* Treaty Establishing the European Community
Economic and Monetary Union (EMU) 70, 128
elections 6, 13, 15, 23, 30, 52, 151; EP, as second order national contests 5, 8, 73, 76, 136; European 7, 24, 68; national 7, 68, 73, 80, 152
end-of-history argument for avoiding accountability 38, 43, 46
EU constitution 38, 47
EU intelligence bodies 97, 104
European agencies 9, 112, 116, 125; as EU executive 123–24
European Central Bank (ECB) 9, 41, 111, 116, 124, 137, 139; as EU executive 121–22; independence of 127–29; transparency of 132–34, 139
European Commission 9, 24, 33, 67, 71, 95, 100, 11[illegible], 115, 123, 141, 146, 150, 156, 160, 167; as EU executive 116–21
European Council 67, 70, 73, 77, 162, 166
European Court of Justice (ECJ) 116, 127
European Parliament (EP) 5, 8, 10, 24, 38, 67, 71, 97, 103, 108, 116, 122, 134, 142, 147, 156, 163, 166
European Security and Defence Policy (ESDP) 98, 100
Europeanisation 25
EUROPOL 98, 99, 101
executive power 9, 111, 112, 117, 123

federalism 38, 43–45, 49

G8 15
game theory 12
globalisation 6, 11, 14

governance 2, 3, 14, 72, 95, 103, 109, 141, 145, 153, 161; deliberative 142, 147; democratic 3, 96; global 6, 11, 14, 20, 51; technocratic 115

Hix, Simon 2, 38, 142, 170

inclusiveness 10, 142, 148, 151; and accountability 153; in policy-making 145
information 11, 29, 69, 77, 98, 105, 122, 144, 155, 162, 163; asymmetries of 12, 85, 113, 134; flows of, and social accountability 165–67; freedom of 37; importance of, for accountability 20, 31, 32, 72, 158
intelligence 8, 96, 99; and accountability 102–3, 106; European 8, 96, 97, 100; European bodies of 97, 101, 103; European cooperation on, and accountability 97, 106–8
Intelligence Division (INTDIV) 98
Intergovernmental Conference (IGC) 8, 67, 69, 79
International Monetary Fund (IMF) 15, 16, 58

judicial review 29, 39

Keohane, Robert 6, 36, 60, 155
Kirchheimer, Otto 46, 47, 174

Laeken declaration 77, 79, 80, 81
legitimacy 2, 6, 16, 20, 22, 50, 111, 112, 116, 120, 127, 129, 131, 139, 141, 173; democratic 54, 55, 115, 120, 140, 143, 145, 153, 154; input 35, 67, 150; output 22, 35, 36, 45, 146, 150; problems of, for the EU 141, 143, 147, 150; procedural 121
legitimation 25, 141, 143
Lijphart, Arend 39, 40, 41, 47
Lisbon strategy 151
Lisbon Treaty *see* Treaty of Lisbon
lobbying 148, 161, 164, 166

Maastricht Treaty *see* Treaty on European Union
Mair, Peter 25, 62, 73, 174
Majone, Giandomenico 41, 42, 43–45, 47, 53, 60, 93, 120, 130
marginal majoritarianism 38, 46, 47, 49
Members of European Parliament (MEPs) 5, 8, 24, 76, 134, 137, 138, 164, 166, 169, 174

mixed polity 39
monitoring 4, 84, 86, 88–90, 100, 103, 114
Moravcsik, Andrew 41–43, 47, 53, 60, 142

nationalism 39, 48, 49
neorealism 12
Nice Treaty *see* Treaty of Nice
non-governmental organisations (NGOs) 10, 16, 20, 149, 155, 158, 160; contribution to EU accountability 155, 156–58, 165, 167
non-majoritarian 25; institutions 112, 114, 116; techniques 40, 41

opposition 7, 10, 34, 45, 46, 68, 73, 80–81; absence of 10, 35, 173–74; classical 46, 48, 174; legitimate 46, 47; of principle 46, 48; waning 46–48

parliamentarisation 120, 124, 141
participation 9, 27, 32, 52, 135, 153, 155; of civil society 10, 141, 143, 145, 149; effective; as the essence of democracy 27, 31
permanent representation (PR) 8, 83, 87, 91, 163
permissive consensus 33, 170–72
politicisation 38, 39, 48, 49, 62, 63, 120
power 1, 20, 21, 37, 44, 49, 56, 60, 83, 102, 111, 137, 156, 157; abuses of 11, 14–18, 19, 21, 30; asymmetries of, in world politics 18; controlled transmission of 1; soft 20
power-sharing 39, 40
principal-agent 4, 53, 57, 60, 68, 84, 86, 102, 126, 140; approach 53, 112; relationship 93, 113, 114; theory 88, 112–15, 130
public interest argument for avoiding accountability 36, 41–45, 47

rational-choice: theory 12, 112; institutionalism 112–15, 119, 121, 124
REACH 147–49; policy-making process on 148, 150; and participatory law-making 147
realism 12
referendum 69, 72, 74–76, 80
responsibility 7, 61, 92, 141, 144, 146, 157
responsiveness 10, 30, 144, 150,151; and accountability 10, 142, 144, 145, 148, 153

Sangiovanni, Andrea 42, 43
Satellite Centre (SATCEN) 98, 100
Scharpf, Fritz 22, 42, 43, 48
self-determination: individual 23; national 38
Situation Centre (SITCEN) 98, 100, 101, 103
societal heterogeneity 31, 32
sovereignty 18, 27, 55; national 14, 121
Statute of the European System of Central Banks and the European Central Bank 128, 132

third transformation 2–4, 171
transparency 6, 20, 76, 81, 132–34, 138, 159; and accountability 9, 10, 122, 127, 131, 140, 142, 144, 153, 155; in information-provision 158, 165
Treaty of Amsterdam 67
Treaty establishing a Constitution for Europe 13, 76, 146
Treaty establishing the European Community (TEC) 105
Treaty on European Union (TEU) 24, 53, 70, 81, 98, 121, 128; article 48 EU 70, 81, 82; article 105.1 EU 130; article 108 EU 128, 137, 138; article 113.3 EU 132
Treaty of Lisbon 70, 146
Treaty of Nice 67
treaty reform 67, 71; and accountability 68, 73, 74, 80; convention method 68, 69–70, 76–80; IGC method 68, 69–71, 72–76

United Nations (UN) 15, 18, 58; Global Compact 17

veto: direct-democratic 32
veto players 32, 64

Weaver, R. Kent 40
Western European Union (WEU) 98
White Paper on European Governance 145, 146, 161, 162
World Bank 15, 16
World Trade Organisation (WTO) 12, 14–16, 58